Hello from all of us in All Time Low, and THANK YOU for picking up a copy of Young Renegades. It's been an absolute dream-come-true to continue building on the themes, narratives, and stories we first conceptualized on our album Last Young Renegade. There was always so much more to explore in the world we created during the LYR era, and in this graphic novel, we get to see some of that realized. Working with this team -- bringing these pages to life -- we couldn't be more excited for you to dive in.

This is a story about destiny, about second chances, about fate reconnecting souls intertwined. What happens when a missed moment or a path not taken sends a ripple into the world that the universe then has to correct? Are we choosing our own fate, or do unknown forces sometimes nudge us in the direction we're meant to go? Do we listen to our surroundings enough, see the writing on the walls to make up for opportunities once lost? Right time, right place, right now. Don't sleep through the clues.

The story told on the pages of this book are extensions of the words, melodies, emotions, and feelings we explored during the LYR era; a companion piece, a visual elaboration, all beautifully tied to some of the most important history that anchors this band to its origins and its growth. This is a work of fiction but it echoes moments of ourselves and the world around us. We hope you find some of yourself in these pages as well.

--Alex Gaskarth

For Kat
-Tres

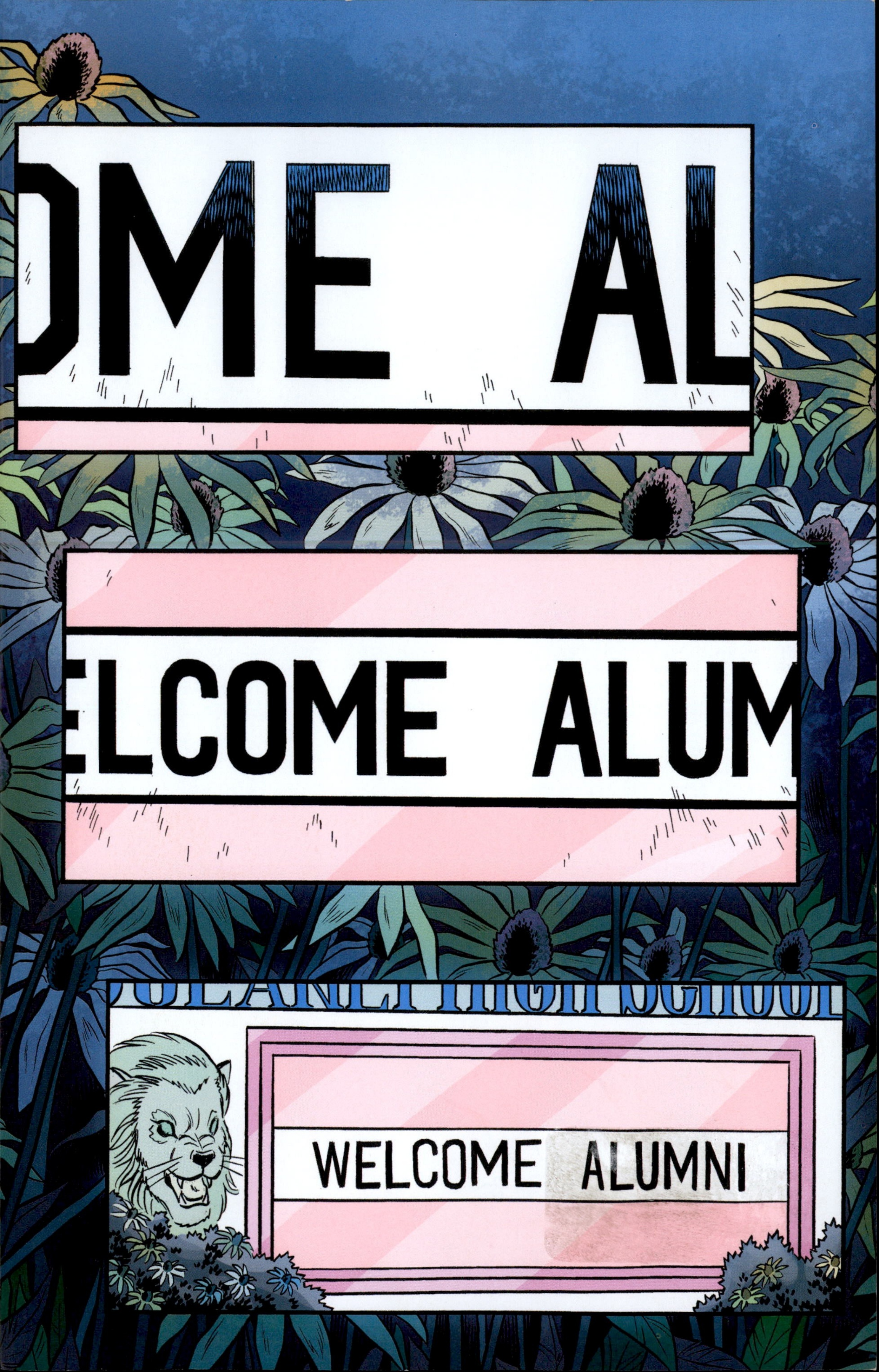
ELCOME ALUM
WELCOME ALUMNI

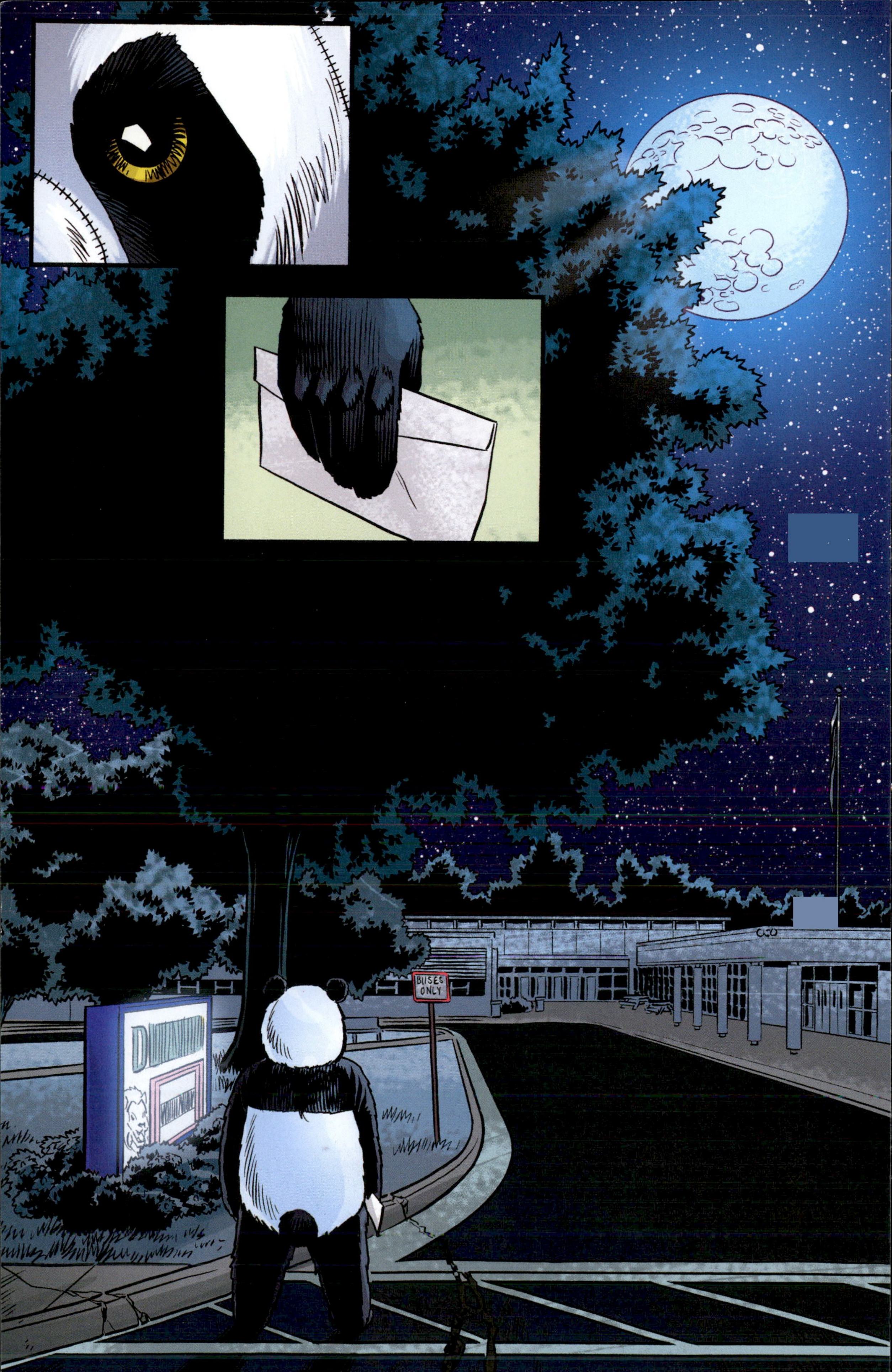
BUSES ONLY

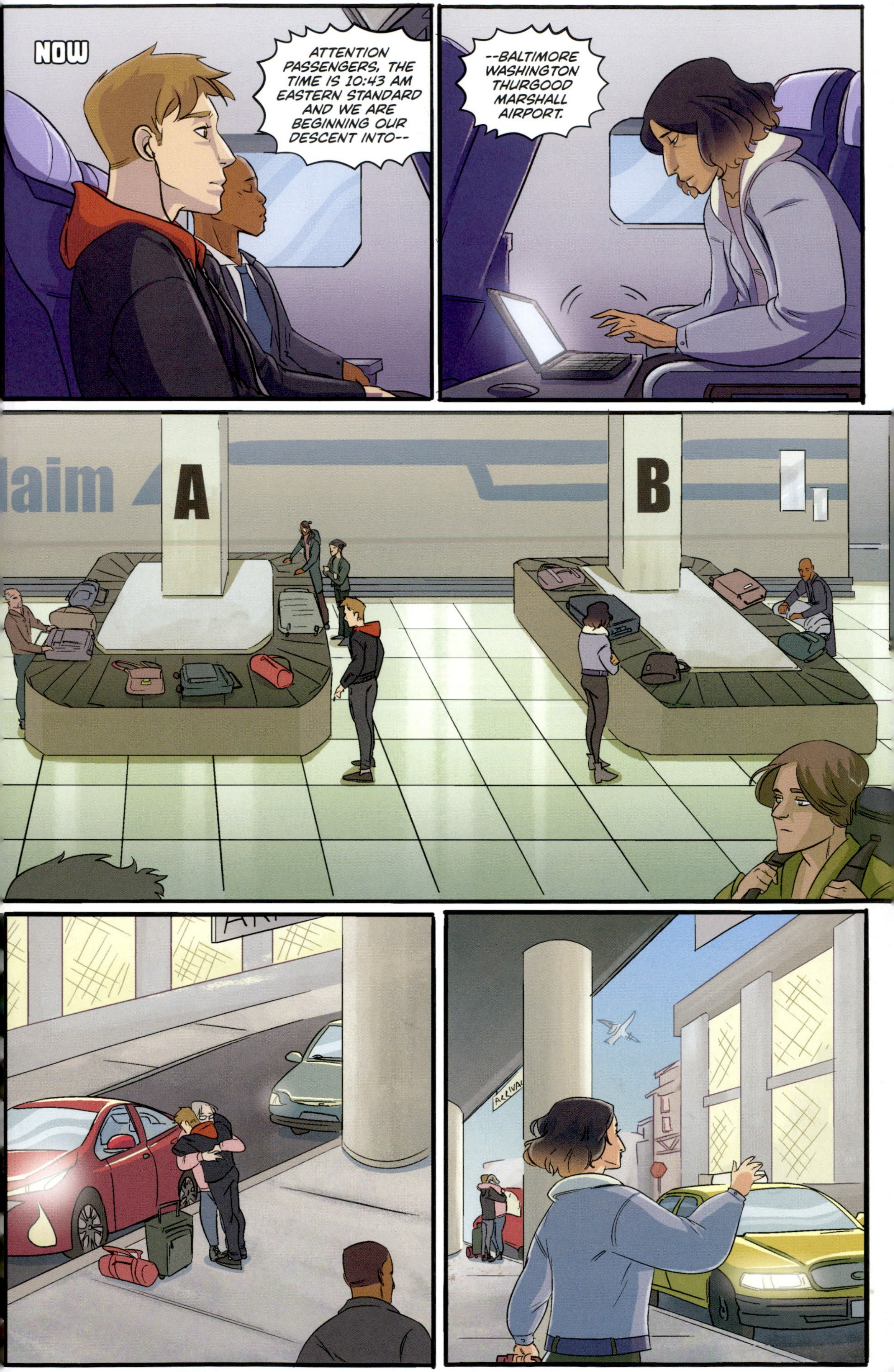
NOW
ATTENTION PASSENGERS, THE TIME IS 10:43 AM EASTERN STANDARD AND WE ARE BEGINNING OUR DESCENT INTO--
--BALTIMORE WASHINGTON THURGOOD MARSHALL AIRPORT.
laim
A
B

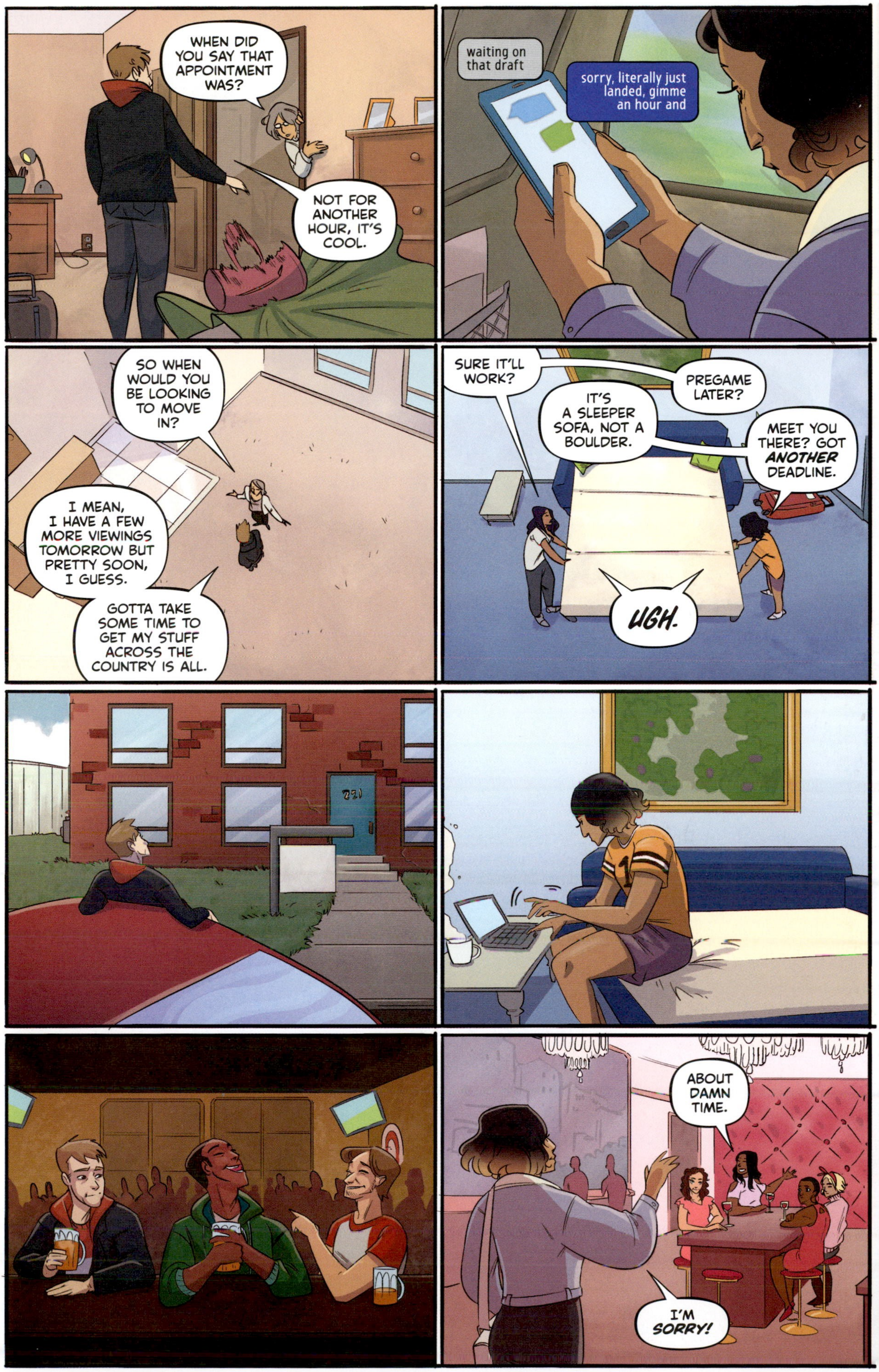
WHEN DID YOU SAY THAT APPOINTMENT WAS?
NOT FOR ANOTHER HOUR, IT'S COOL.
waiting on that draft
sorry, literally just landed, gimme an hour and
SO WHEN WOULD YOU BE LOOKING TO MOVE IN?
I MEAN, I HAVE A FEW MORE VIEWINGS TOMORROW BUT PRETTY SOON, I GUESS.
GOTTA TAKE SOME TIME TO GET MY STUFF ACROSS THE COUNTRY IS ALL.
SURE IT'LL WORK?
IT'S A SLEEPER SOFA, NOT A BOULDER.
PREGAME LATER?
MEET YOU THERE? GOT ANOTHER DEADLINE.
UGH.
ABOUT DAMN TIME.
I'M SORRY!

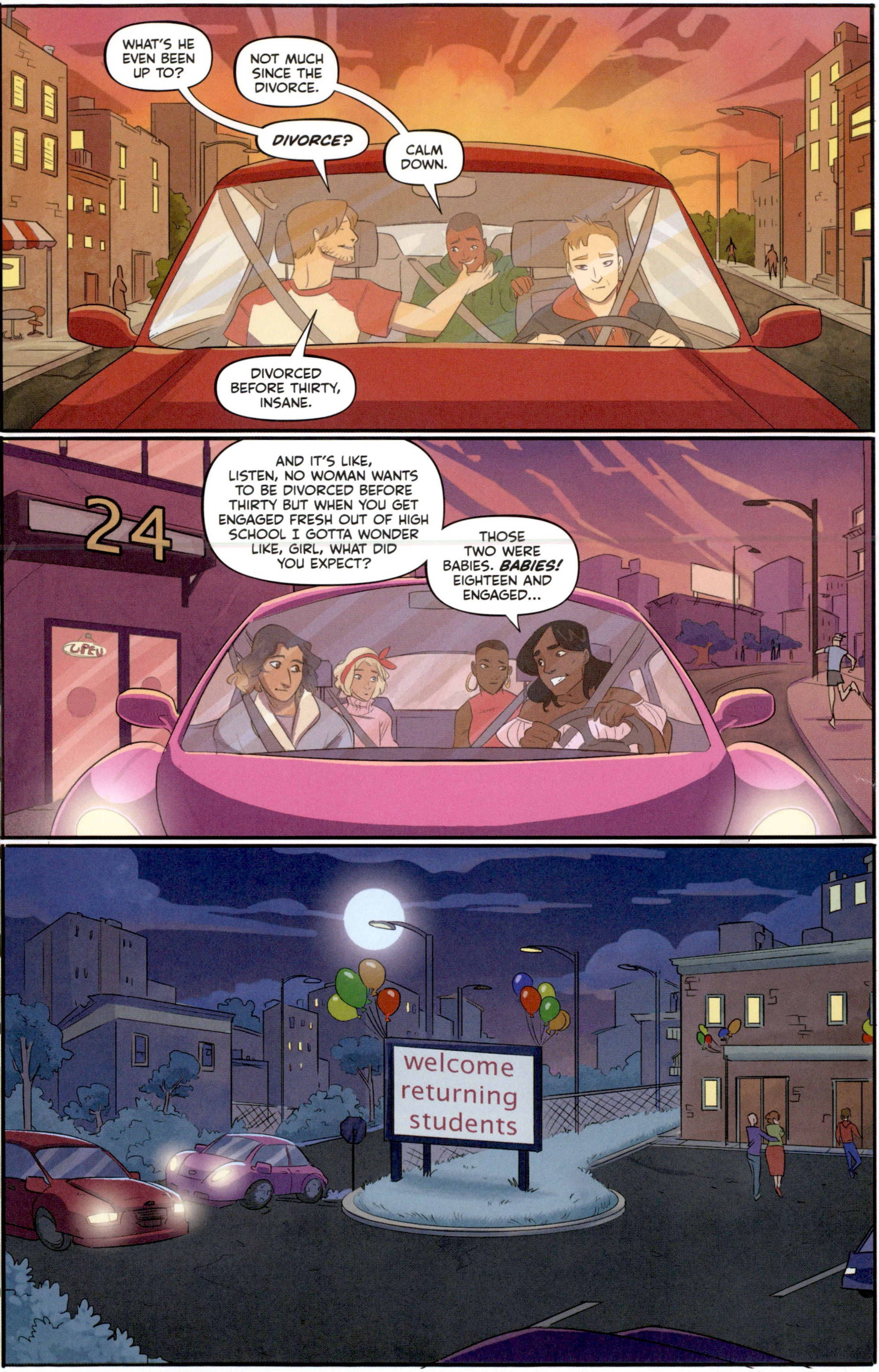
WHAT'S HE EVEN BEEN UP TO?
NOT MUCH SINCE THE DIVORCE.
DIVORCE?
CALM DOWN.
DIVORCED BEFORE THIRTY, INSANE.
24
OPEN
AND IT'S LIKE, LISTEN, NO WOMAN WANTS TO BE DIVORCED BEFORE THIRTY BUT WHEN YOU GET ENGAGED FRESH OUT OF HIGH SCHOOL I GOTTA WONDER LIKE, GIRL, WHAT DID YOU EXPECT?
THOSE TWO WERE BABIES. BABIES! EIGHTEEN AND ENGAGED...
welcome returning students

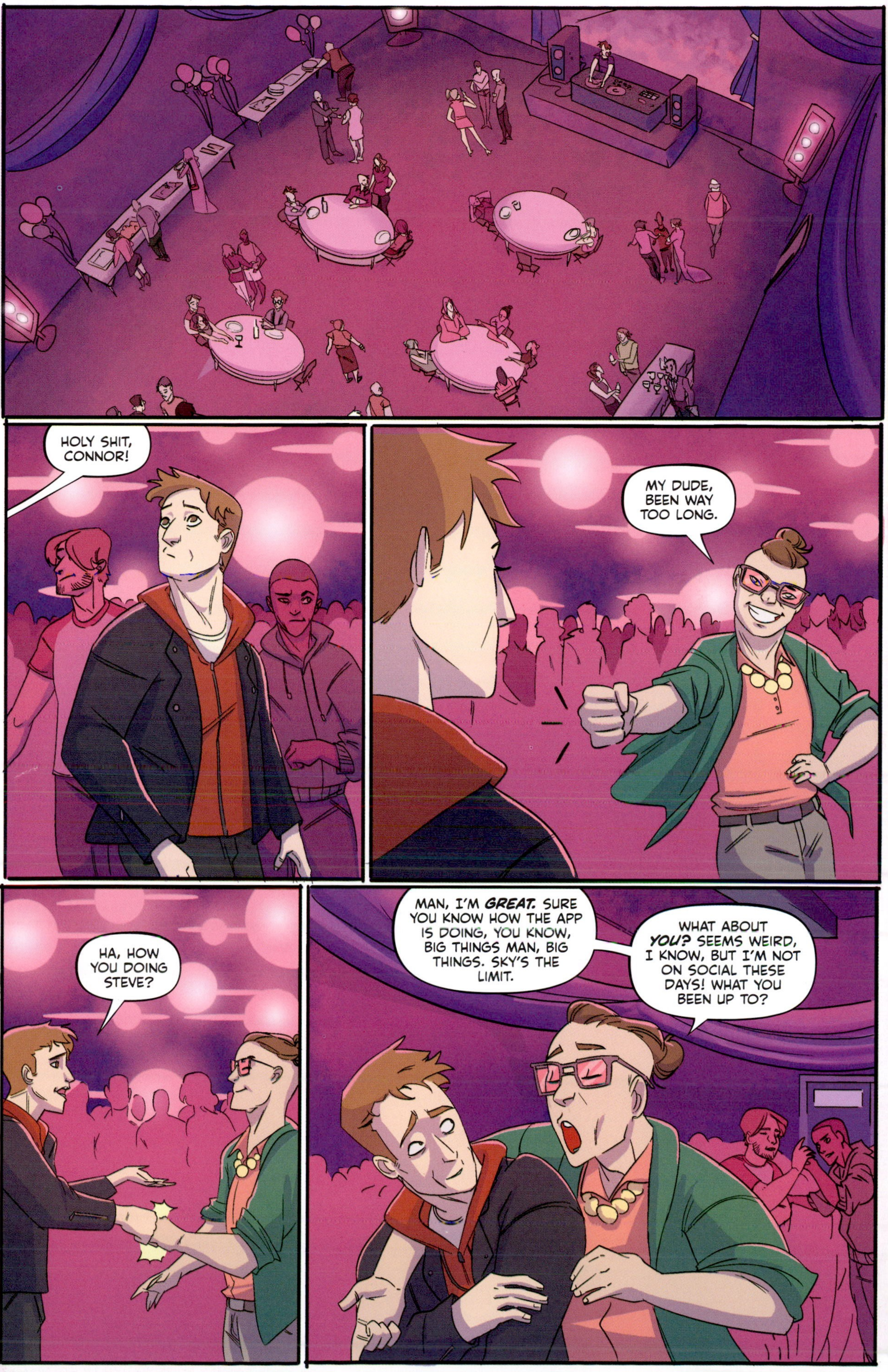
HOLY SHIT, CONNOR!
MY DUDE, BEEN WAY TOO LONG.
HA, HOW YOU DOING STEVE?
MAN, I'M **GREAT.** SURE YOU KNOW HOW THE APP IS DOING, YOU KNOW, BIG THINGS MAN, BIG THINGS. SKY'S THE LIMIT.
WHAT ABOUT ***YOU?*** SEEMS WEIRD, I KNOW, BUT I'M NOT ON SOCIAL THESE DAYS! WHAT YOU BEEN UP TO?

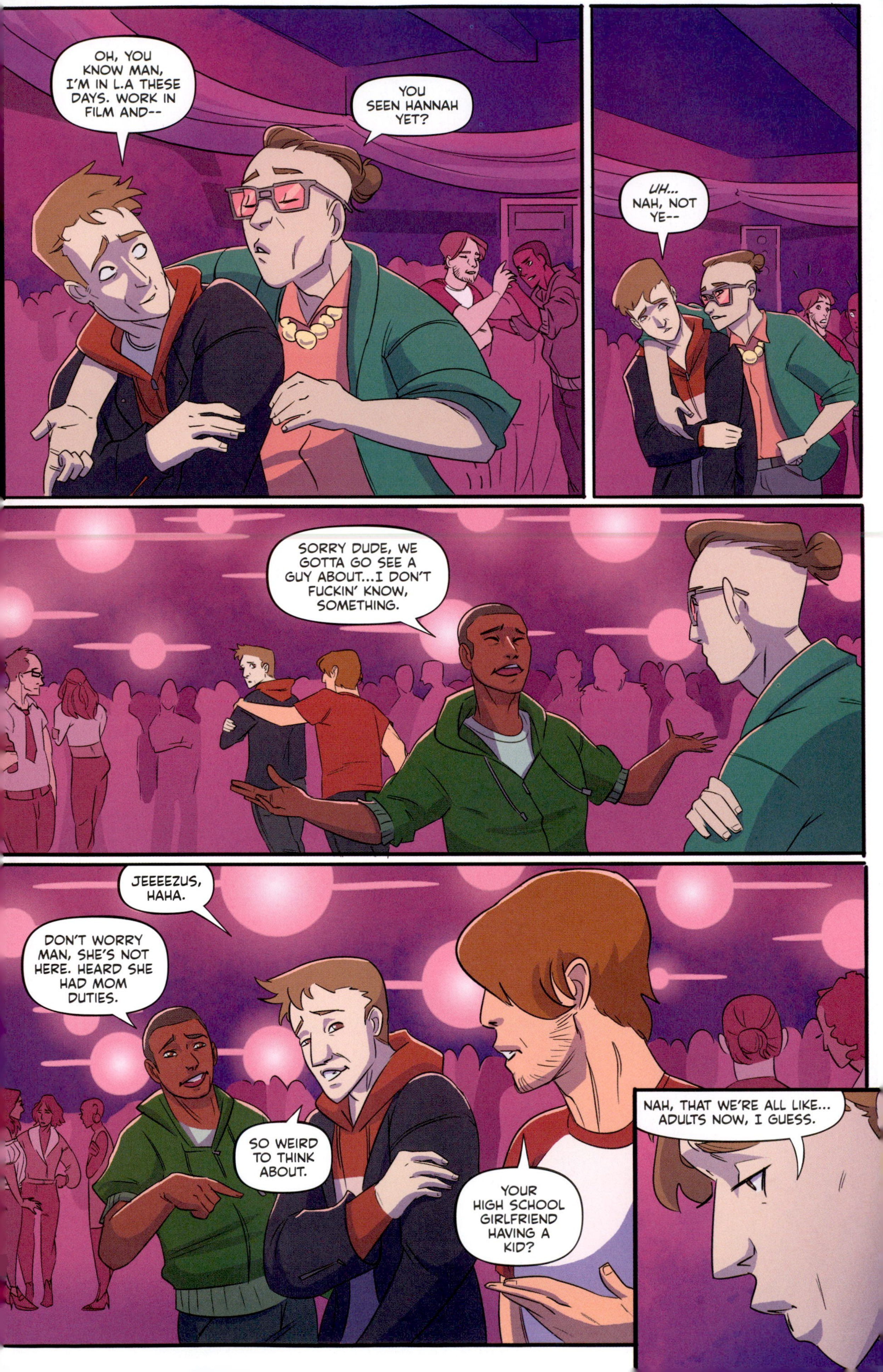
OH, YOU KNOW MAN, I'M IN L.A THESE DAYS. WORK IN FILM AND--
YOU SEEN HANNAH YET?
UH... NAH, NOT YE--
SORRY DUDE, WE GOTTA GO SEE A GUY ABOUT...I DON'T FUCKIN' KNOW, SOMETHING.
JEEEEZUS, HAHA.
DON'T WORRY MAN, SHE'S NOT HERE. HEARD SHE HAD MOM DUTIES.
SO WEIRD TO THINK ABOUT.
YOUR HIGH SCHOOL GIRLFRIEND HAVING A KID?
NAH, THAT WE'RE ALL LIKE... ADULTS NOW, I GUESS.

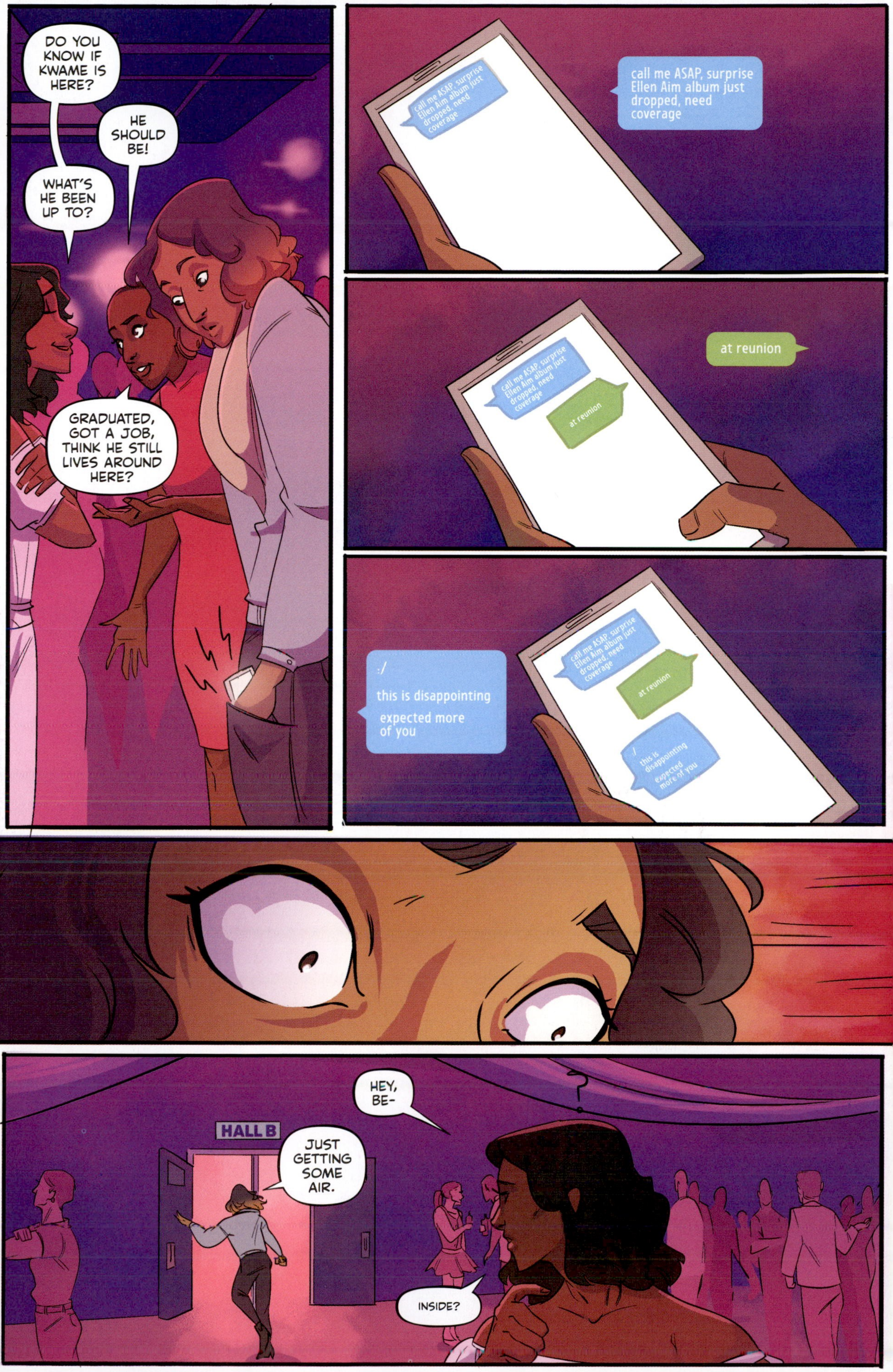
DO YOU KNOW IF KWAME IS HERE?
HE SHOULD BE!
WHAT'S HE BEEN UP TO?
GRADUATED, GOT A JOB, THINK HE STILL LIVES AROUND HERE?
call me ASAP, surprise Ellen Aim album just dropped, need coverage
at reunion
:/
this is disappointing
expected more of you
HEY, BE-
HALL B
JUST GETTING SOME AIR.
INSIDE?

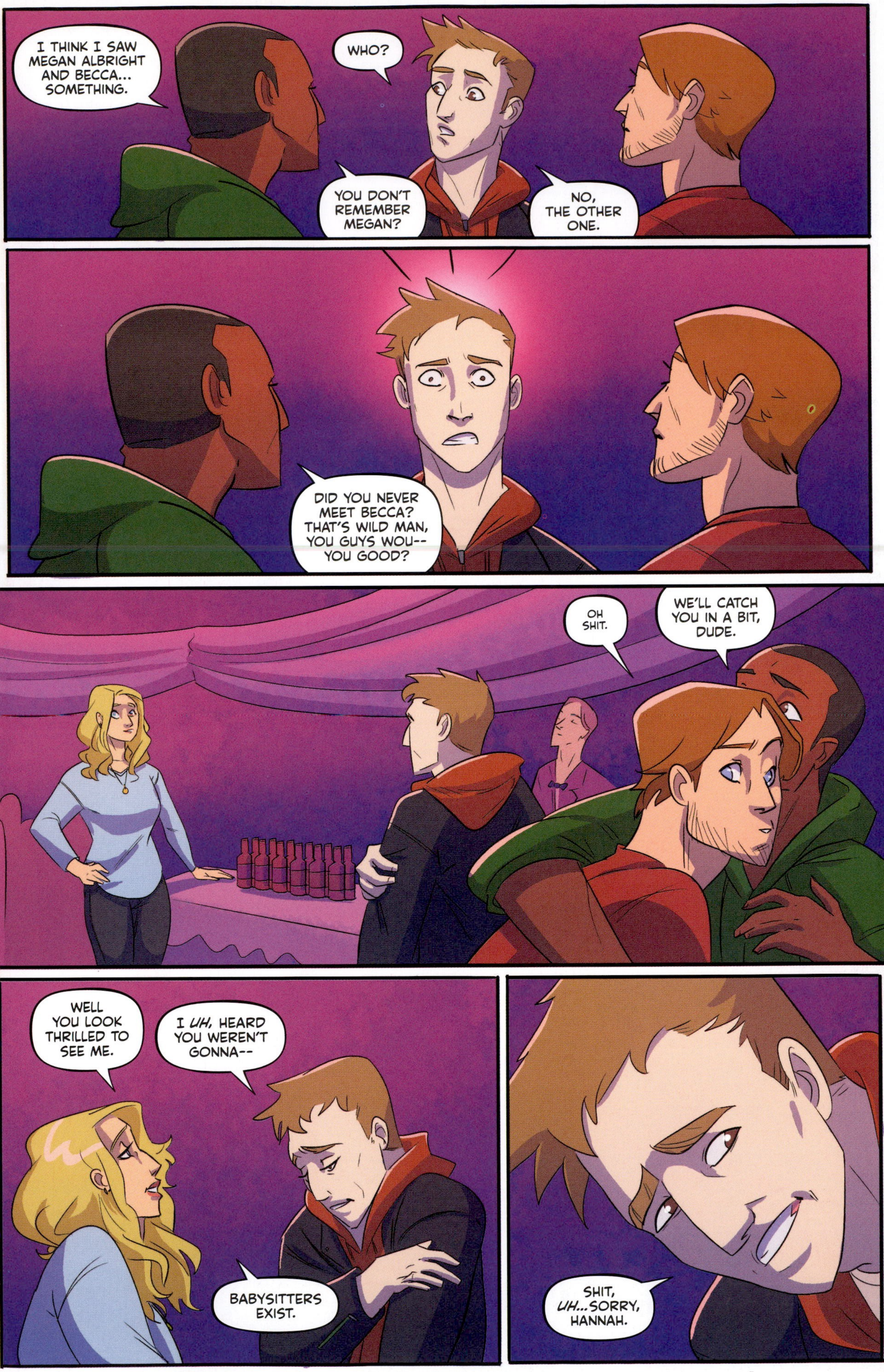
I THINK I SAW MEGAN ALBRIGHT AND BECCA... SOMETHING.
WHO?
YOU DON'T REMEMBER MEGAN?
NO, THE OTHER ONE.
DID YOU NEVER MEET BECCA? THAT'S WILD MAN, YOU GUYS WOU-- YOU GOOD?
OH SHIT.
WE'LL CATCH YOU IN A BIT, DUDE.
WELL YOU LOOK THRILLED TO SEE ME.
I *UH,* HEARD YOU WEREN'T GONNA--
BABYSITTERS EXIST.
SHIT, *UH*...SORRY, HANNAH.

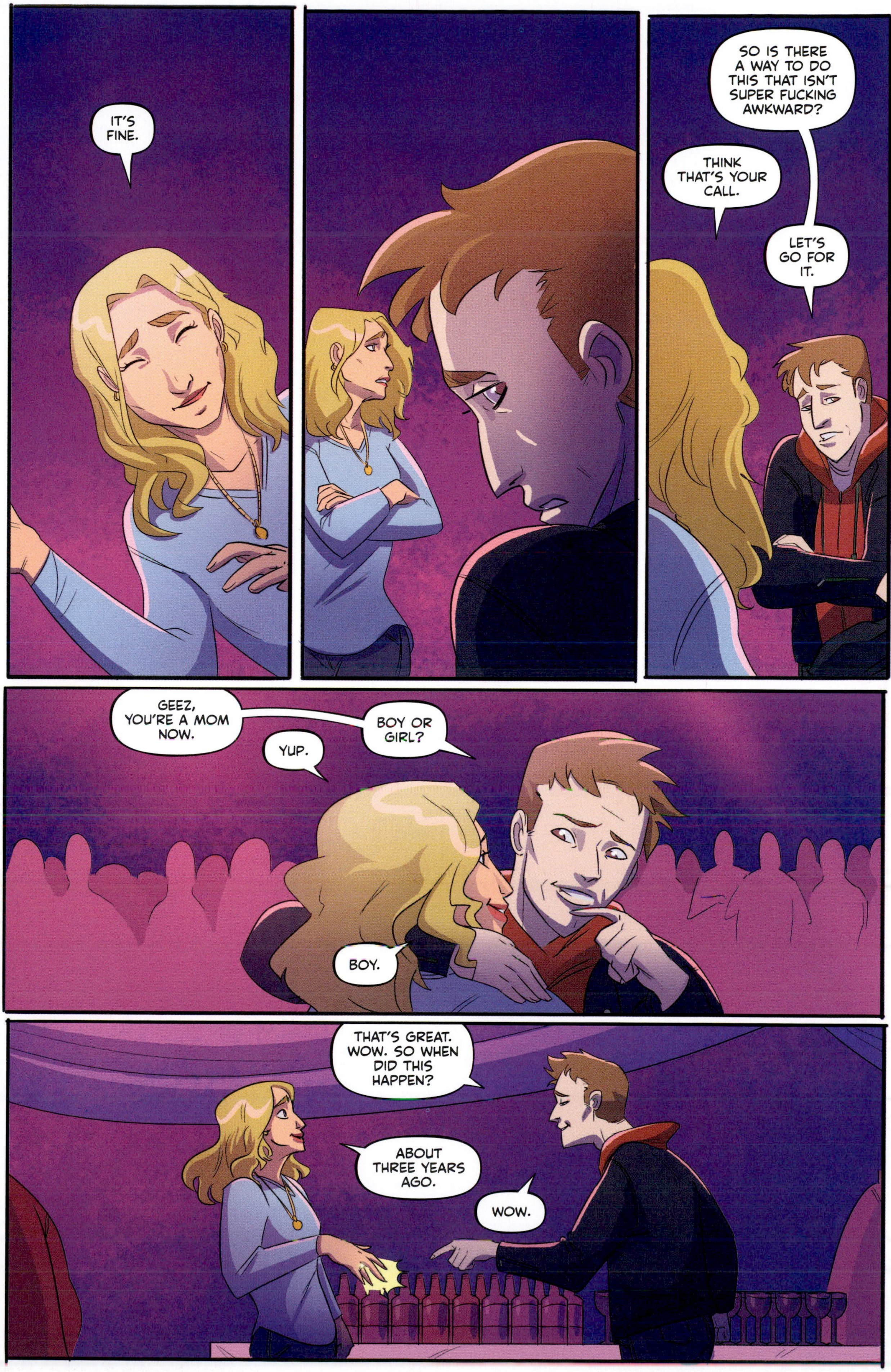
IT'S FINE.
SO IS THERE A WAY TO DO THIS THAT ISN'T SUPER FUCKING AWKWARD?
THINK THAT'S YOUR CALL.
LET'S GO FOR IT.
GEEZ, YOU'RE A MOM NOW.
YUP.
BOY OR GIRL?
BOY.
THAT'S GREAT. WOW. SO WHEN DID THIS HAPPEN?
ABOUT THREE YEARS AGO.
WOW.

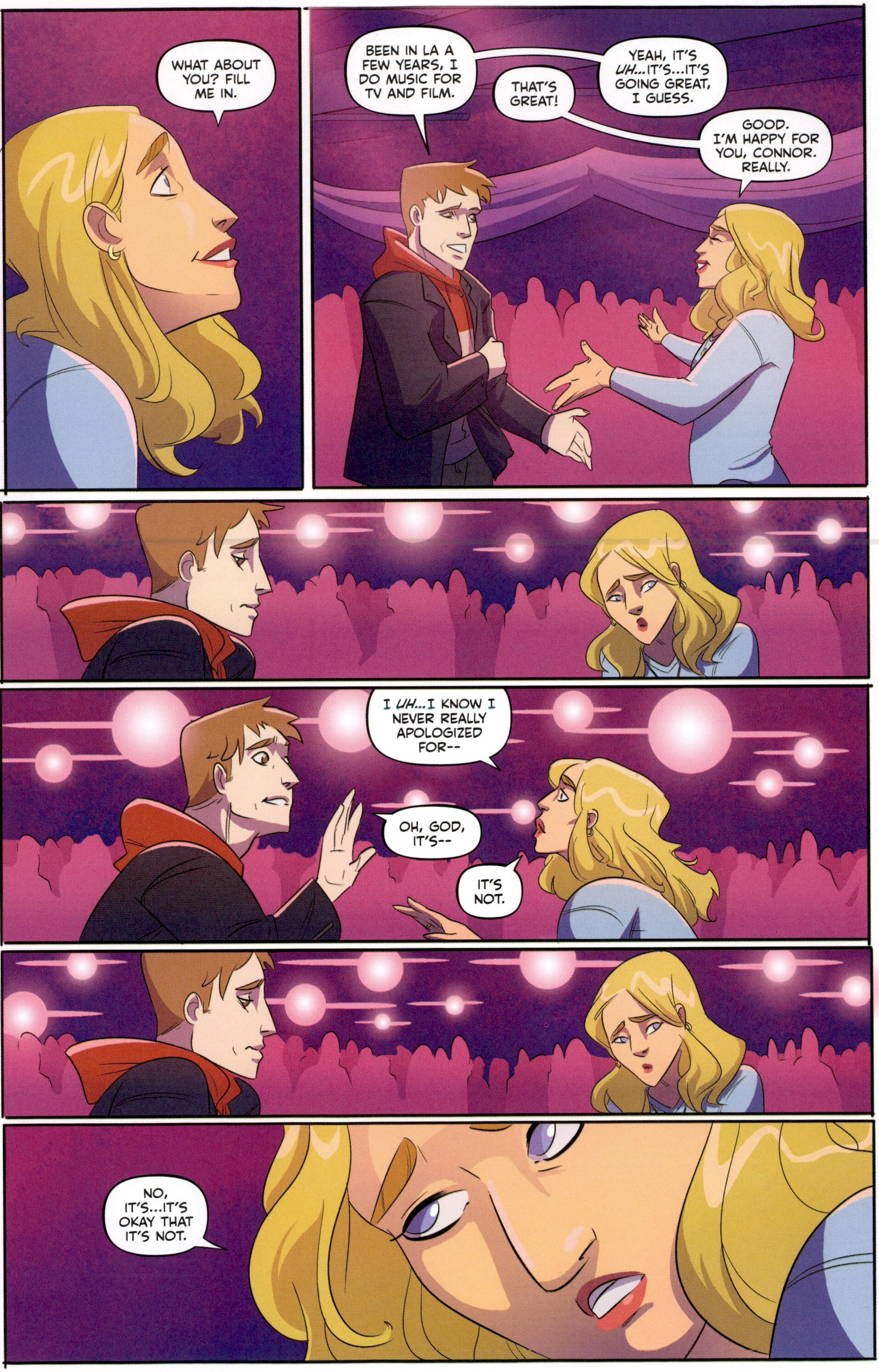
WHAT ABOUT YOU? FILL ME IN.
BEEN IN LA A FEW YEARS, I DO MUSIC FOR TV AND FILM.
THAT'S GREAT!
YEAH, IT'S *UH*...IT'S...IT'S GOING GREAT, I GUESS.
GOOD. I'M HAPPY FOR YOU, CONNOR. REALLY.
I *UH*...I KNOW I NEVER REALLY APOLOGIZED FOR--
OH, GOD, IT'S--
IT'S NOT.
NO, IT'S...IT'S OKAY THAT IT'S NOT.

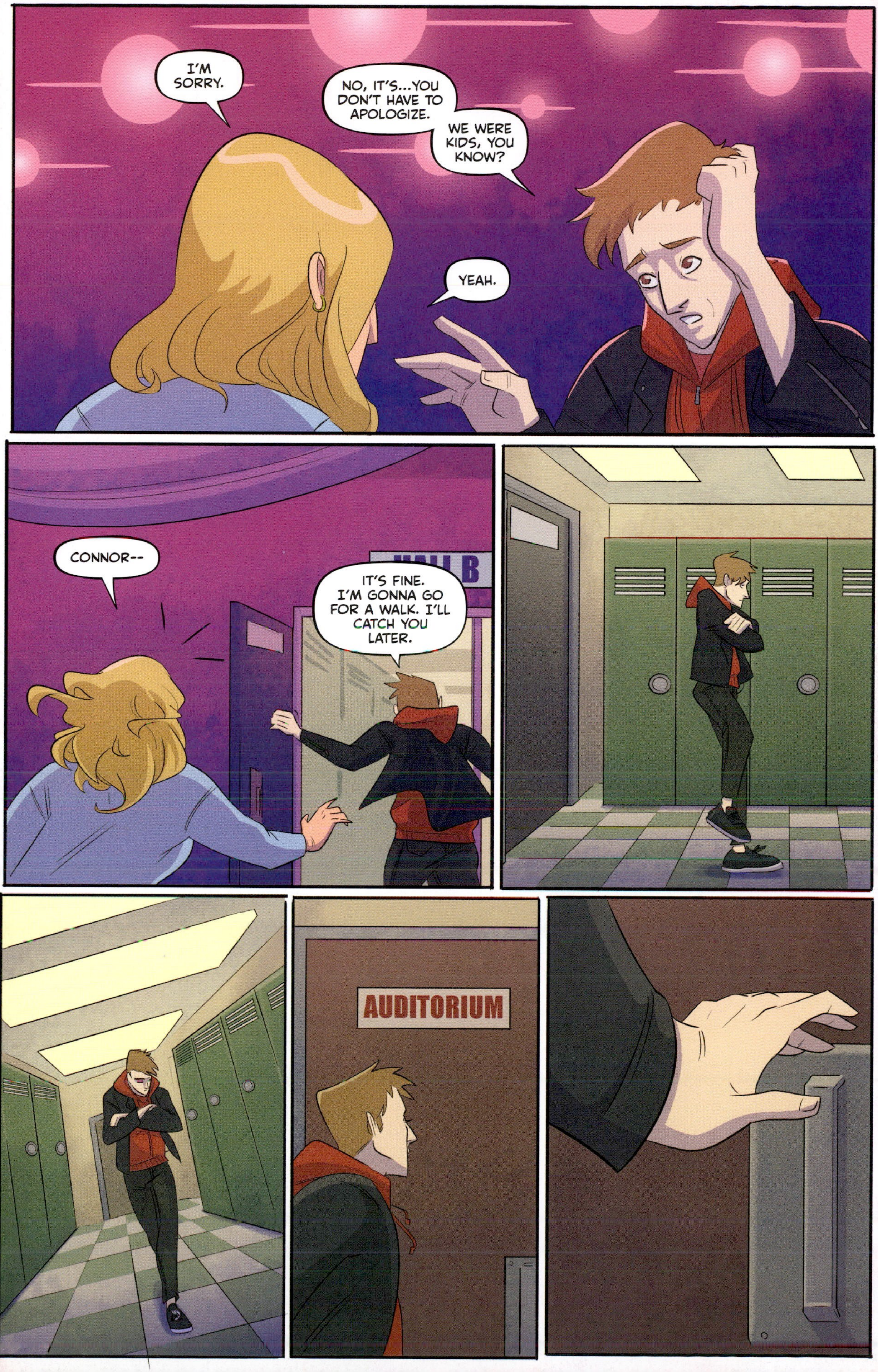
I'M SORRY.
NO, IT'S...YOU DON'T HAVE TO APOLOGIZE.
WE WERE KIDS, YOU KNOW?
YEAH.
CONNOR--
HALL B
IT'S FINE. I'M GONNA GO FOR A WALK. I'LL CATCH YOU LATER.
AUDITORIUM

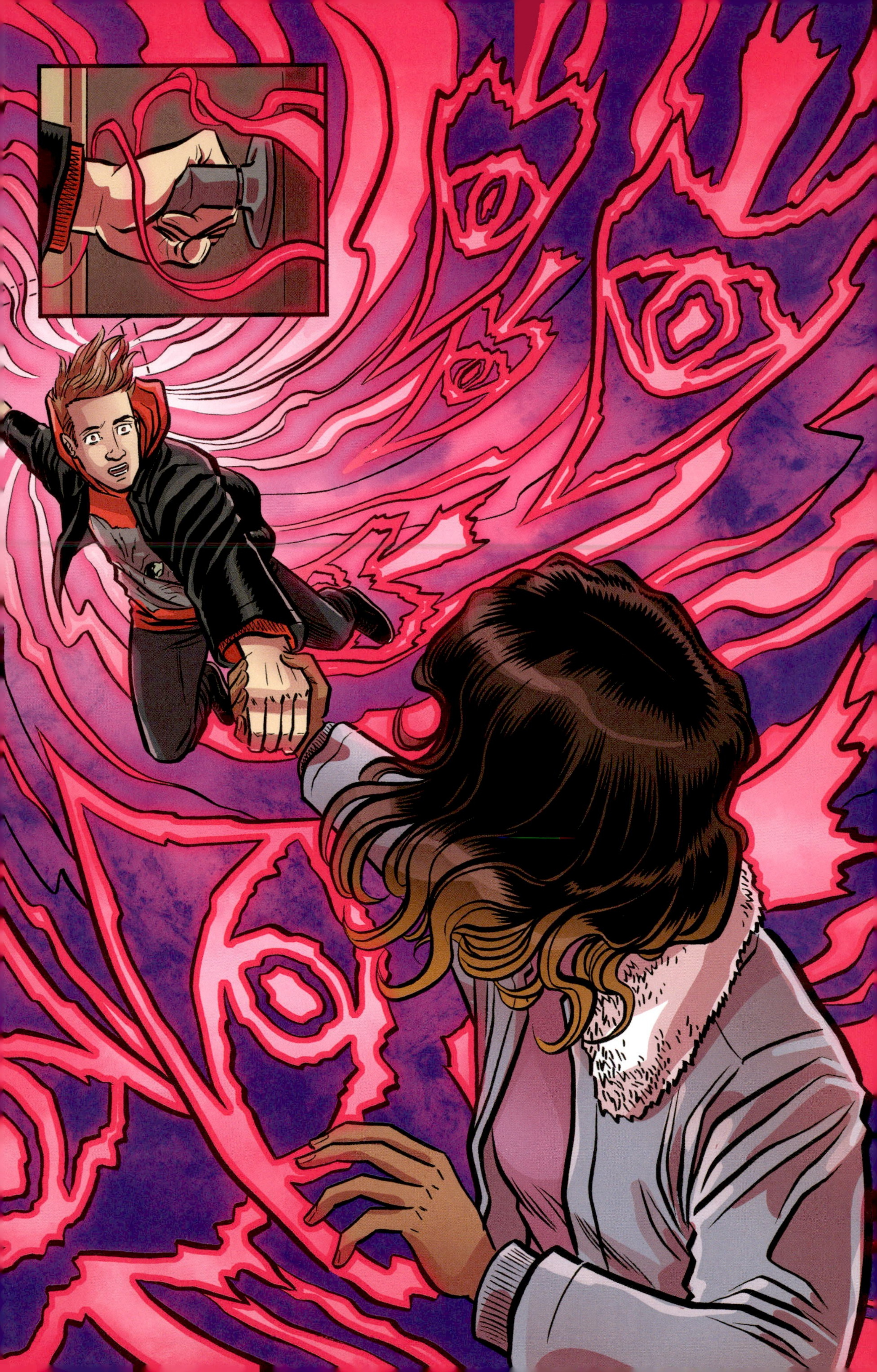

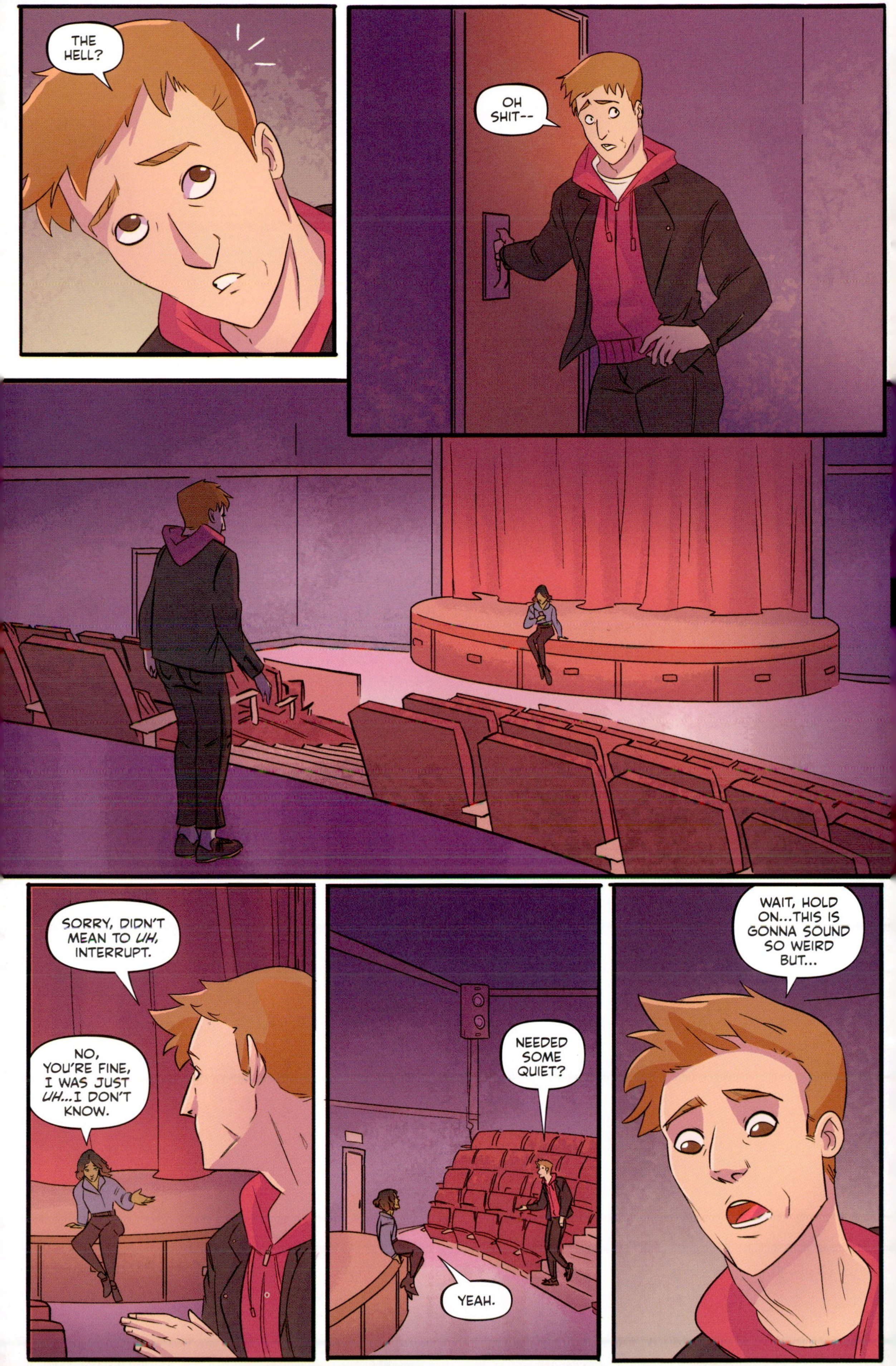
THE HELL?
OH SHIT--
SORRY, DIDN'T MEAN TO *UH*, INTERRUPT.
NO, YOU'RE FINE, I WAS JUST *UH*...I DON'T KNOW.
NEEDED SOME QUIET?
YEAH.
WAIT, HOLD ON...THIS IS GONNA SOUND SO WEIRD BUT...

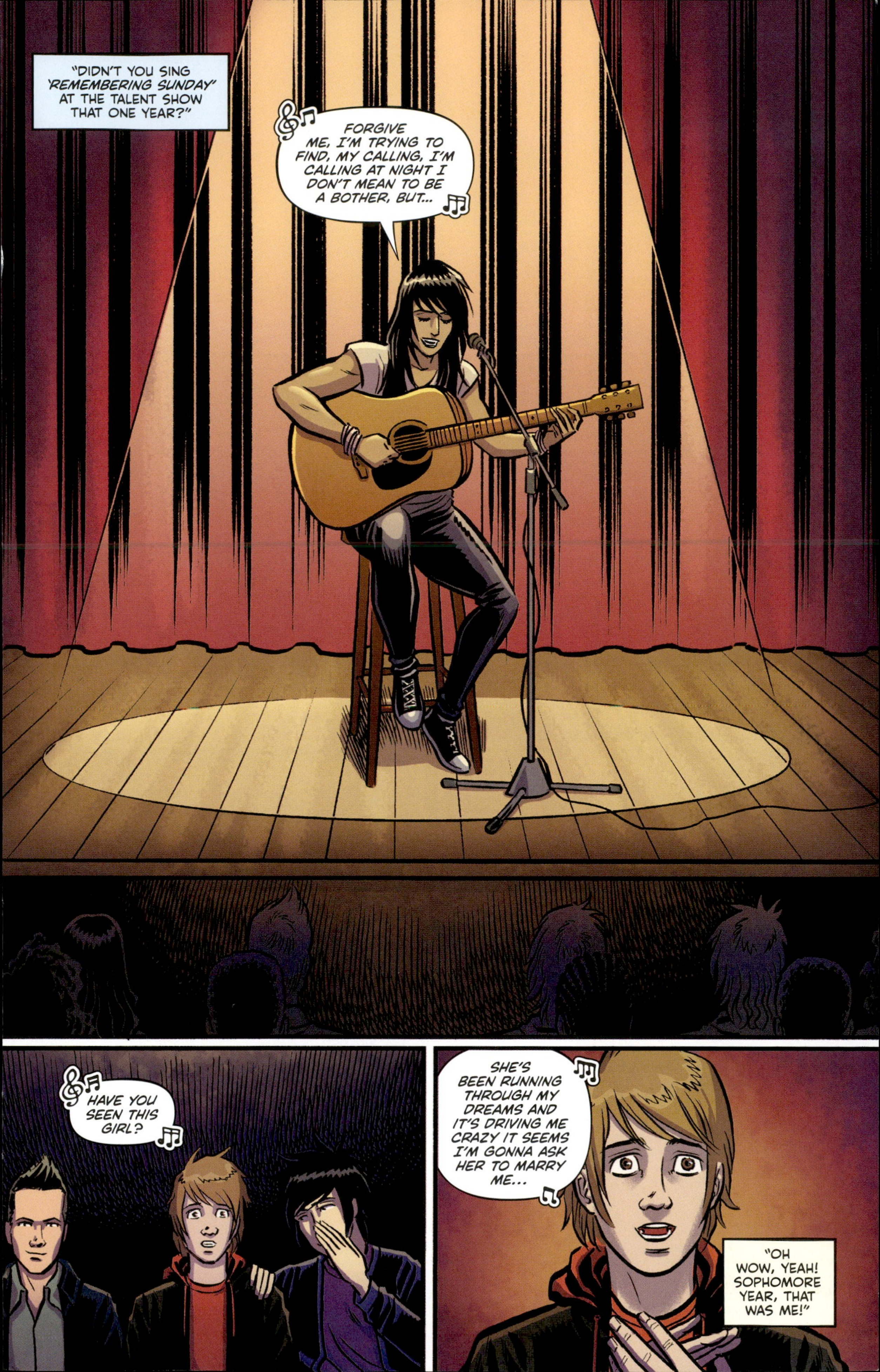
"DIDN'T YOU SING 'REMEMBERING SUNDAY' AT THE TALENT SHOW THAT ONE YEAR?"
FORGIVE ME, I'M TRYING TO FIND, MY CALLING, I'M CALLING AT NIGHT I DON'T MEAN TO BE A BOTHER, BUT...
HAVE YOU SEEN THIS GIRL?
SHE'S BEEN RUNNING THROUGH MY DREAMS AND IT'S DRIVING ME CRAZY IT SEEMS I'M GONNA ASK HER TO MARRY ME...
"OH WOW, YEAH! SOPHOMORE YEAR, THAT WAS ME!"

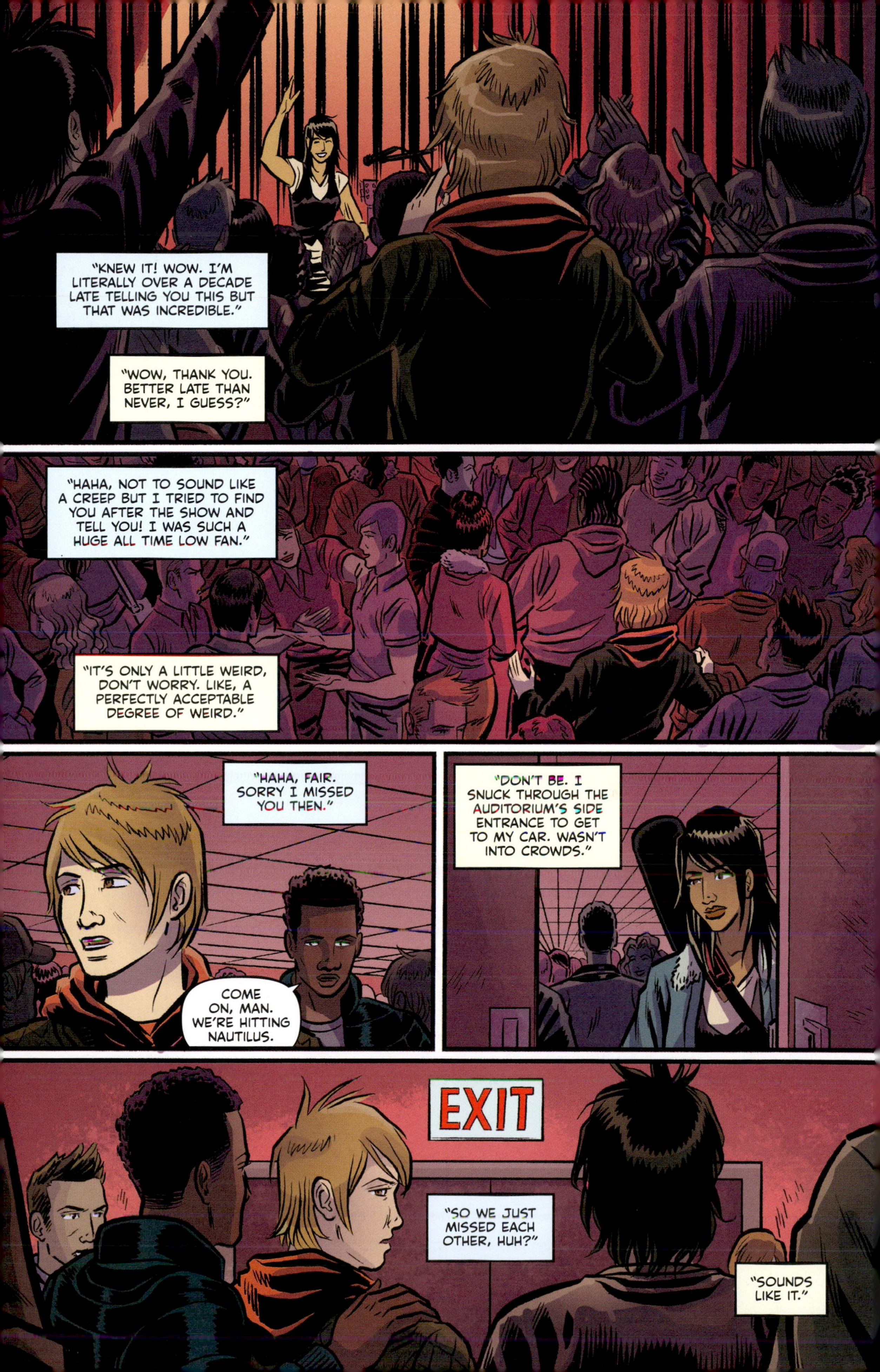
"KNEW IT! WOW. I'M LITERALLY OVER A DECADE LATE TELLING YOU THIS BUT THAT WAS INCREDIBLE."
"WOW, THANK YOU. BETTER LATE THAN NEVER, I GUESS?"
"HAHA, NOT TO SOUND LIKE A CREEP BUT I TRIED TO FIND YOU AFTER THE SHOW AND TELL YOU! I WAS SUCH A HUGE ALL TIME LOW FAN."
"IT'S ONLY A LITTLE WEIRD, DON'T WORRY. LIKE, A PERFECTLY ACCEPTABLE DEGREE OF WEIRD."
"HAHA, FAIR. SORRY I MISSED YOU THEN."
COME ON, MAN. WE'RE HITTING NAUTILUS.
"DON'T BE. I SNUCK THROUGH THE AUDITORIUM'S SIDE ENTRANCE TO GET TO MY CAR. WASN'T INTO CROWDS."
EXIT
"SO WE JUST MISSED EACH OTHER, HUH?"
"SOUNDS LIKE IT."

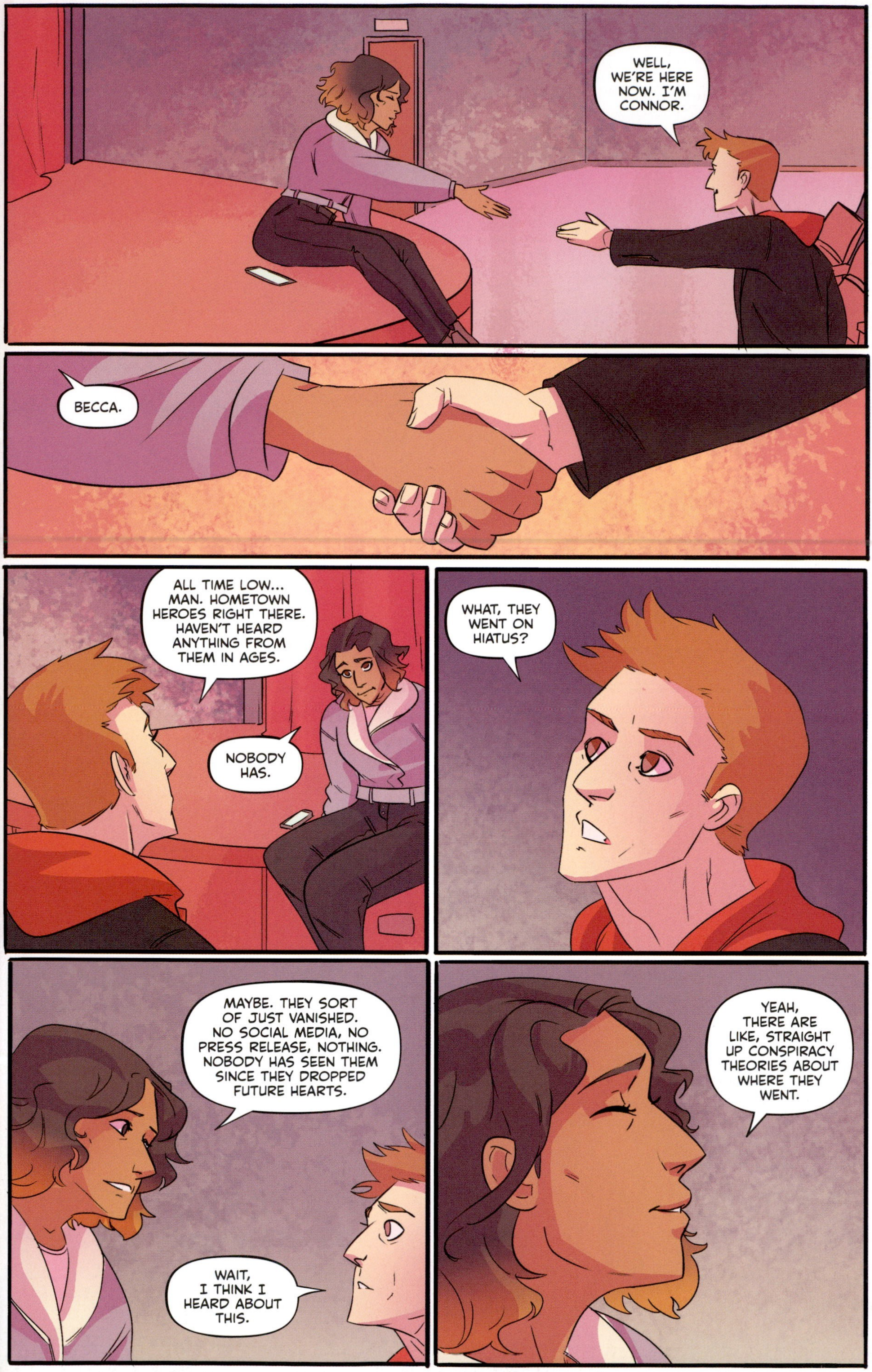
WELL, WE'RE HERE NOW. I'M CONNOR.
BECCA.
ALL TIME LOW... MAN. HOMETOWN HEROES RIGHT THERE. HAVEN'T HEARD ANYTHING FROM THEM IN AGES.
NOBODY HAS.
WHAT, THEY WENT ON HIATUS?
MAYBE. THEY SORT OF JUST VANISHED. NO SOCIAL MEDIA, NO PRESS RELEASE, NOTHING. NOBODY HAS SEEN THEM SINCE THEY DROPPED FUTURE HEARTS.
WAIT, I THINK I HEARD ABOUT THIS.
YEAH, THERE ARE LIKE, STRAIGHT UP CONSPIRACY THEORIES ABOUT WHERE THEY WENT.

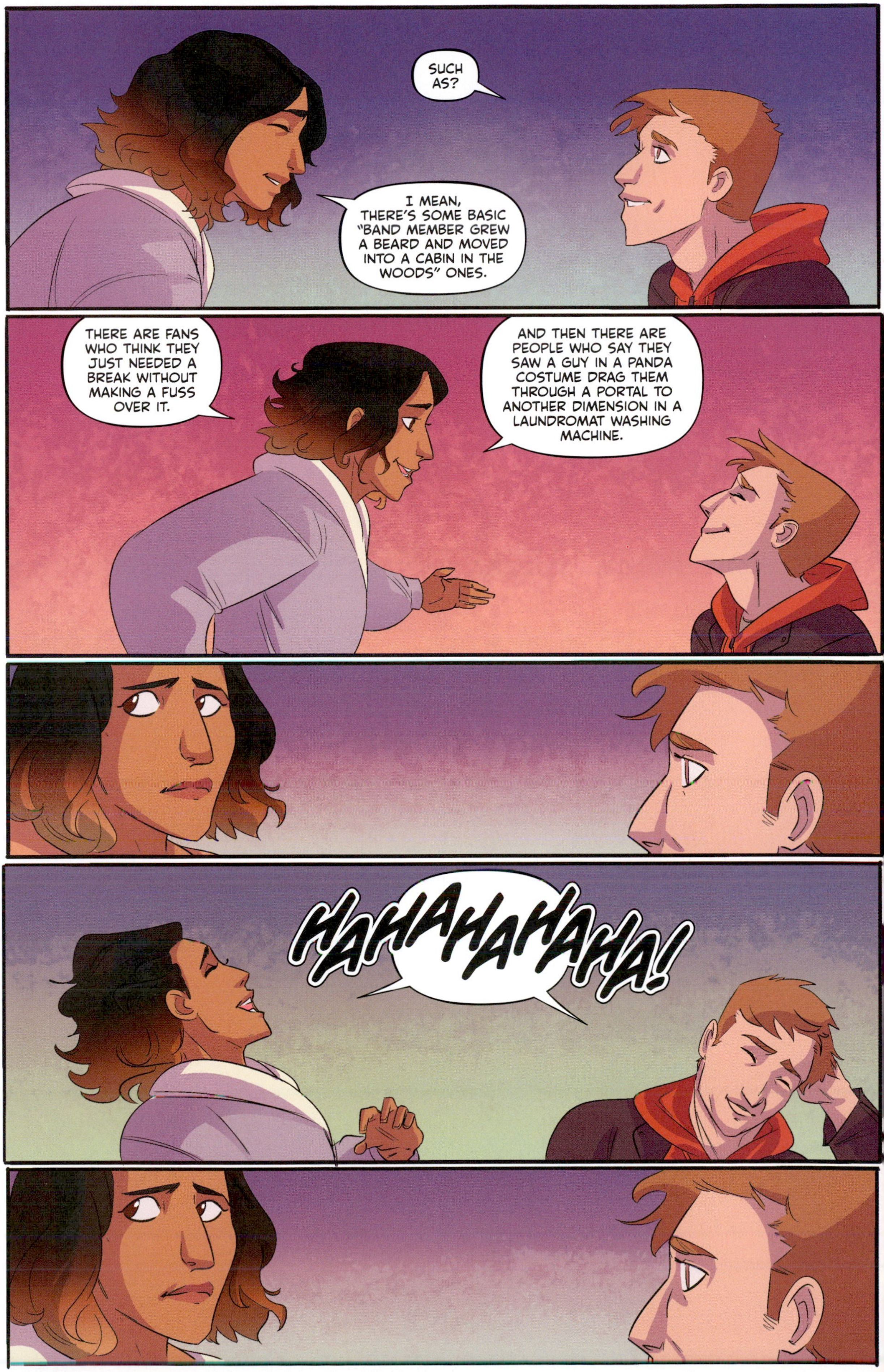
SUCH AS?
I MEAN, THERE'S SOME BASIC "BAND MEMBER GREW A BEARD AND MOVED INTO A CABIN IN THE WOODS" ONES.
THERE ARE FANS WHO THINK THEY JUST NEEDED A BREAK WITHOUT MAKING A FUSS OVER IT.
AND THEN THERE ARE PEOPLE WHO SAY THEY SAW A GUY IN A PANDA COSTUME DRAG THEM THROUGH A PORTAL TO ANOTHER DIMENSION IN A LAUNDROMAT WASHING MACHINE.
HAHAHAHAHAHA!

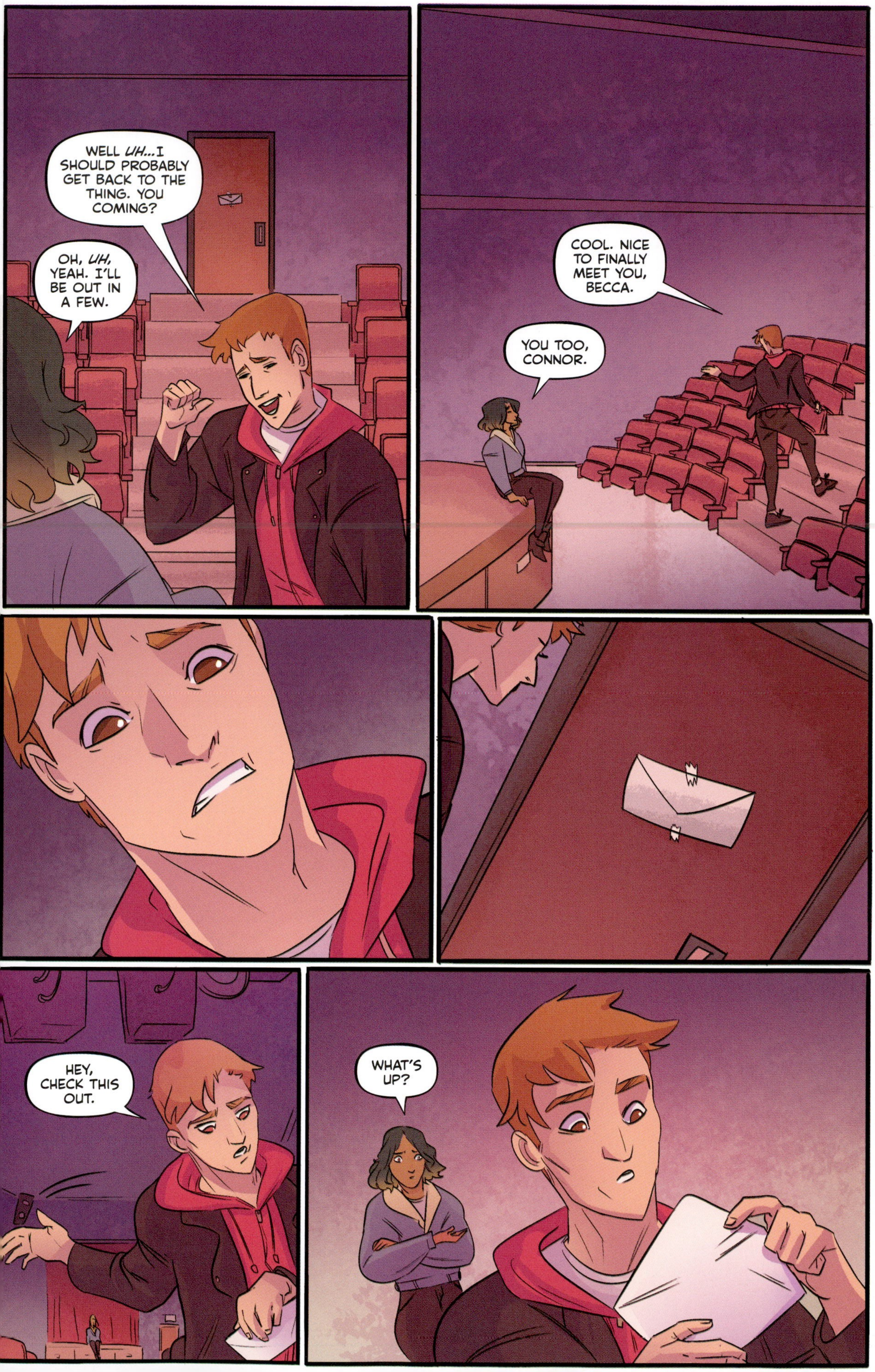
WELL *UH*...I SHOULD PROBABLY GET BACK TO THE THING. YOU COMING?
OH, *UH*, YEAH. I'LL BE OUT IN A FEW.
COOL. NICE TO FINALLY MEET YOU, BECCA.
YOU TOO, CONNOR.
HEY, CHECK THIS OUT.
WHAT'S UP?

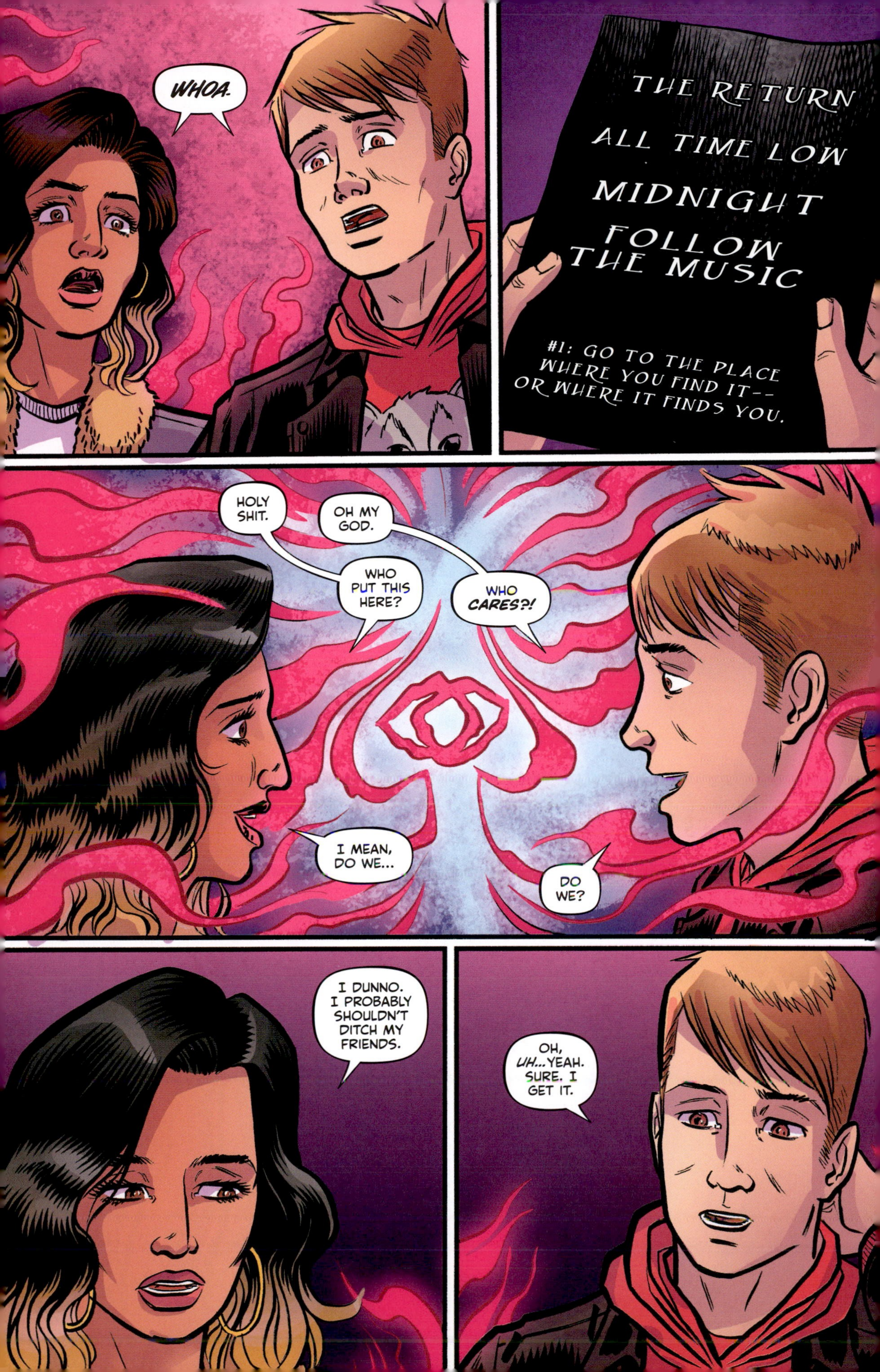
WHOA.
THE RETURN
ALL TIME LOW
MIDNIGHT
FOLLOW THE MUSIC
#1: GO TO THE PLACE WHERE YOU FIND IT-- OR WHERE IT FINDS YOU.
HOLY SHIT.
OH MY GOD.
WHO PUT THIS HERE?
WHO CARES?!
I MEAN, DO WE...
DO WE?
I DUNNO. I PROBABLY SHOULDN'T DITCH MY FRIENDS.
OH, UH...YEAH. SURE. I GET IT.

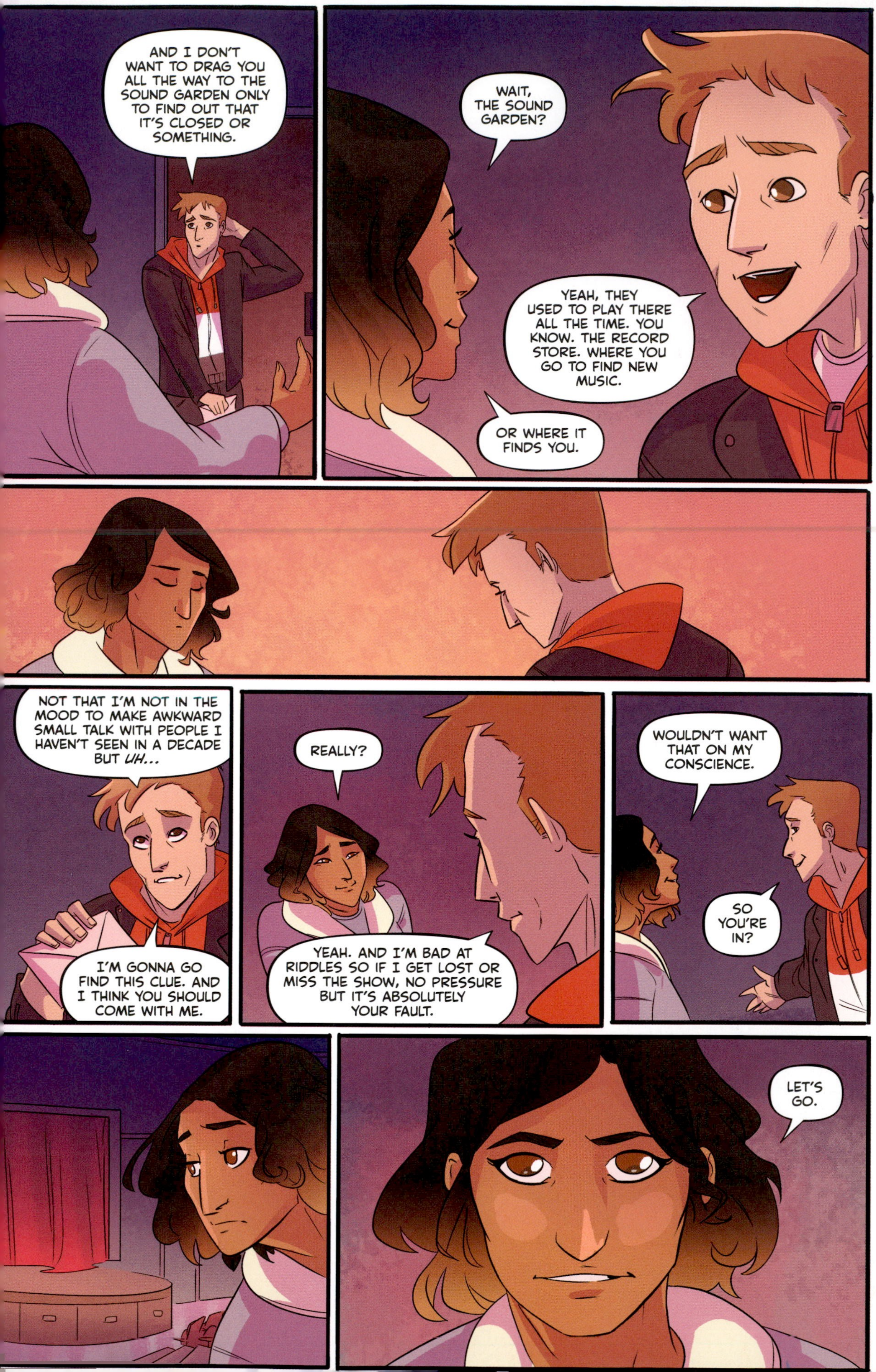
AND I DON'T WANT TO DRAG YOU ALL THE WAY TO THE SOUND GARDEN ONLY TO FIND OUT THAT IT'S CLOSED OR SOMETHING.
WAIT, THE SOUND GARDEN?
YEAH, THEY USED TO PLAY THERE ALL THE TIME. YOU KNOW. THE RECORD STORE. WHERE YOU GO TO FIND NEW MUSIC.
OR WHERE IT FINDS YOU.
NOT THAT I'M NOT IN THE MOOD TO MAKE AWKWARD SMALL TALK WITH PEOPLE I HAVEN'T SEEN IN A DECADE BUT *UH...*
I'M GONNA GO FIND THIS CLUE. AND I THINK YOU SHOULD COME WITH ME.
REALLY?
YEAH. AND I'M BAD AT RIDDLES SO IF I GET LOST OR MISS THE SHOW, NO PRESSURE BUT IT'S ABSOLUTELY YOUR FAULT.
WOULDN'T WANT THAT ON MY CONSCIENCE.
SO YOU'RE IN?
LET'S GO.

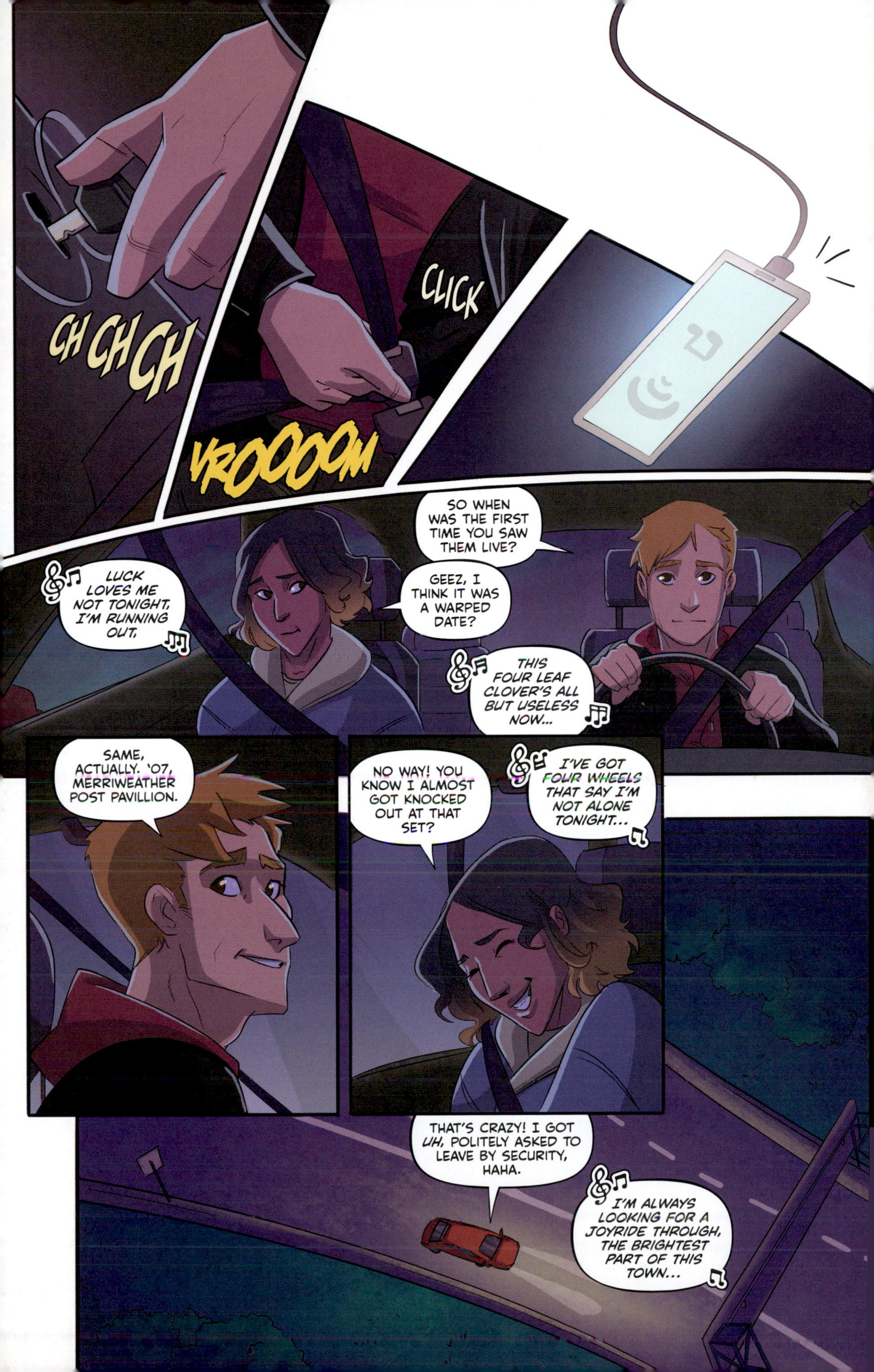
CH CH CH
CLICK
VROOOOM
SO WHEN WAS THE FIRST TIME YOU SAW THEM LIVE?
LUCK LOVES ME NOT TONIGHT, I'M RUNNING OUT,
GEEZ, I THINK IT WAS A WARPED DATE?
THIS FOUR LEAF CLOVER'S ALL BUT USELESS NOW...
SAME, ACTUALLY. '07, MERRIWEATHER POST PAVILLION.
NO WAY! YOU KNOW I ALMOST GOT KNOCKED OUT AT THAT SET?
I'VE GOT FOUR WHEELS THAT SAY I'M NOT ALONE TONIGHT...
THAT'S CRAZY! I GOT UH, POLITELY ASKED TO LEAVE BY SECURITY, HAHA.
I'M ALWAYS LOOKING FOR A JOYRIDE THROUGH, THE BRIGHTEST PART OF THIS TOWN...

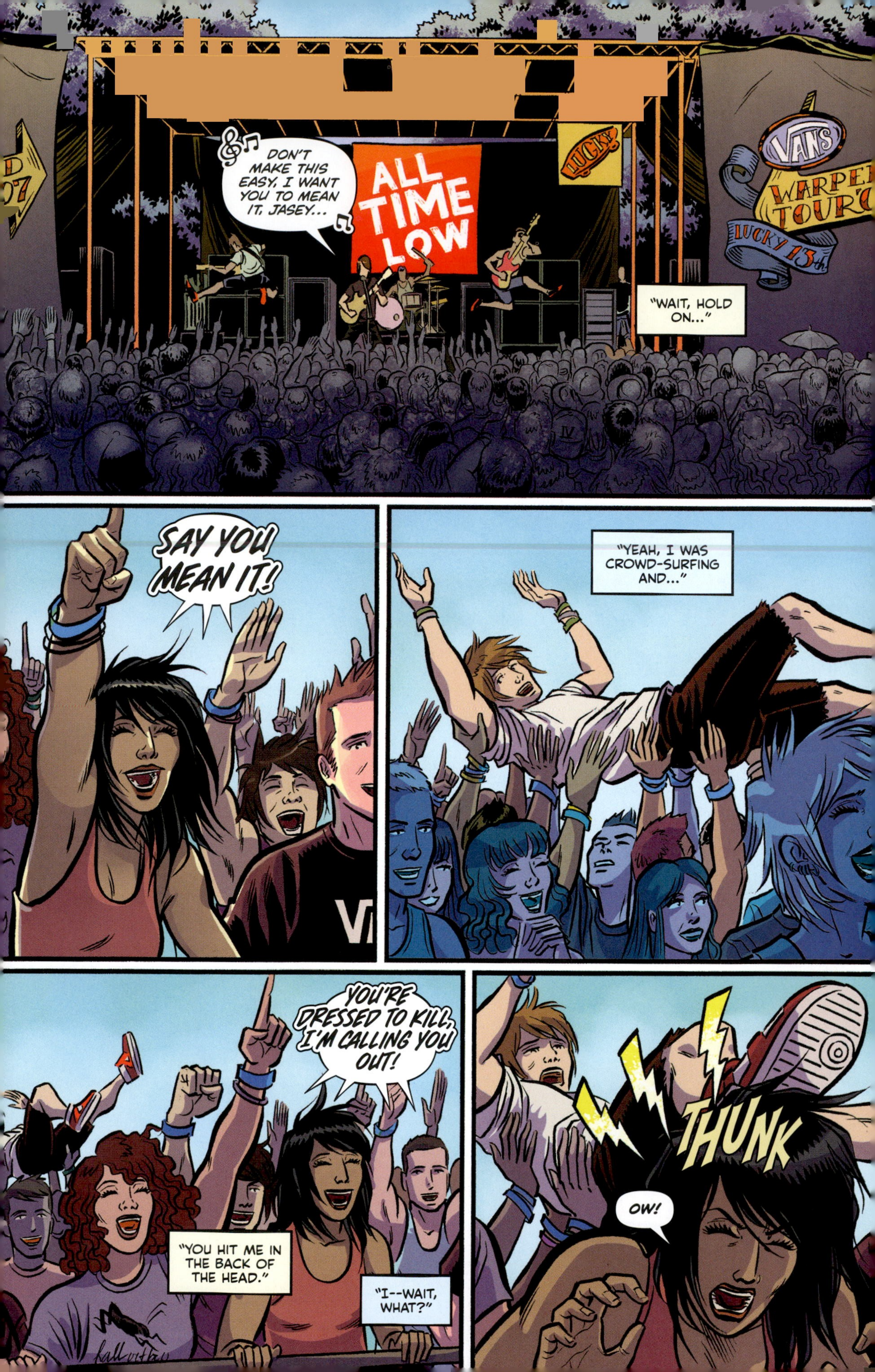

DON'T MAKE THIS EASY, I WANT YOU TO MEAN IT, JASEY...
ALL TIME LOW
LUCKY
VANS
"WAIT, HOLD ON..."
SAY YOU MEAN IT!
"YEAH, I WAS CROWD-SURFING AND..."
YOU'RE DRESSED TO KILL, I'M CALLING YOU OUT!
"YOU HIT ME IN THE BACK OF THE HEAD."
"I--WAIT, WHAT?"
THUNK
OW!

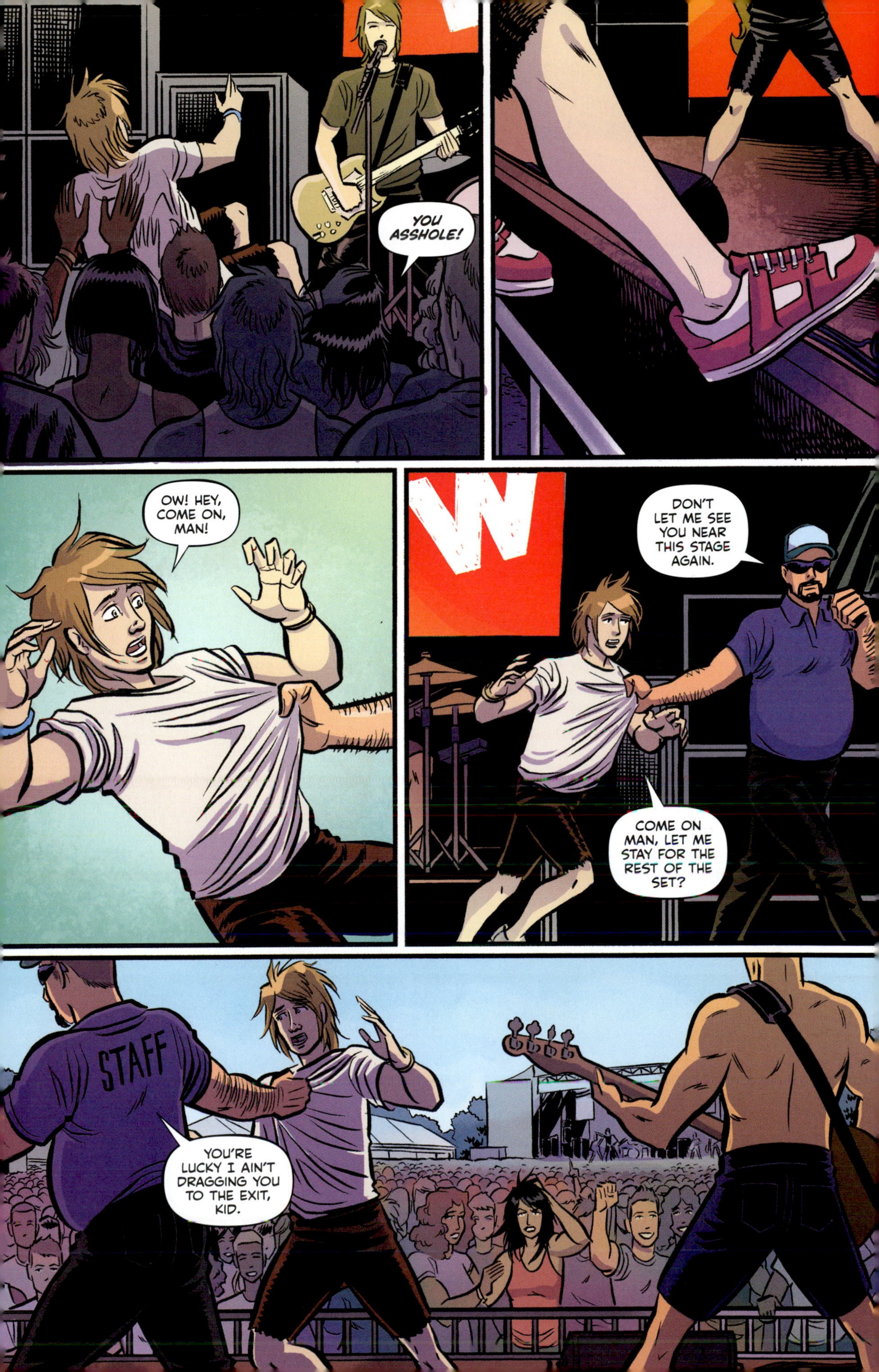
YOU ASSHOLE!
OW! HEY, COME ON, MAN!
W
DON'T LET ME SEE YOU NEAR THIS STAGE AGAIN.
COME ON MAN, LET ME STAY FOR THE REST OF THE SET?
STAFF
YOU'RE LUCKY I AIN'T DRAGGING YOU TO THE EXIT, KID.

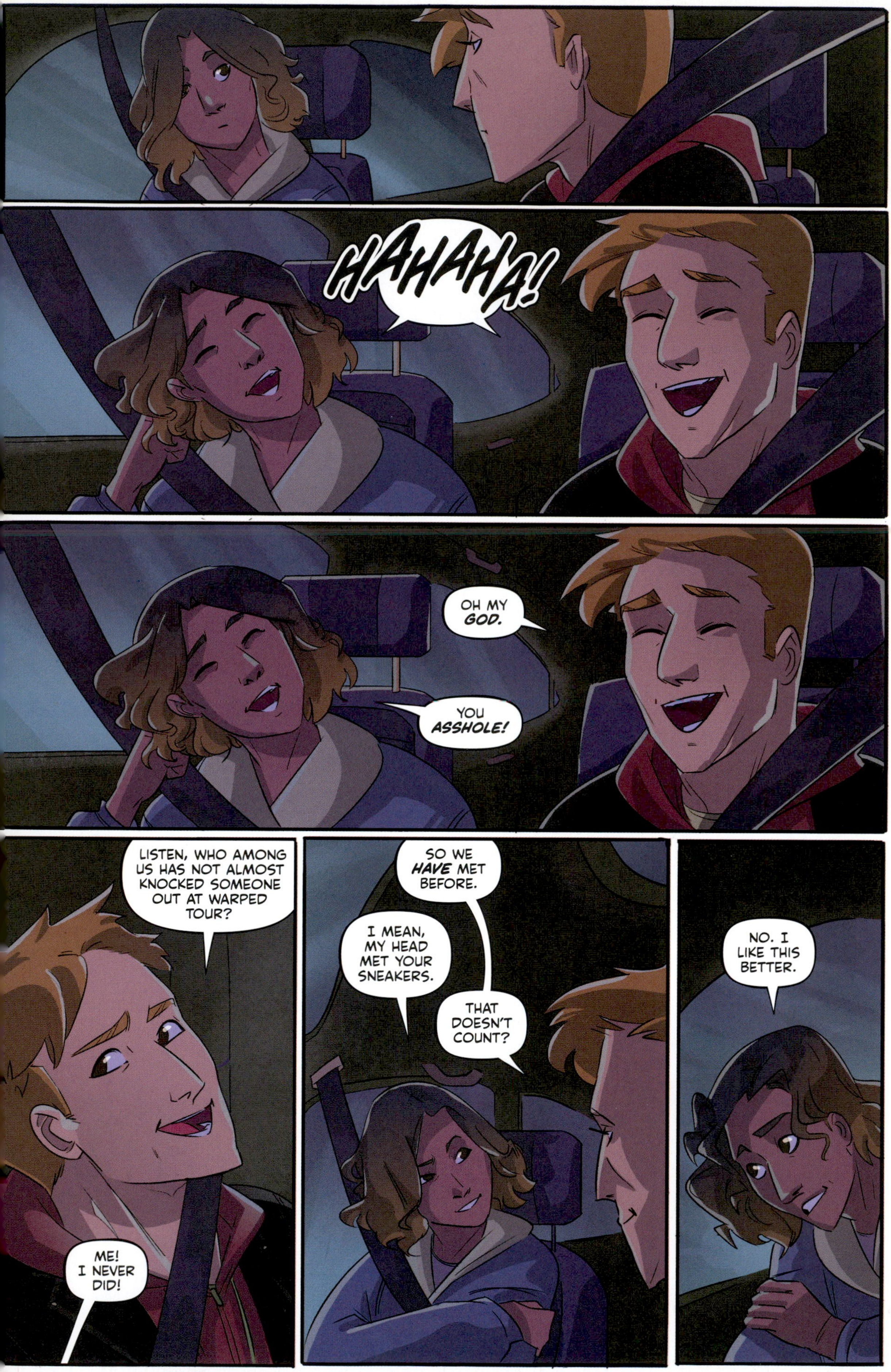
HAHAHA!
OH MY GOD.
YOU ASSHOLE!
LISTEN, WHO AMONG US HAS NOT ALMOST KNOCKED SOMEONE OUT AT WARPED TOUR?
ME! I NEVER DID!
SO WE HAVE MET BEFORE.
I MEAN, MY HEAD MET YOUR SNEAKERS.
THAT DOESN'T COUNT?
NO. I LIKE THIS BETTER.

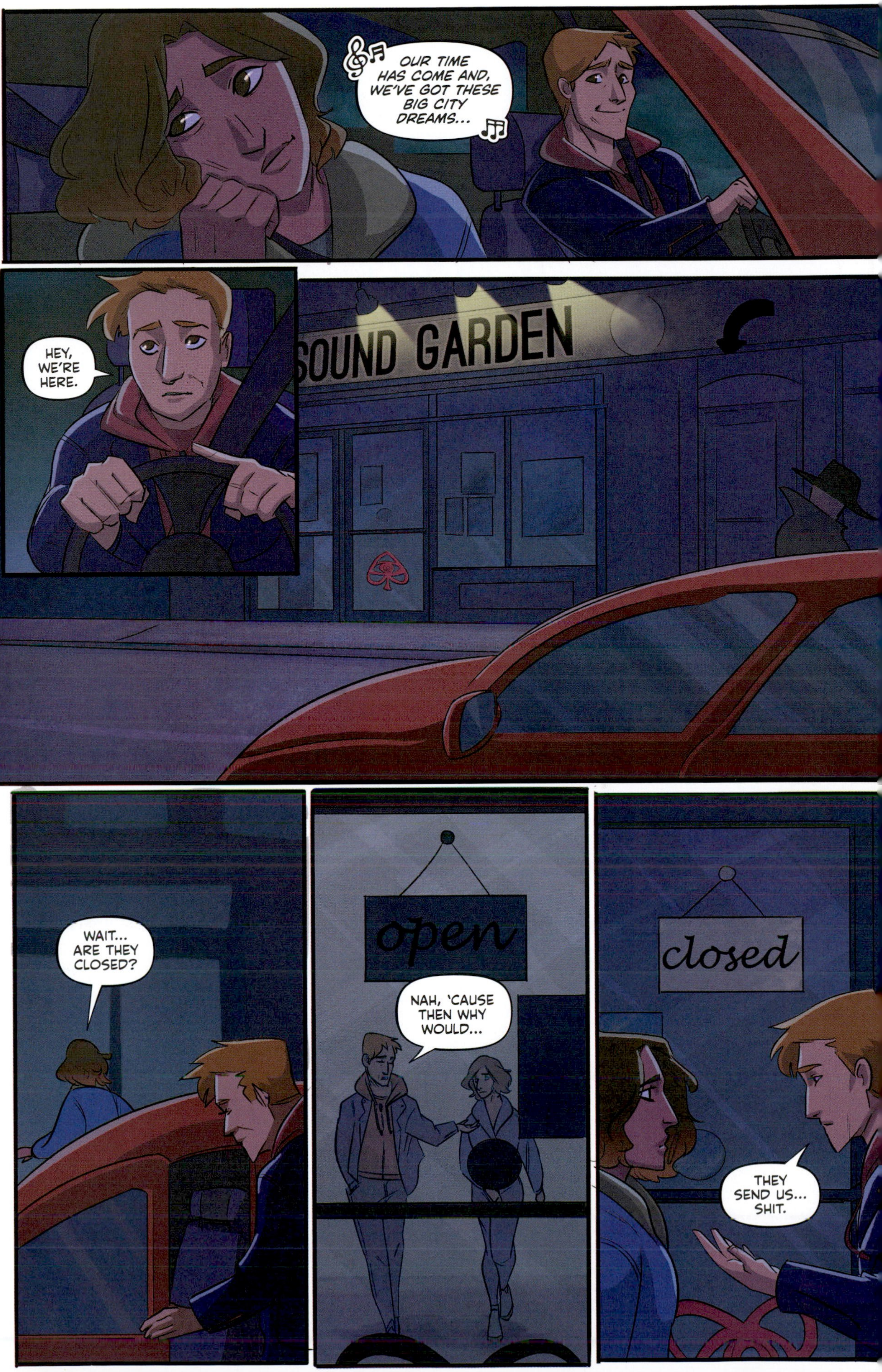
OUR TIME HAS COME AND, WE'VE GOT THESE BIG CITY DREAMS...
HEY, WE'RE HERE.
SOUND GARDEN
WAIT... ARE THEY CLOSED?
open
NAH, 'CAUSE THEN WHY WOULD...
closed
THEY SEND US... SHIT.

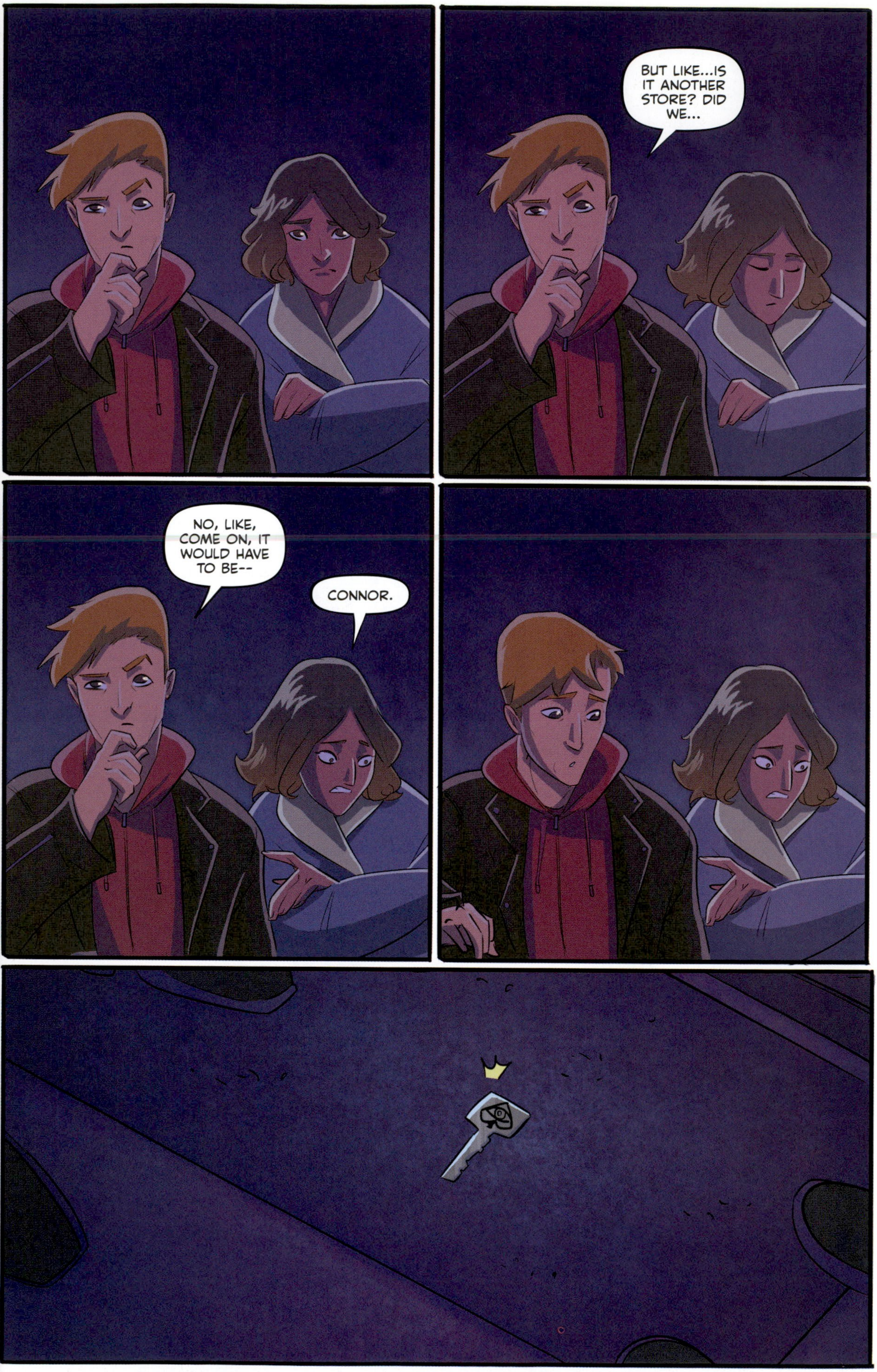
BUT LIKE...IS IT ANOTHER STORE? DID WE...
NO, LIKE, COME ON, IT WOULD HAVE TO BE--
CONNOR.

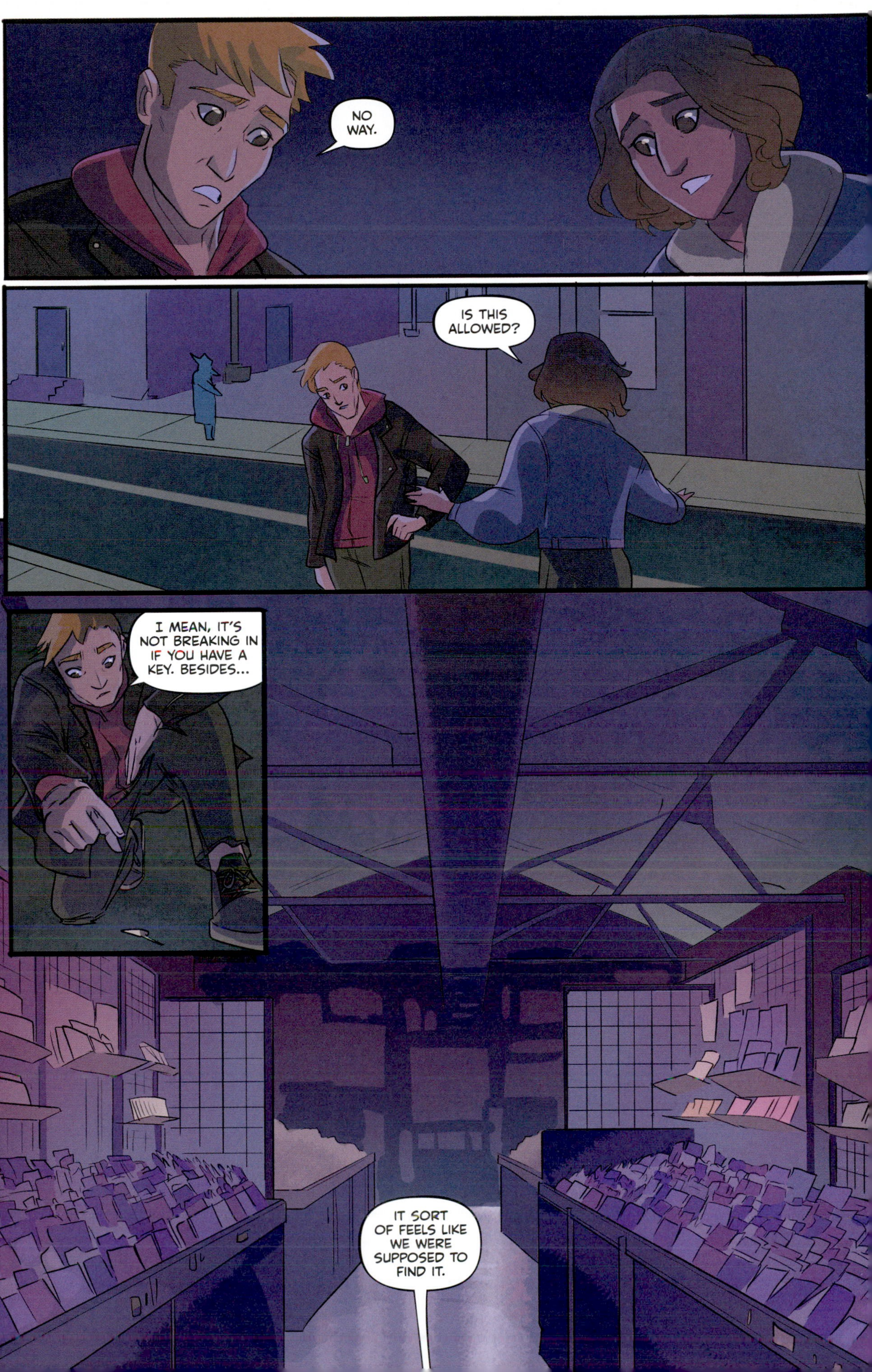
NO WAY.
IS THIS ALLOWED?
I MEAN, IT'S NOT BREAKING IN IF YOU HAVE A KEY. BESIDES...
IT SORT OF FEELS LIKE WE WERE SUPPOSED TO FIND IT.

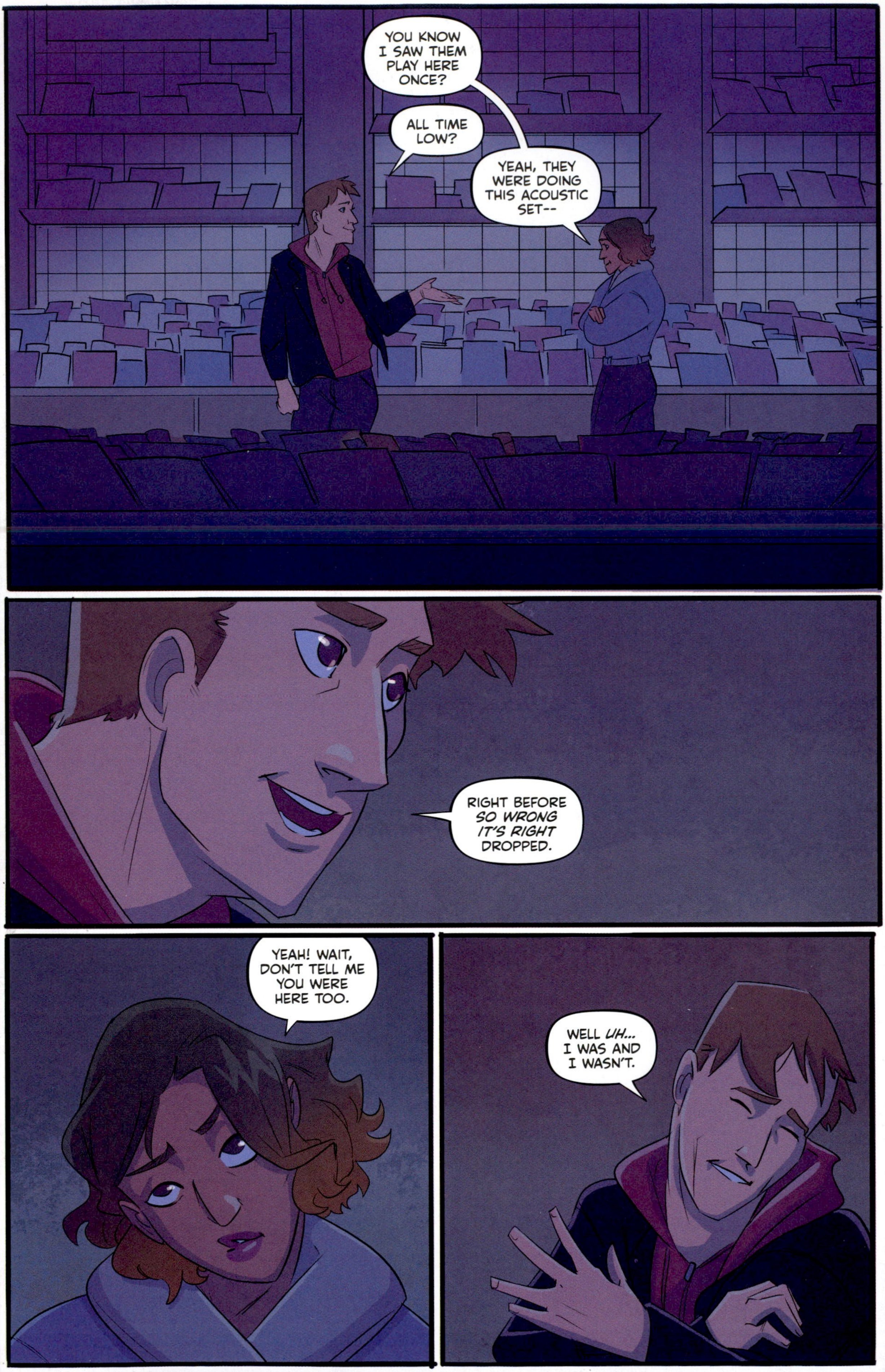
YOU KNOW I SAW THEM PLAY HERE ONCE?
ALL TIME LOW?
YEAH, THEY WERE DOING THIS ACOUSTIC SET--
RIGHT BEFORE *SO WRONG IT'S RIGHT* DROPPED.
YEAH! WAIT, DON'T TELL ME YOU WERE HERE TOO.
WELL *UH*... I WAS AND I WASN'T.

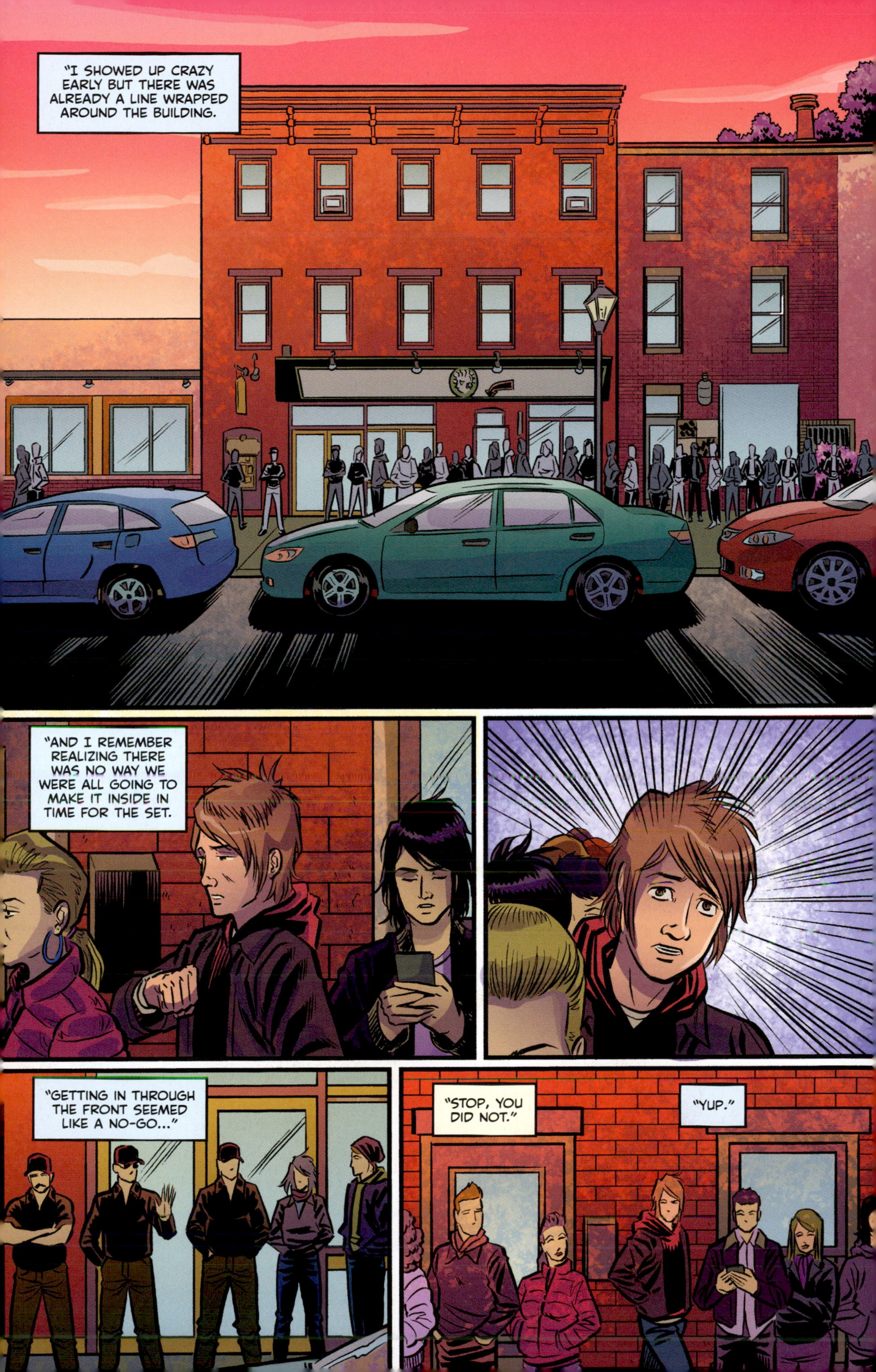
"I SHOWED UP CRAZY EARLY BUT THERE WAS ALREADY A LINE WRAPPED AROUND THE BUILDING.
"AND I REMEMBER REALIZING THERE WAS NO WAY WE WERE ALL GOING TO MAKE IT INSIDE IN TIME FOR THE SET.
"GETTING IN THROUGH THE FRONT SEEMED LIKE A NO-GO..."
"STOP, YOU DID NOT."
"YUP."

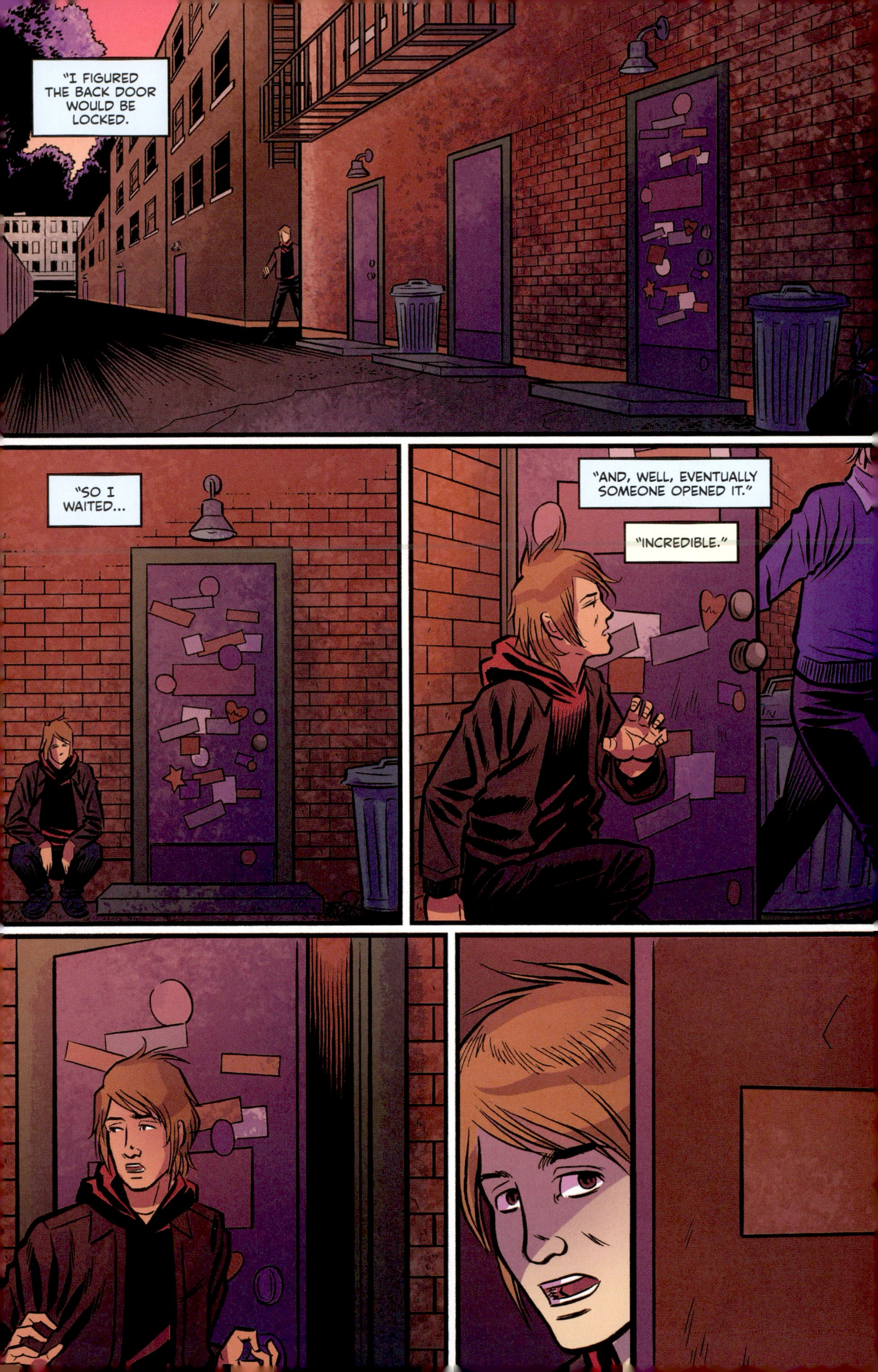
"I FIGURED THE BACK DOOR WOULD BE LOCKED.
"SO I WAITED...
"AND, WELL, EVENTUALLY SOMEONE OPENED IT."
"INCREDIBLE."

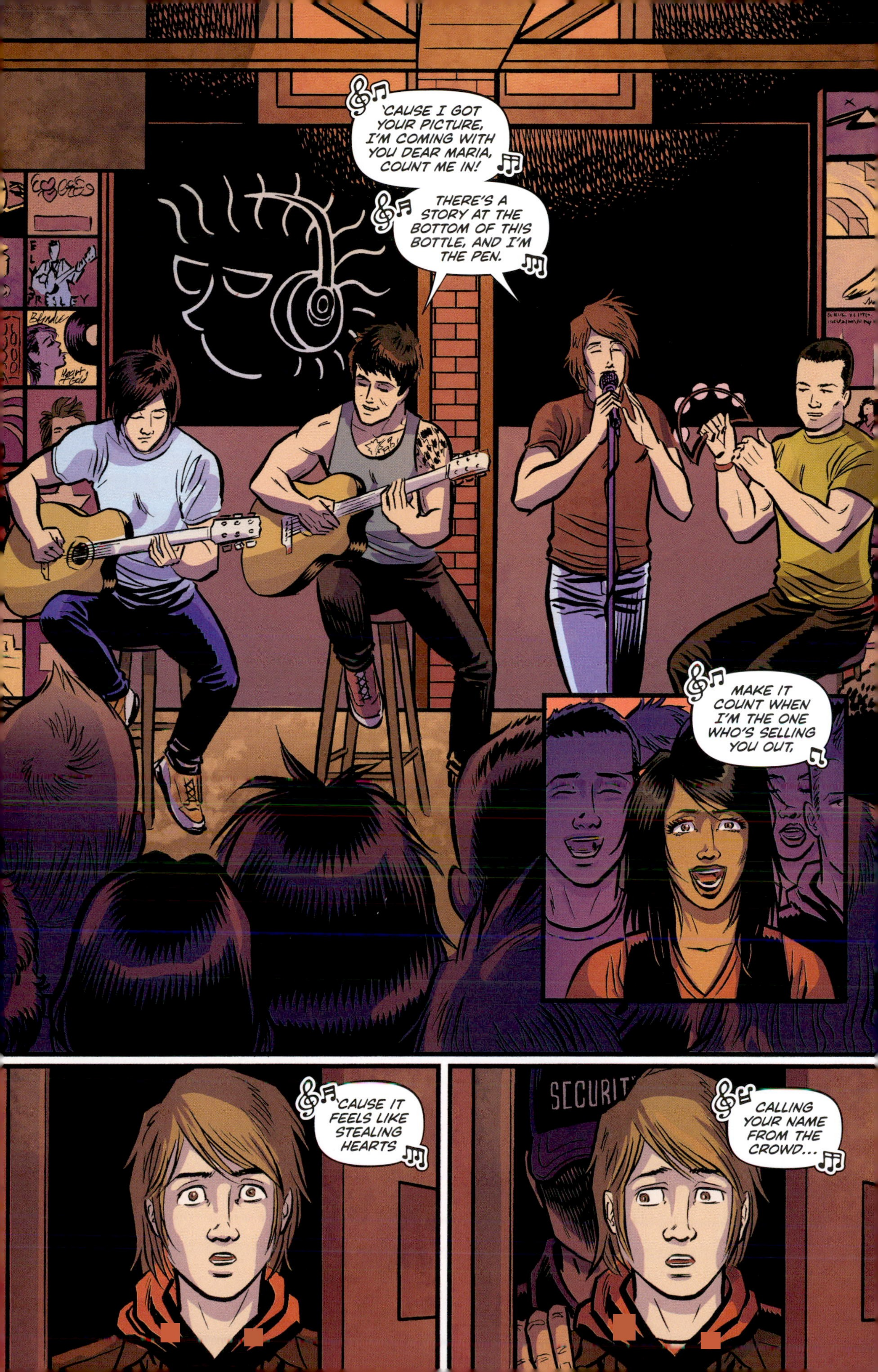
'CAUSE I GOT YOUR PICTURE, I'M COMING WITH YOU DEAR MARIA, COUNT ME IN!
THERE'S A STORY AT THE BOTTOM OF THIS BOTTLE, AND I'M THE PEN.
MAKE IT COUNT WHEN I'M THE ONE WHO'S SELLING YOU OUT,
'CAUSE IT FEELS LIKE STEALING HEARTS
CALLING YOUR NAME FROM THE CROWD...

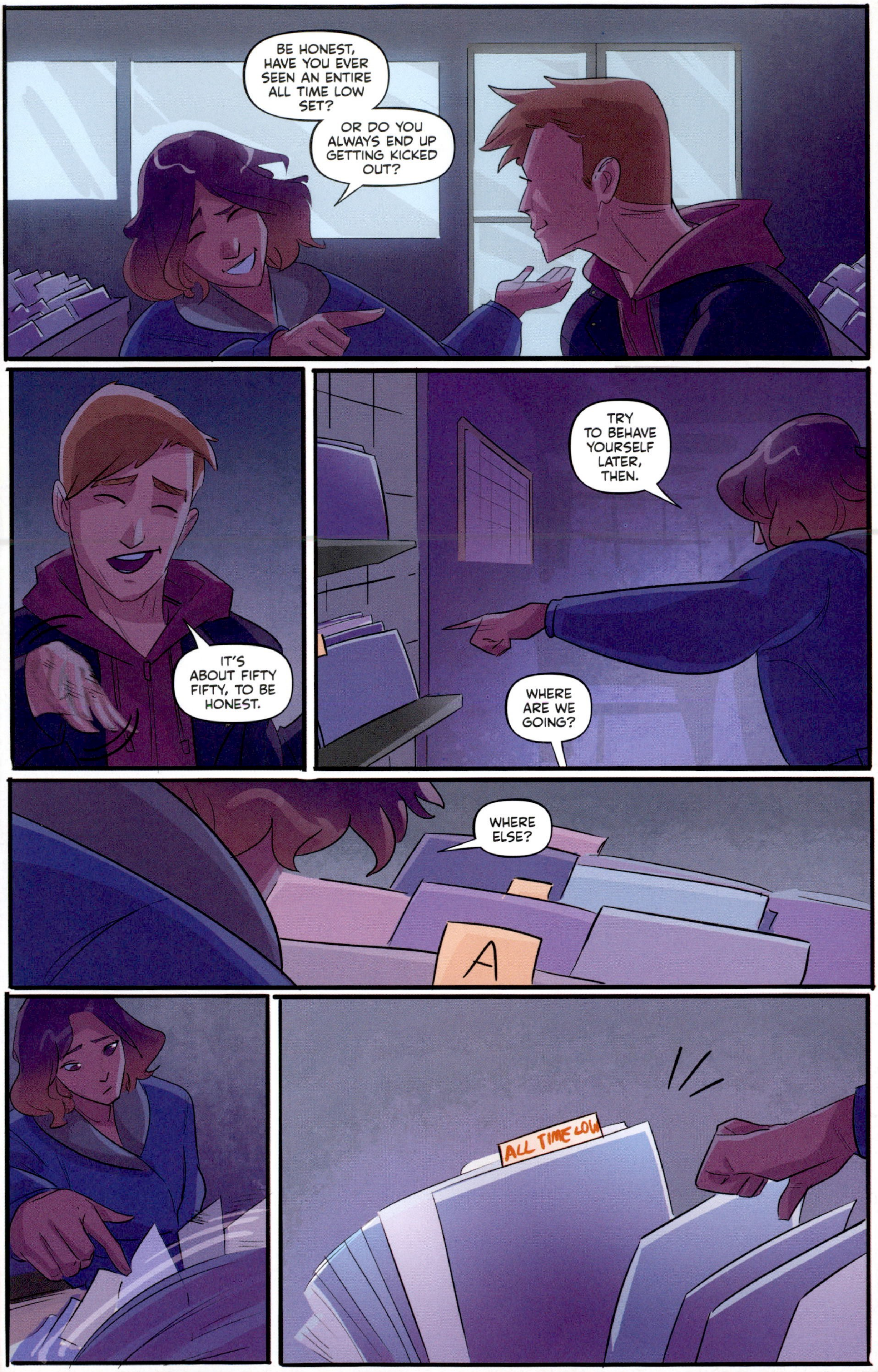
BE HONEST, HAVE YOU EVER SEEN AN ENTIRE ALL TIME LOW SET?
OR DO YOU ALWAYS END UP GETTING KICKED OUT?
IT'S ABOUT FIFTY FIFTY, TO BE HONEST.
TRY TO BEHAVE YOURSELF LATER, THEN.
WHERE ARE WE GOING?
WHERE ELSE?
A
ALL TIME LOW

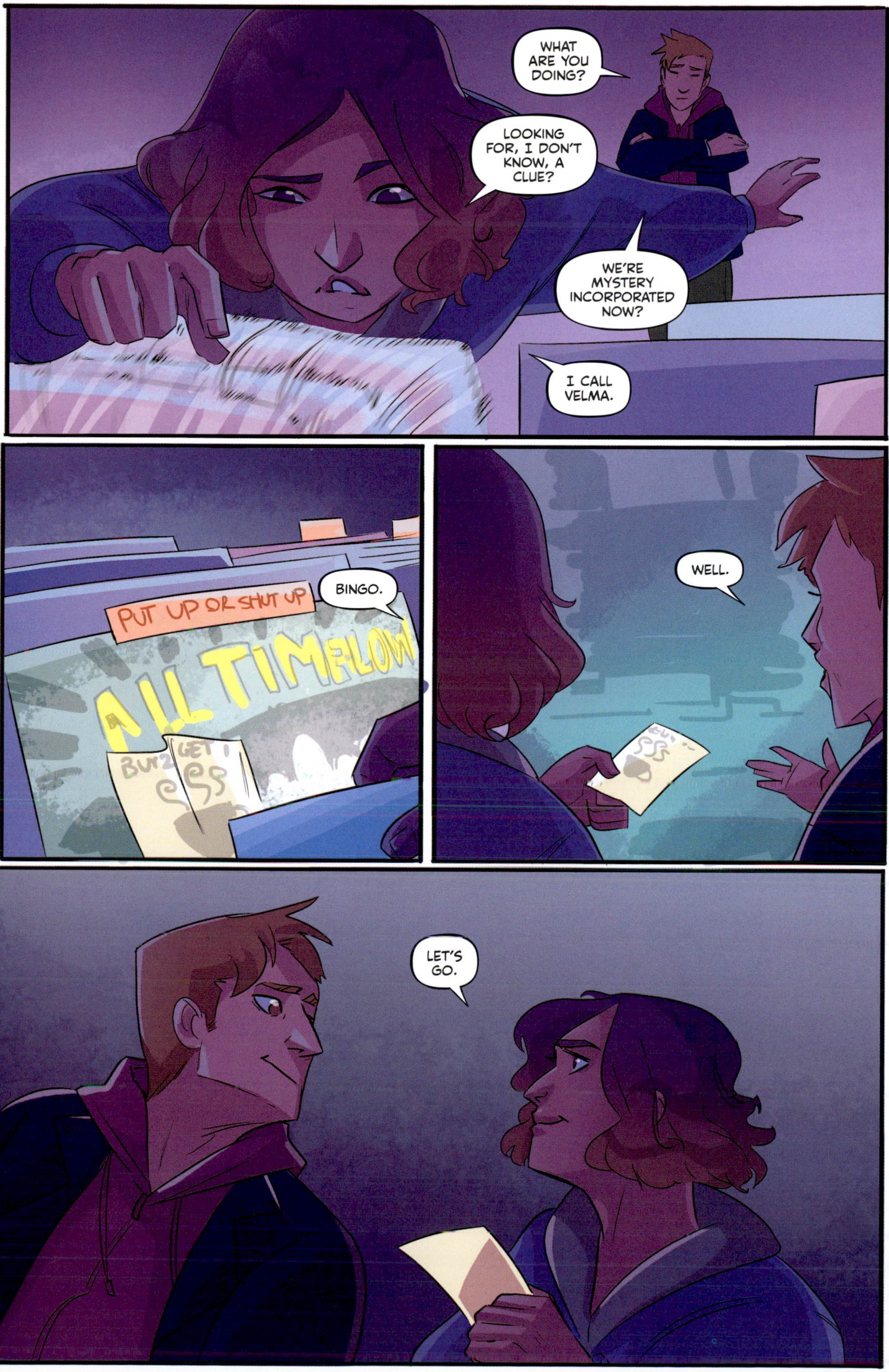
WHAT ARE YOU DOING?
LOOKING FOR, I DON'T KNOW, A CLUE?
WE'RE MYSTERY INCORPORATED NOW?
I CALL VELMA.
PUT UP OR SHUT UP
ALL TIME LOW
BINGO.
WELL.
LET'S GO.

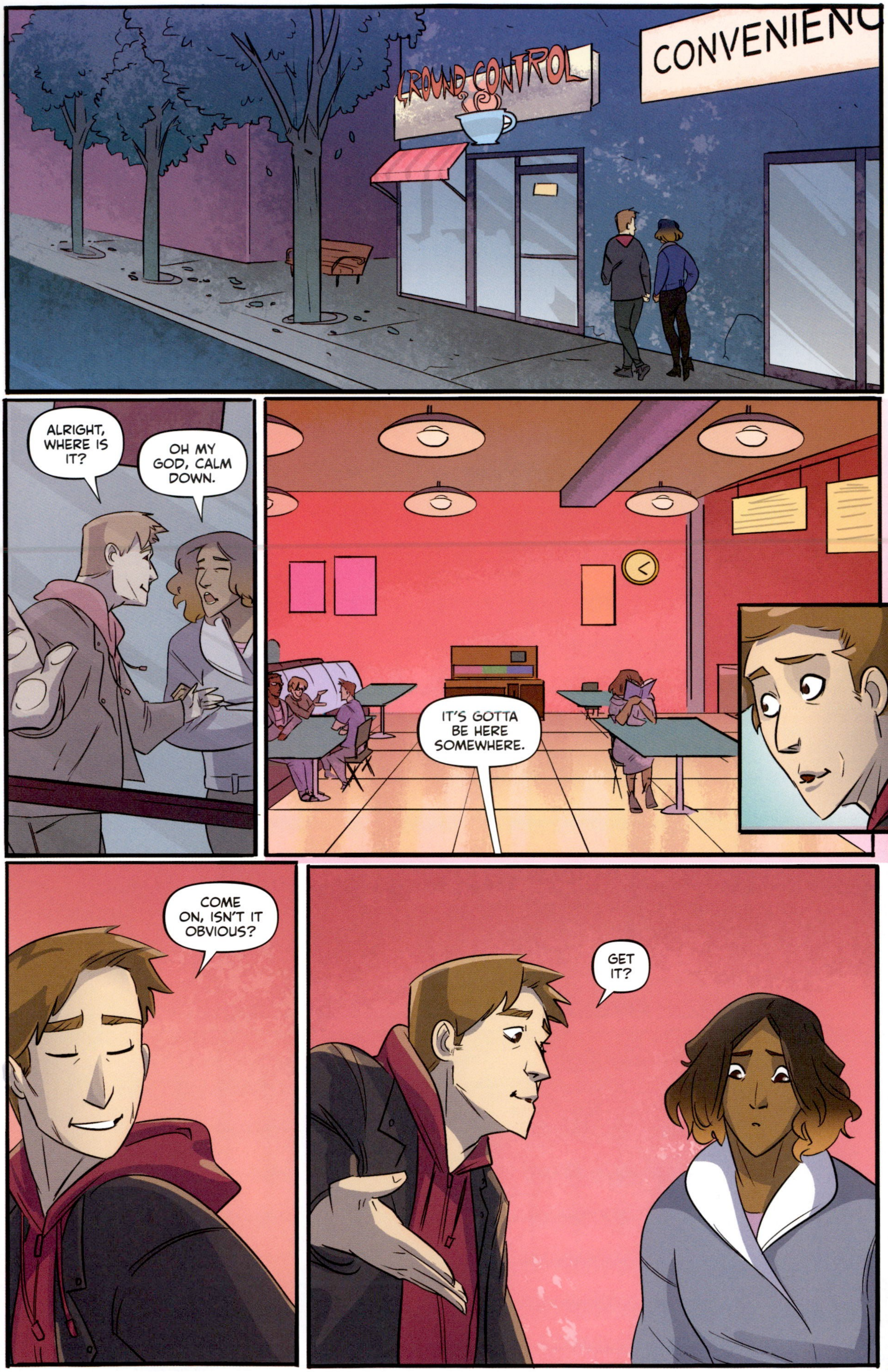

CROUND CONTROL
CONVENIENC
ALRIGHT, WHERE IS IT?
OH MY GOD, CALM DOWN.
IT'S GOTTA BE HERE SOMEWHERE.
COME ON, ISN'T IT OBVIOUS?
GET IT?

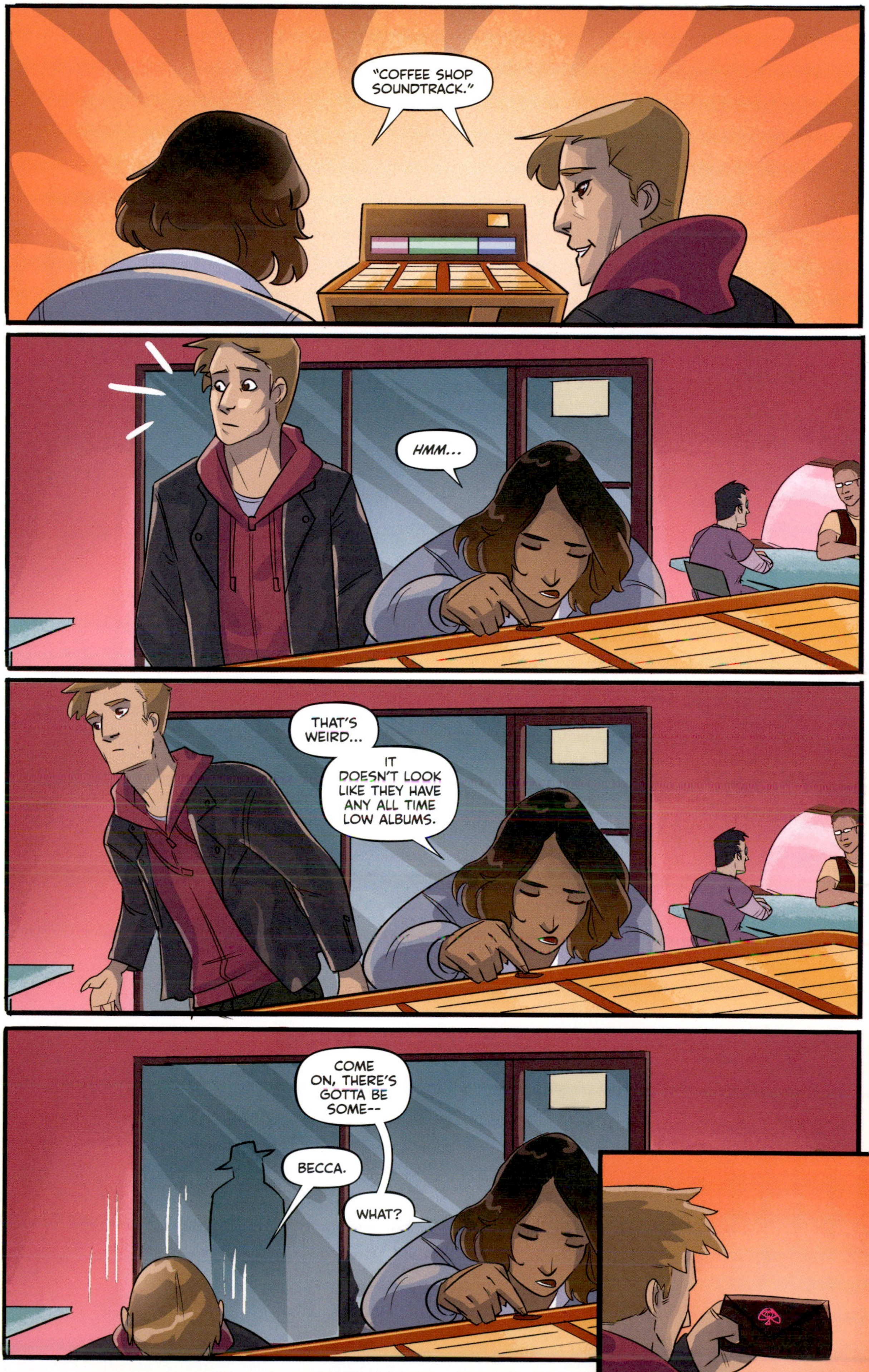
"COFFEE SHOP SOUNDTRACK."
HMM...
THAT'S WEIRD...
IT DOESN'T LOOK LIKE THEY HAVE ANY ALL TIME LOW ALBUMS.
COME ON, THERE'S GOTTA BE SOME--
BECCA.
WHAT?

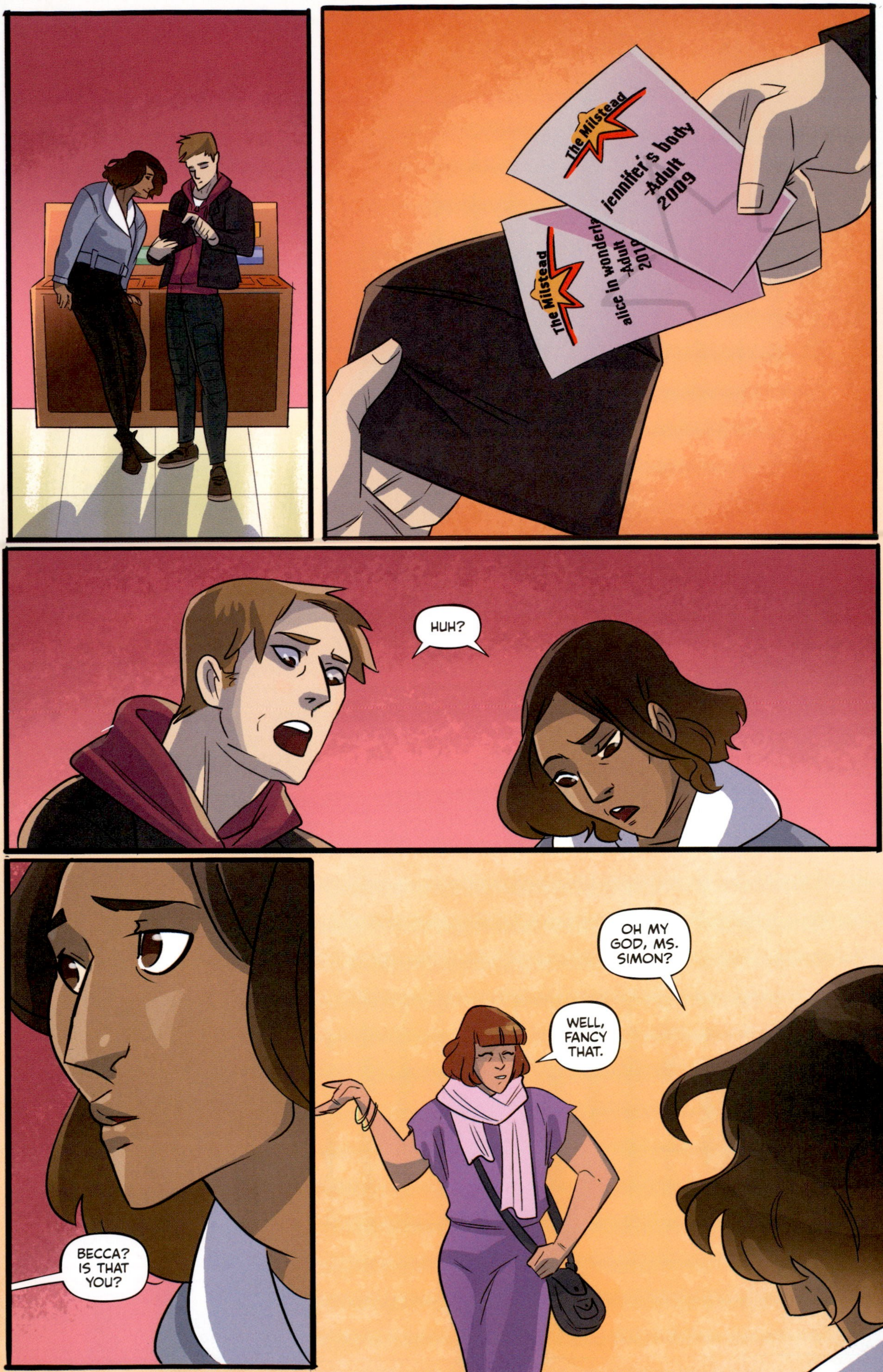

The Milstead
jennifer's body
-Adult
2009
The Milstead
alice in wonderla
-Adult
201
HUH?
BECCA? IS THAT YOU?
OH MY GOD, MS. SIMON?
WELL, FANCY THAT.

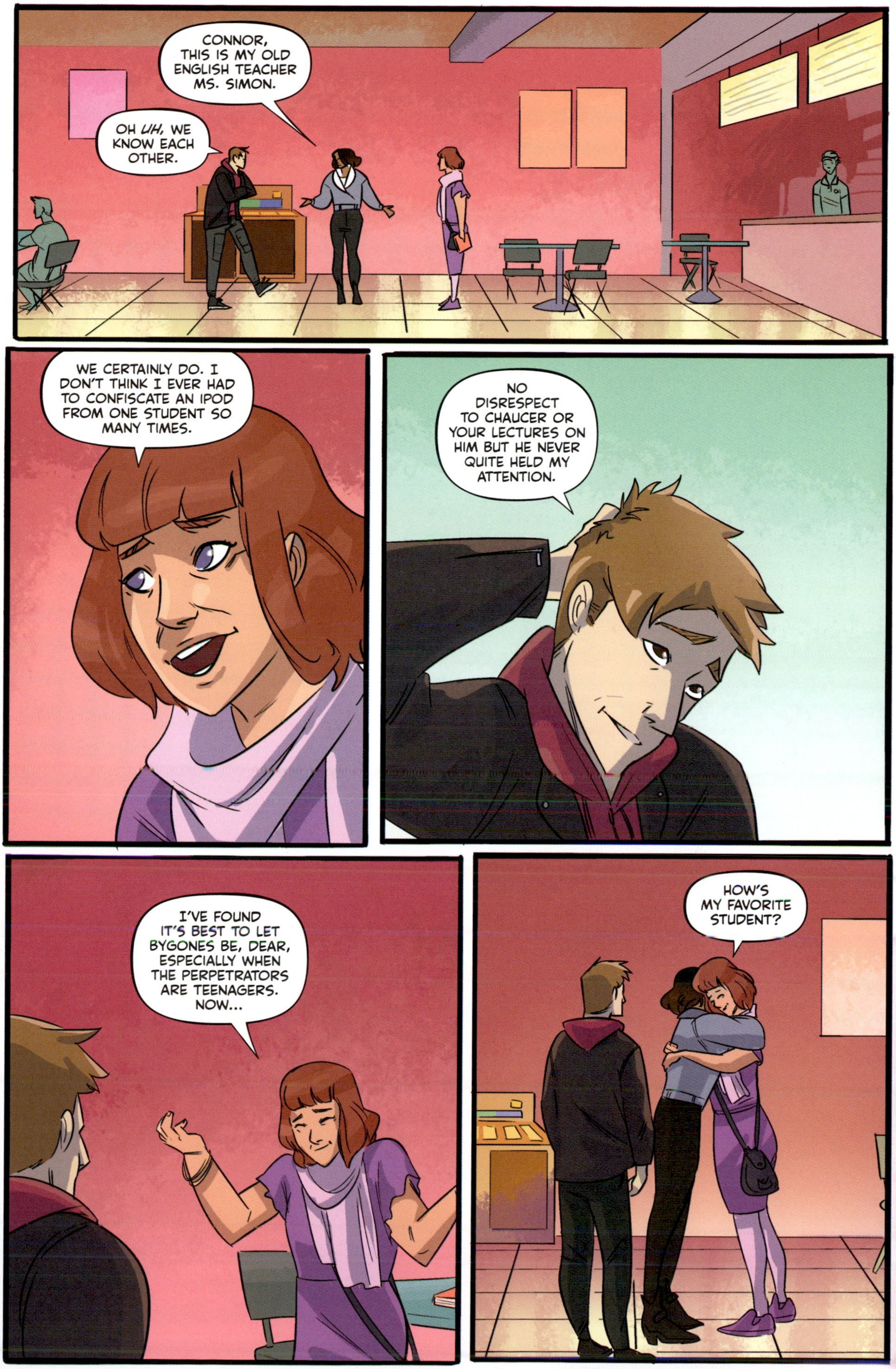
CONNOR, THIS IS MY OLD ENGLISH TEACHER MS. SIMON.
OH *UH*, WE KNOW EACH OTHER.
WE CERTAINLY DO. I DON'T THINK I EVER HAD TO CONFISCATE AN IPOD FROM ONE STUDENT SO MANY TIMES.
NO DISRESPECT TO CHAUCER OR YOUR LECTURES ON HIM BUT HE NEVER QUITE HELD MY ATTENTION.
I'VE FOUND IT'S BEST TO LET BYGONES BE, DEAR, ESPECIALLY WHEN THE PERPETRATORS ARE TEENAGERS. NOW...
HOW'S MY FAVORITE STUDENT?

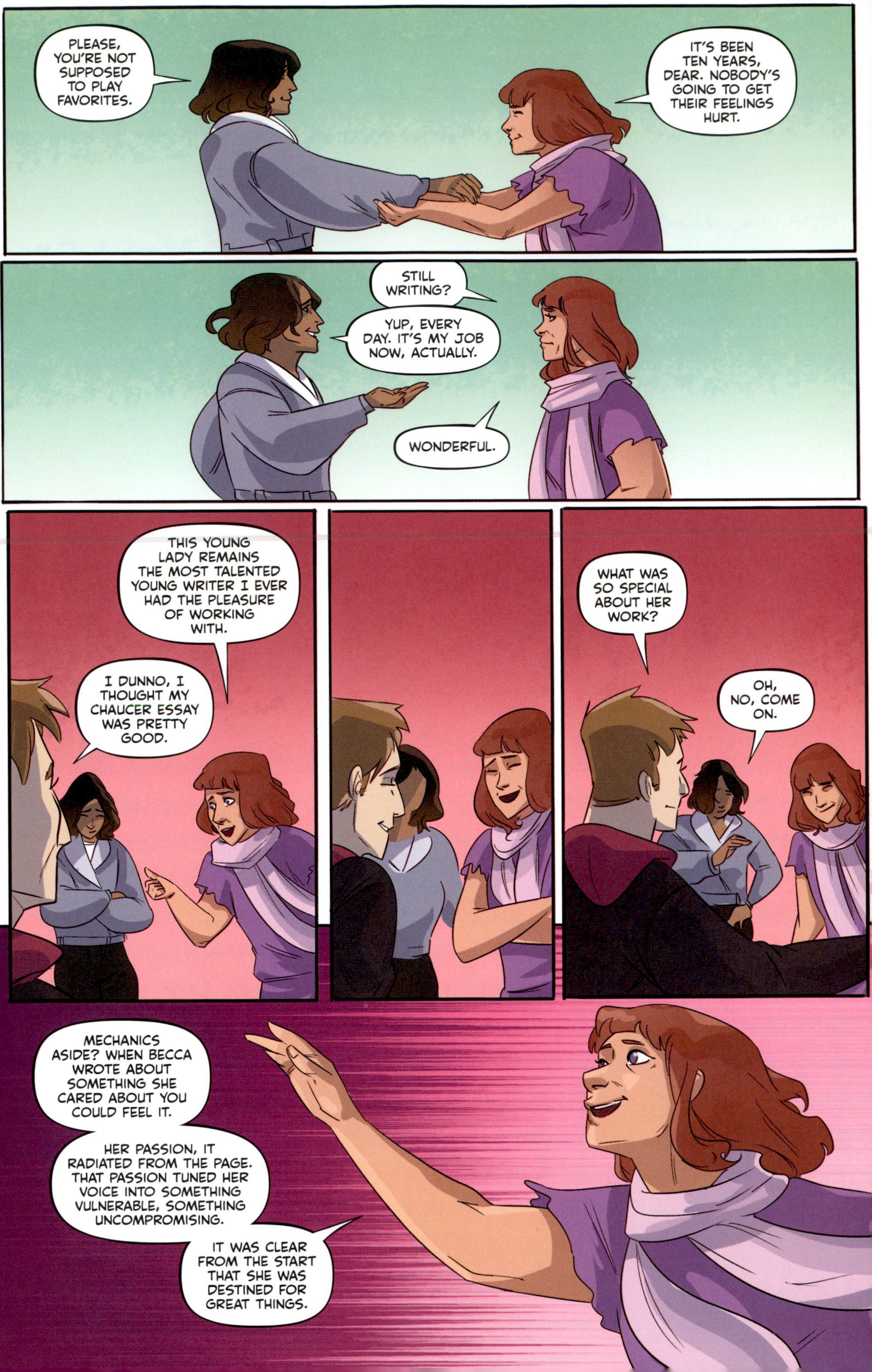
PLEASE, YOU'RE NOT SUPPOSED TO PLAY FAVORITES.
IT'S BEEN TEN YEARS, DEAR. NOBODY'S GOING TO GET THEIR FEELINGS HURT.
STILL WRITING?
YUP, EVERY DAY. IT'S MY JOB NOW, ACTUALLY.
WONDERFUL.
THIS YOUNG LADY REMAINS THE MOST TALENTED YOUNG WRITER I EVER HAD THE PLEASURE OF WORKING WITH.
I DUNNO, I THOUGHT MY CHAUCER ESSAY WAS PRETTY GOOD.
WHAT WAS SO SPECIAL ABOUT HER WORK?
OH, NO, COME ON.
MECHANICS ASIDE? WHEN BECCA WROTE ABOUT SOMETHING SHE CARED ABOUT YOU COULD FEEL IT.
HER PASSION, IT RADIATED FROM THE PAGE. THAT PASSION TUNED HER VOICE INTO SOMETHING VULNERABLE, SOMETHING UNCOMPROMISING.
IT WAS CLEAR FROM THE START THAT SHE WAS DESTINED FOR GREAT THINGS.

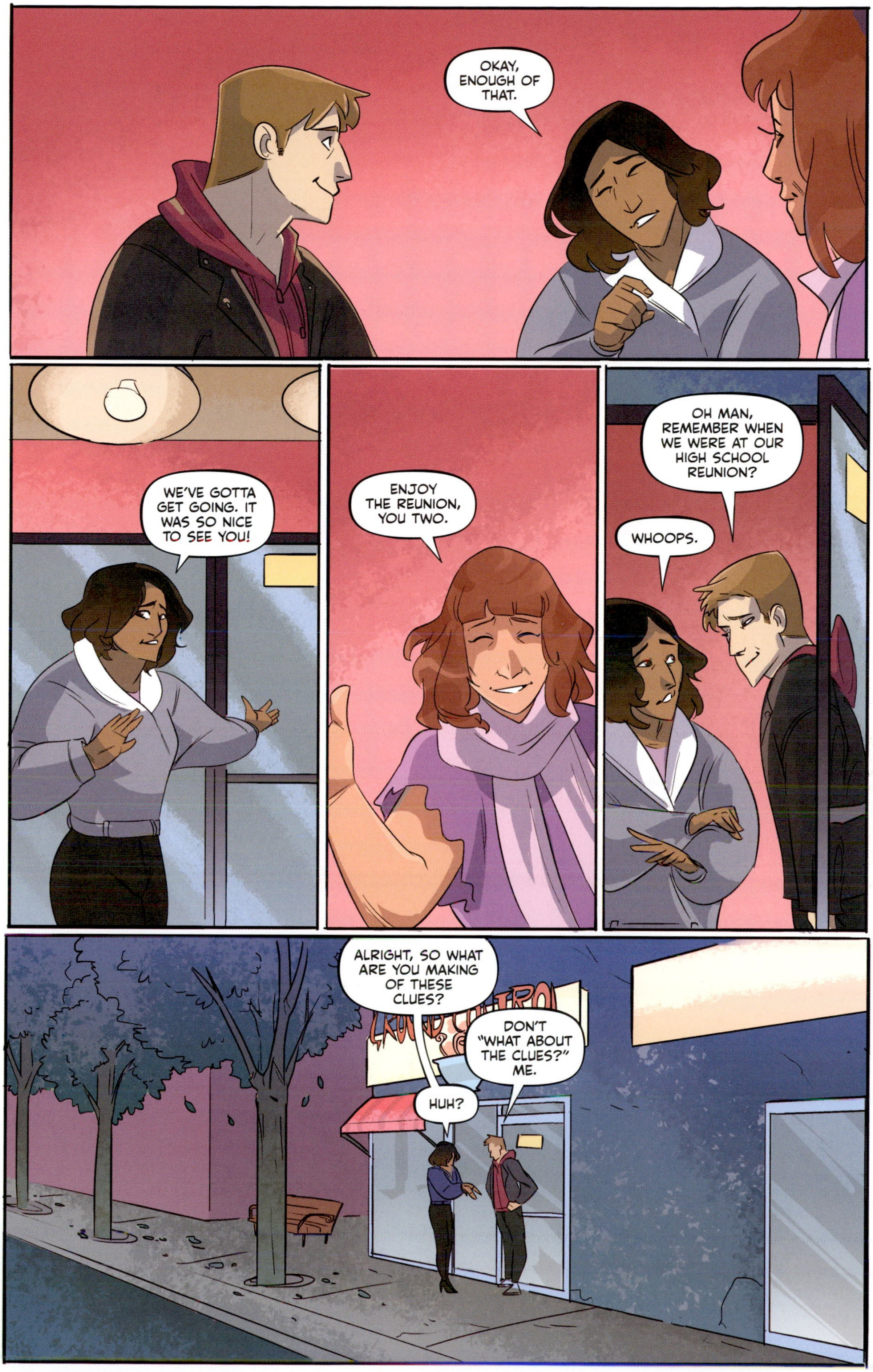
OKAY, ENOUGH OF THAT.
WE'VE GOTTA GET GOING. IT WAS SO NICE TO SEE YOU!
ENJOY THE REUNION, YOU TWO.
OH MAN, REMEMBER WHEN WE WERE AT OUR HIGH SCHOOL REUNION?
WHOOPS.
ALRIGHT, SO WHAT ARE YOU MAKING OF THESE CLUES?
HUH?
DON'T "WHAT ABOUT THE CLUES?" ME.

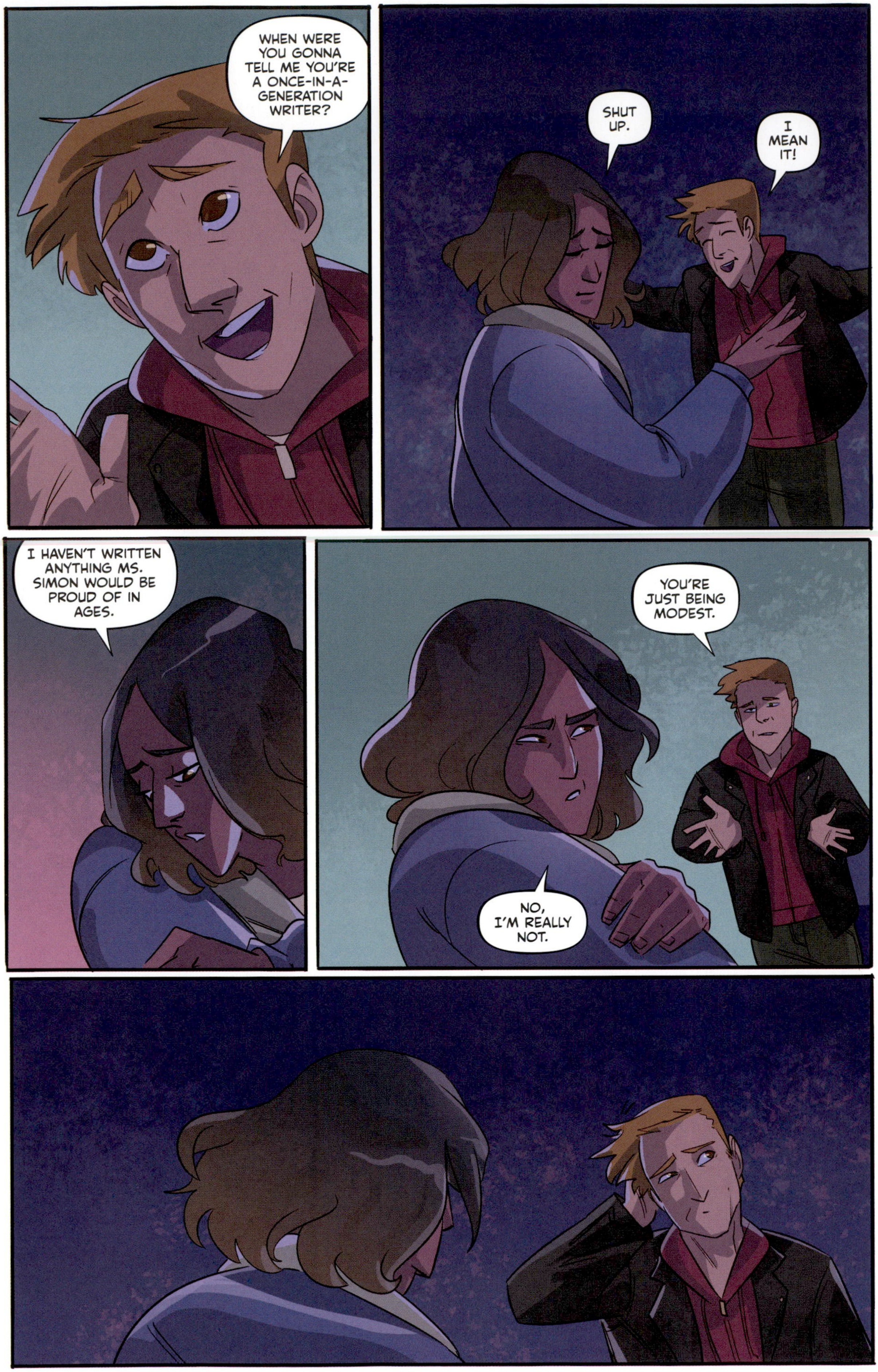
WHEN WERE YOU GONNA TELL ME YOU'RE A ONCE-IN-A-GENERATION WRITER?
SHUT UP.
I MEAN IT!
I HAVEN'T WRITTEN ANYTHING MS. SIMON WOULD BE PROUD OF IN AGES.
YOU'RE JUST BEING MODEST.
NO, I'M REALLY NOT.

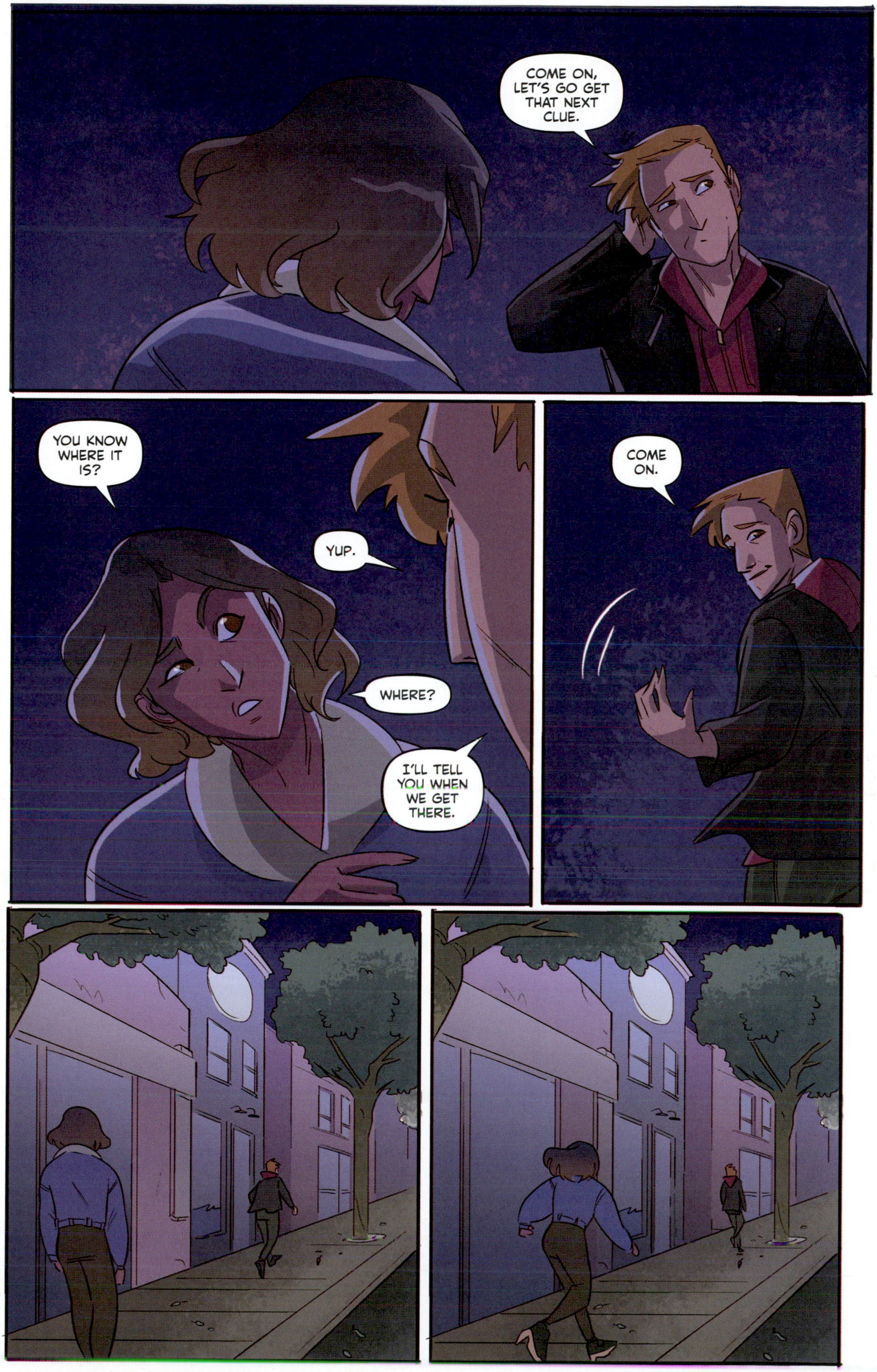
COME ON, LET'S GO GET THAT NEXT CLUE.
YOU KNOW WHERE IT IS?
YUP.
WHERE?
I'LL TELL YOU WHEN WE GET THERE.
COME ON.

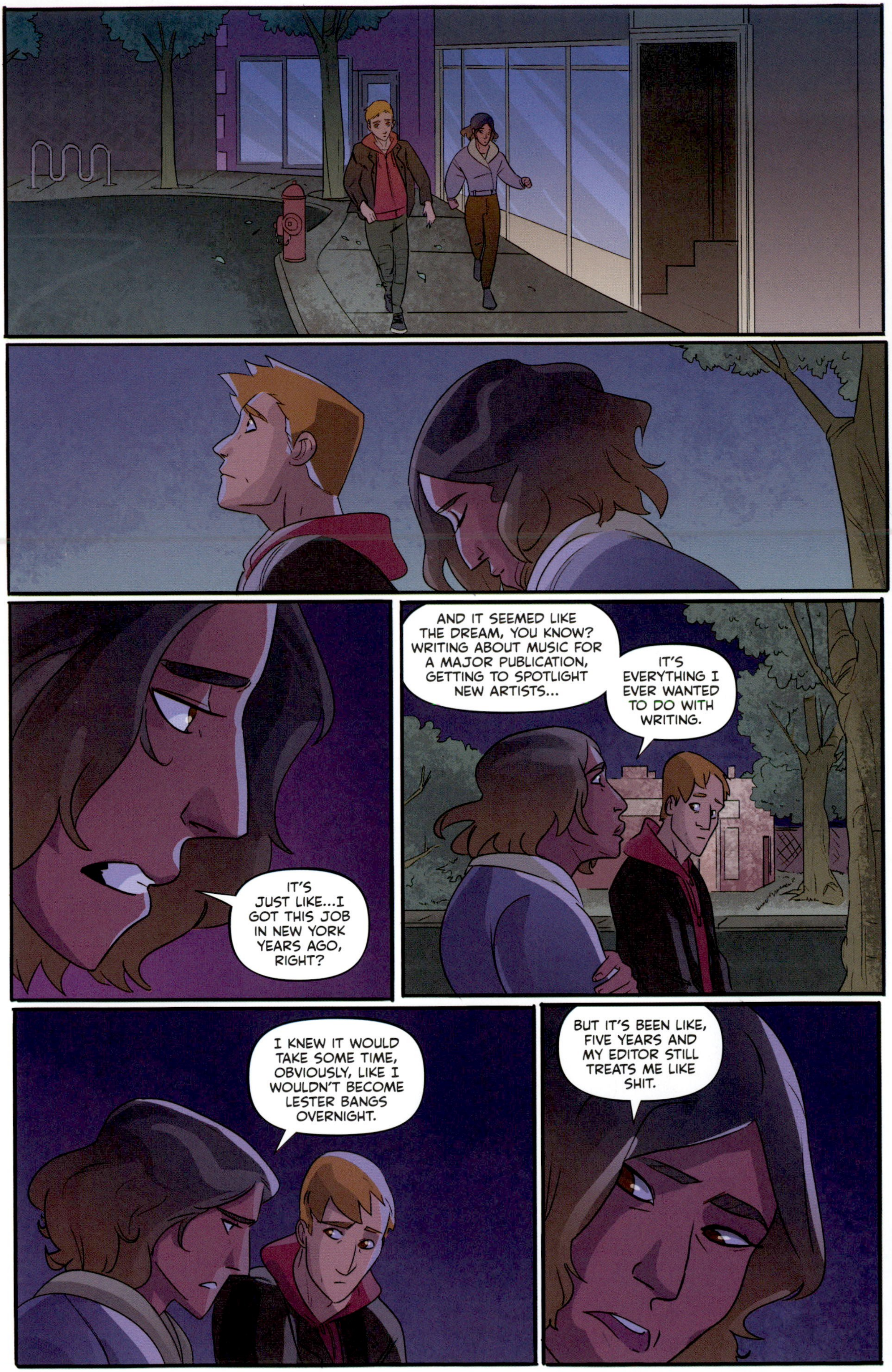
IT'S JUST LIKE...I GOT THIS JOB IN NEW YORK YEARS AGO, RIGHT?
AND IT SEEMED LIKE THE DREAM, YOU KNOW? WRITING ABOUT MUSIC FOR A MAJOR PUBLICATION, GETTING TO SPOTLIGHT NEW ARTISTS...
IT'S EVERYTHING I EVER WANTED TO DO WITH WRITING.
I KNEW IT WOULD TAKE SOME TIME, OBVIOUSLY, LIKE I WOULDN'T BECOME LESTER BANGS OVERNIGHT.
BUT IT'S BEEN LIKE, FIVE YEARS AND MY EDITOR STILL TREATS ME LIKE SHIT.

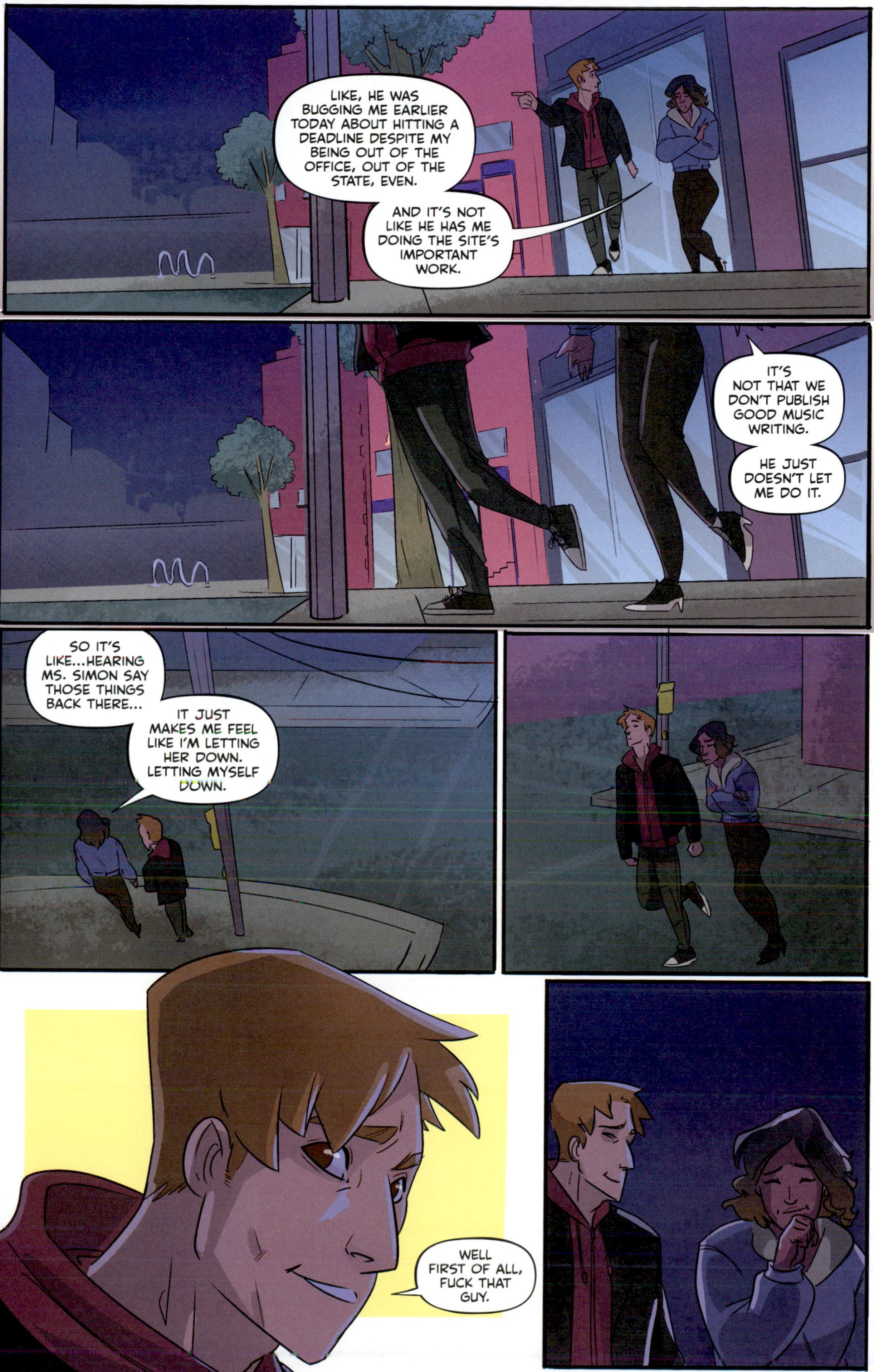
LIKE, HE WAS BUGGING ME EARLIER TODAY ABOUT HITTING A DEADLINE DESPITE MY BEING OUT OF THE OFFICE, OUT OF THE STATE, EVEN.
AND IT'S NOT LIKE HE HAS ME DOING THE SITE'S IMPORTANT WORK.
IT'S NOT THAT WE DON'T PUBLISH GOOD MUSIC WRITING.
HE JUST DOESN'T LET ME DO IT.
SO IT'S LIKE...HEARING MS. SIMON SAY THOSE THINGS BACK THERE...
IT JUST MAKES ME FEEL LIKE I'M LETTING HER DOWN. LETTING MYSELF DOWN.
WELL FIRST OF ALL, FUCK THAT GUY.

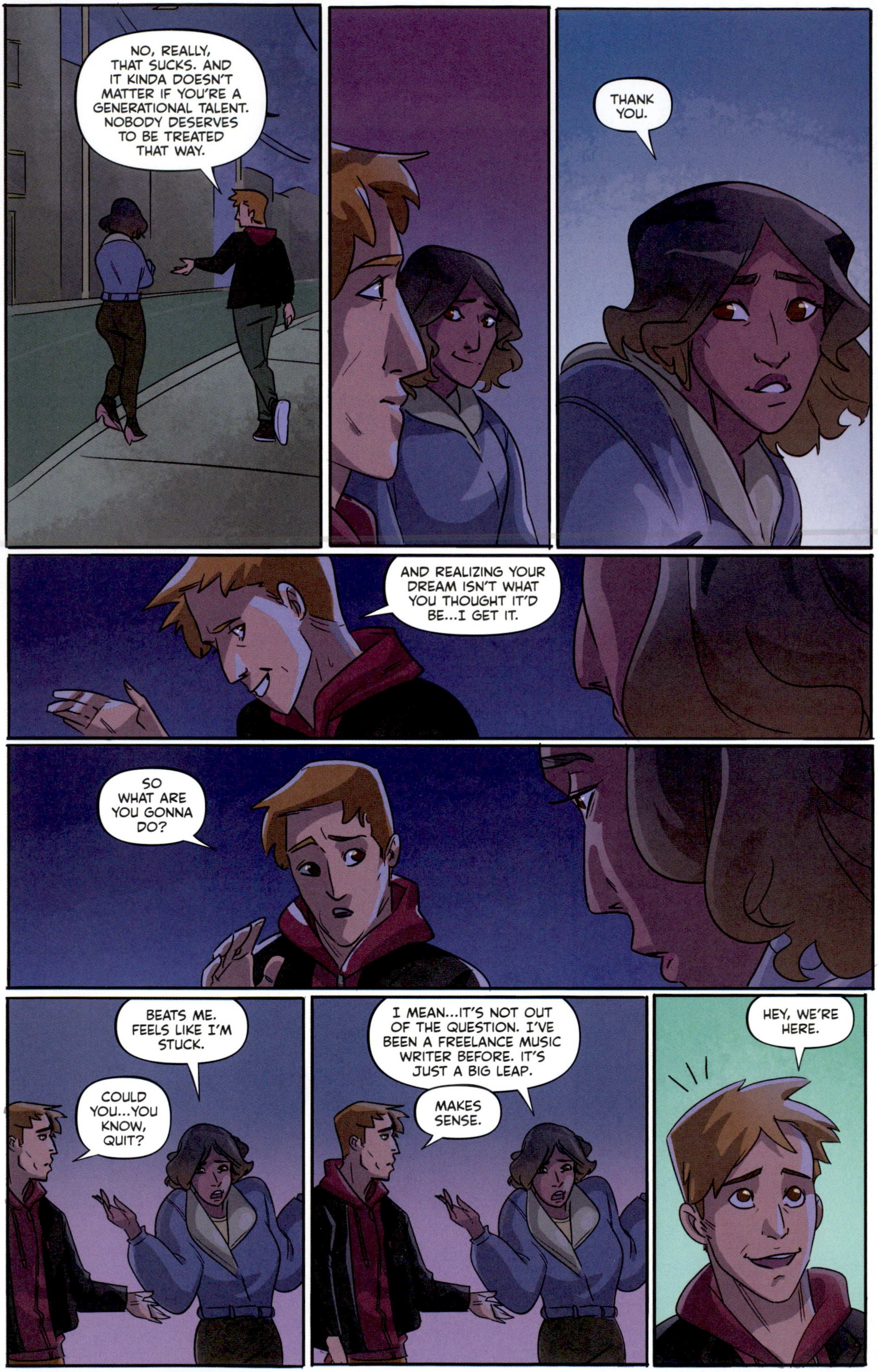
NO, REALLY, THAT SUCKS. AND IT KINDA DOESN'T MATTER IF YOU'RE A GENERATIONAL TALENT. NOBODY DESERVES TO BE TREATED THAT WAY.
THANK YOU.
AND REALIZING YOUR DREAM ISN'T WHAT YOU THOUGHT IT'D BE...I GET IT.
SO WHAT ARE YOU GONNA DO?
BEATS ME. FEELS LIKE I'M STUCK.
COULD YOU...YOU KNOW, QUIT?
I MEAN...IT'S NOT OUT OF THE QUESTION. I'VE BEEN A FREELANCE MUSIC WRITER BEFORE. IT'S JUST A BIG LEAP.
MAKES SENSE.
HEY, WE'RE HERE.

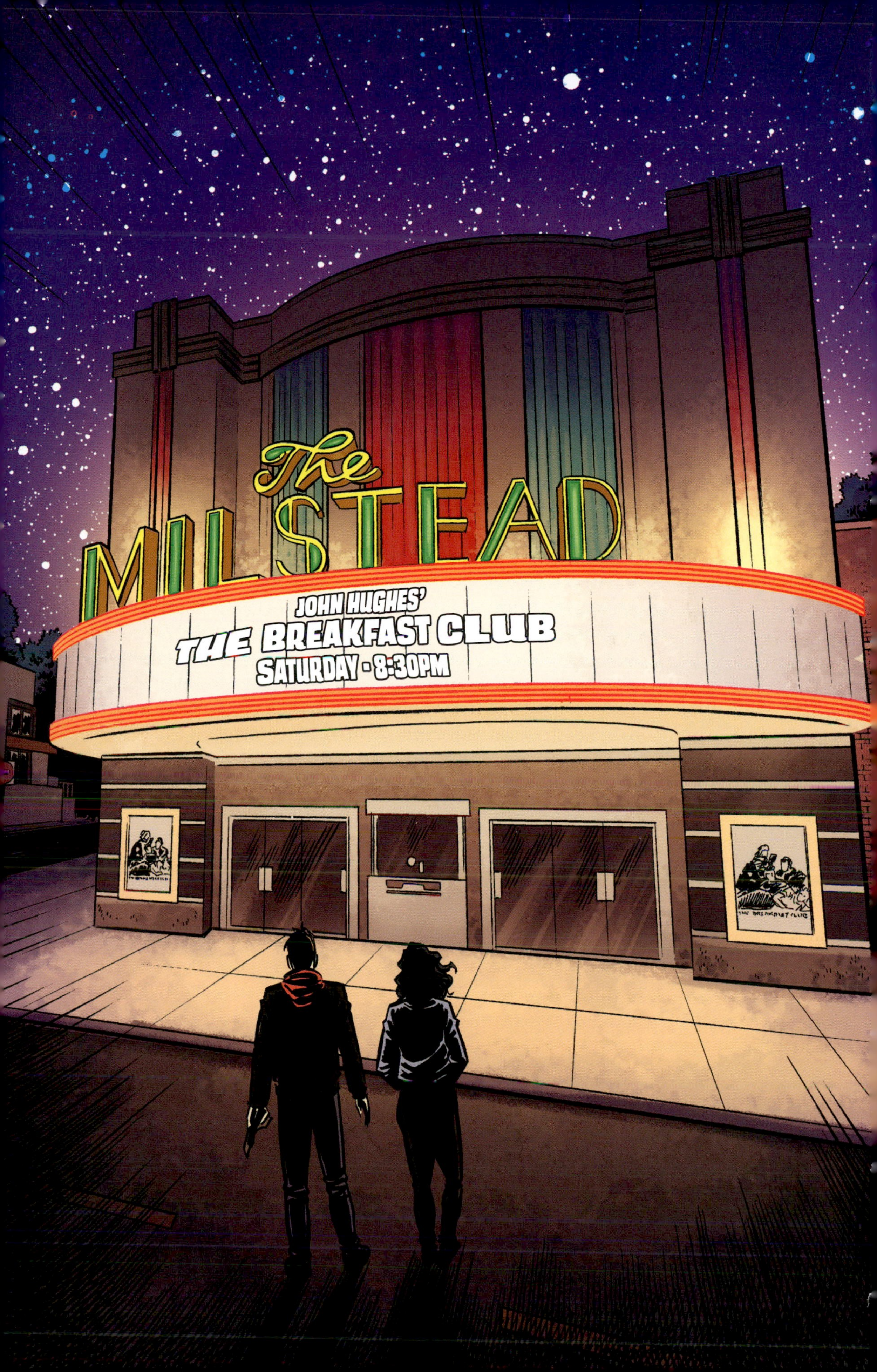
The
MILSTEAD
JOHN HUGHES'
THE BREAKFAST CLUB
SATURDAY - 8:30PM

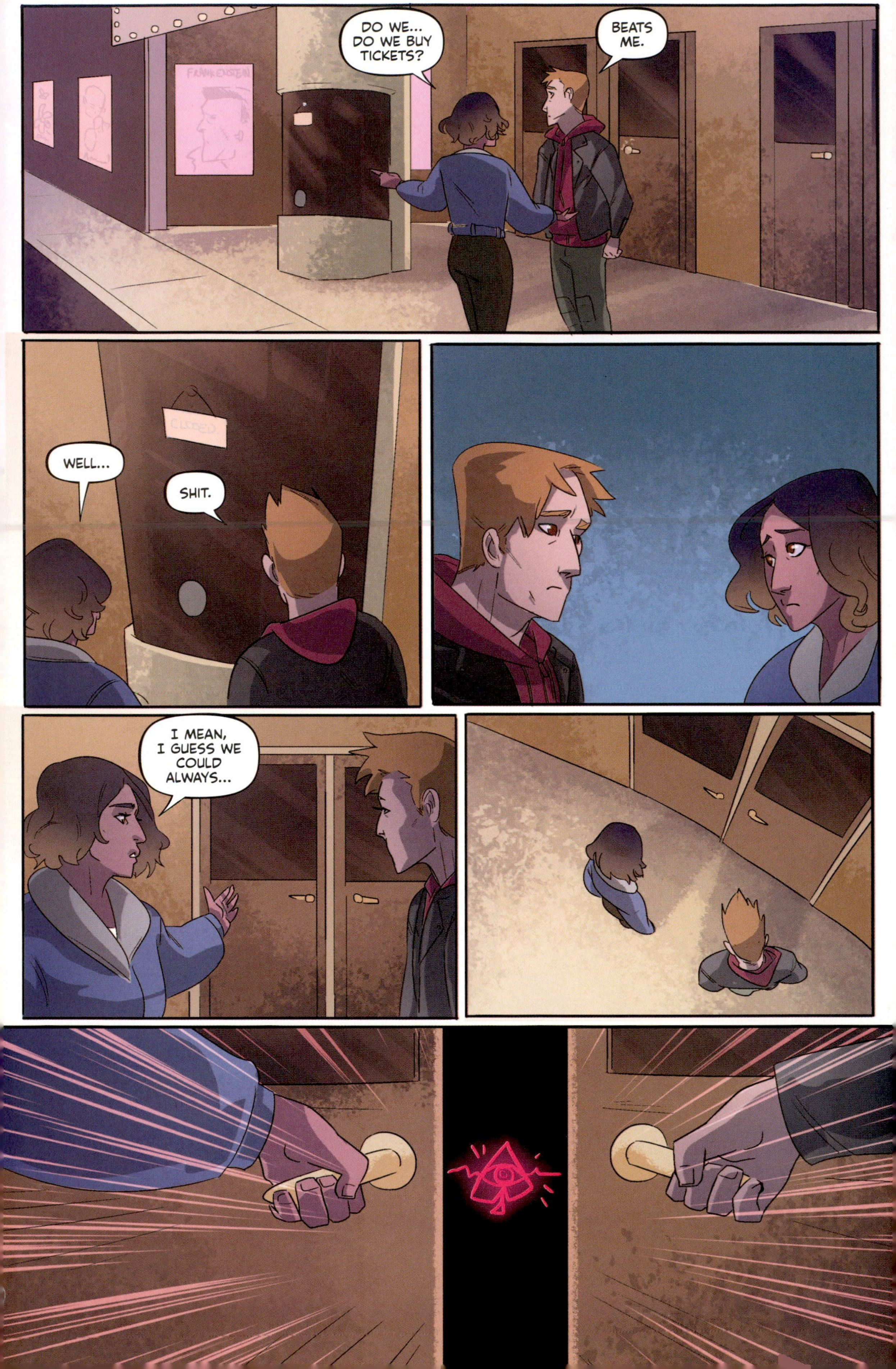
DO WE... DO WE BUY TICKETS?
BEATS ME.
WELL...
SHIT.
I MEAN, I GUESS WE COULD ALWAYS...

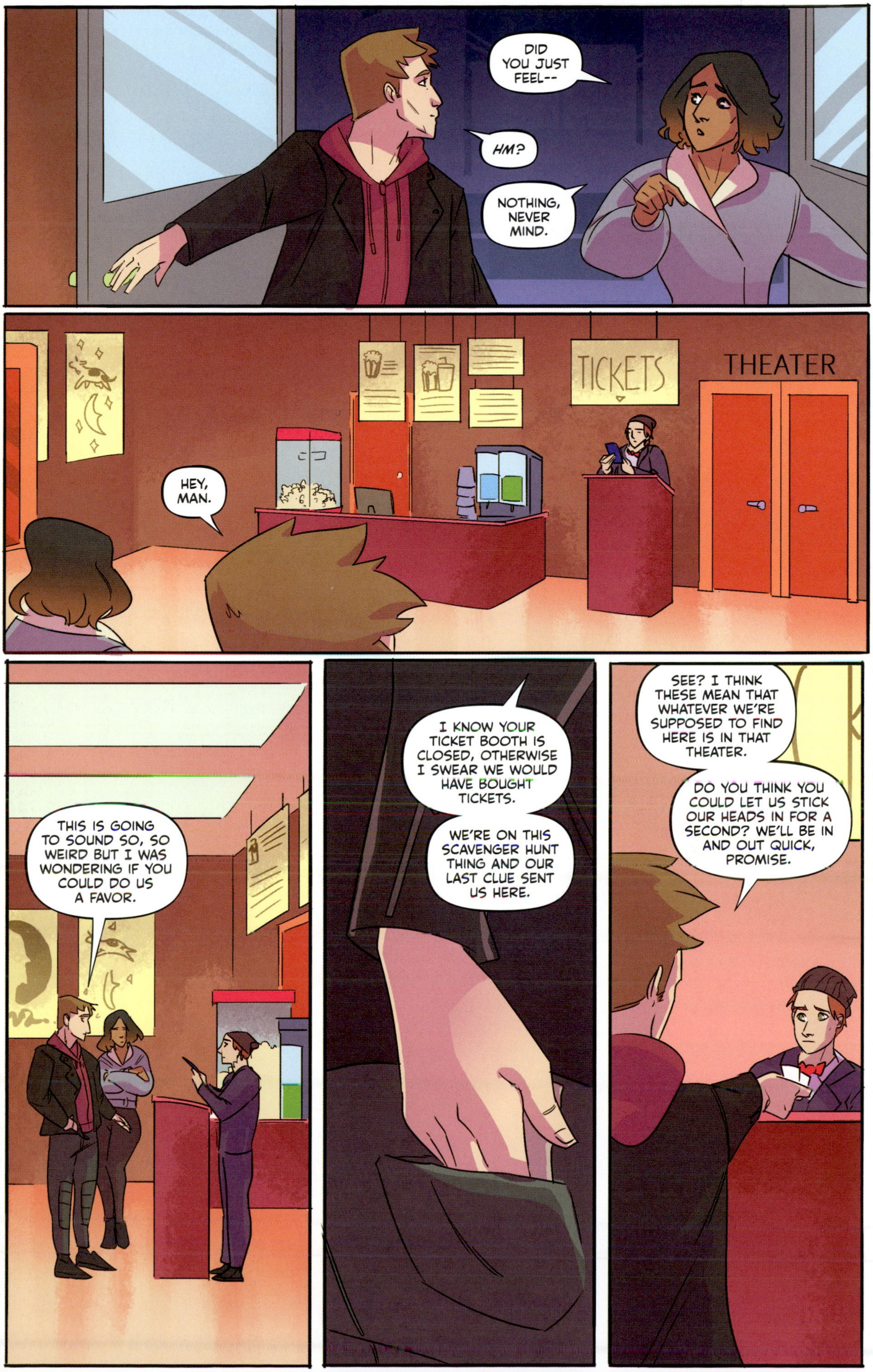
DID YOU JUST FEEL--
HM?
NOTHING, NEVER MIND.
TICKETS
THEATER
HEY, MAN.
THIS IS GOING TO SOUND SO, SO WEIRD BUT I WAS WONDERING IF YOU COULD DO US A FAVOR.
I KNOW YOUR TICKET BOOTH IS CLOSED, OTHERWISE I SWEAR WE WOULD HAVE BOUGHT TICKETS.
WE'RE ON THIS SCAVENGER HUNT THING AND OUR LAST CLUE SENT US HERE.
SEE? I THINK THESE MEAN THAT WHATEVER WE'RE SUPPOSED TO FIND HERE IS IN THAT THEATER.
DO YOU THINK YOU COULD LET US STICK OUR HEADS IN FOR A SECOND? WE'LL BE IN AND OUT QUICK, PROMISE.

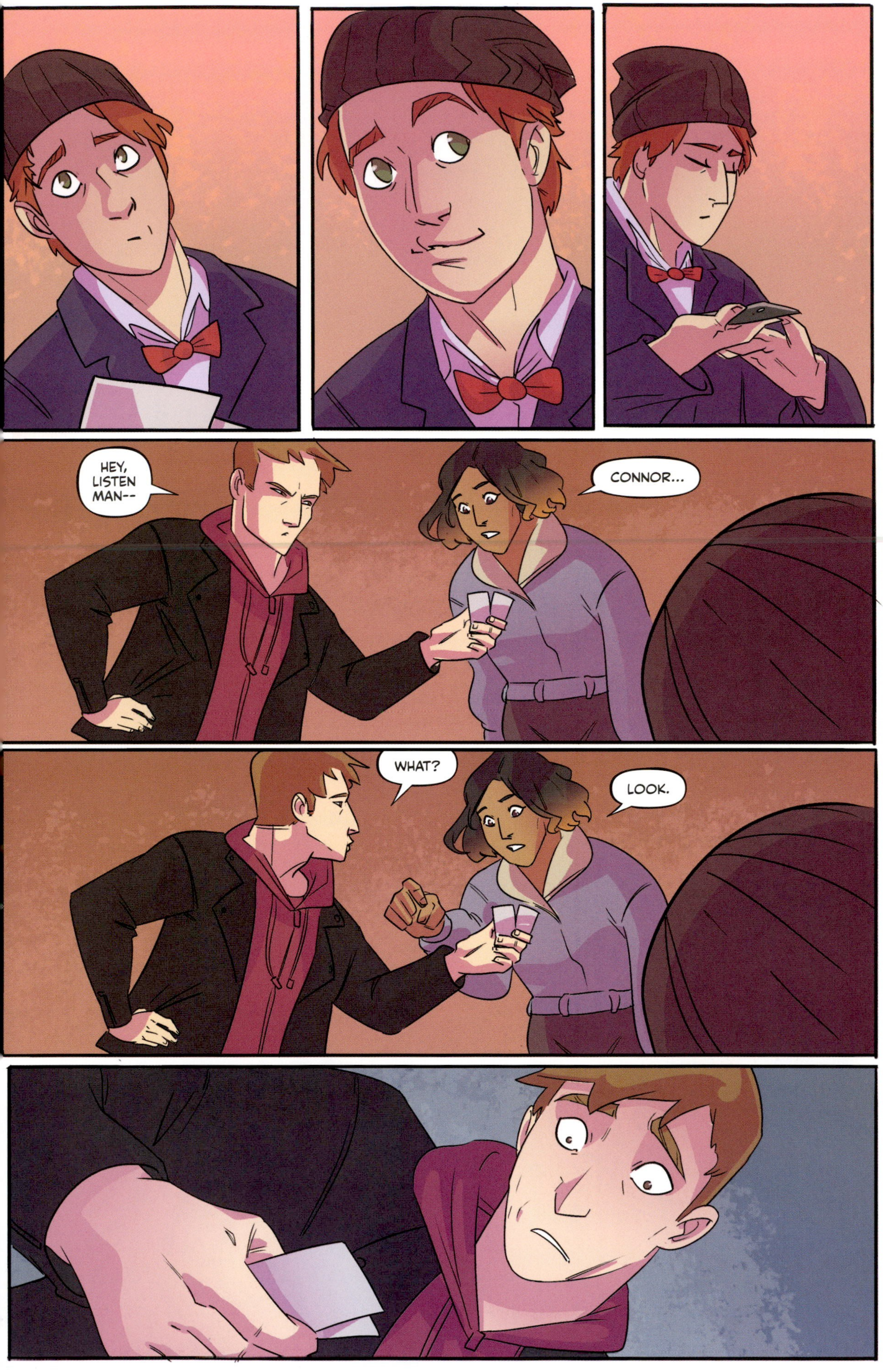
HEY, LISTEN MAN--
CONNOR...
WHAT?
LOOK.

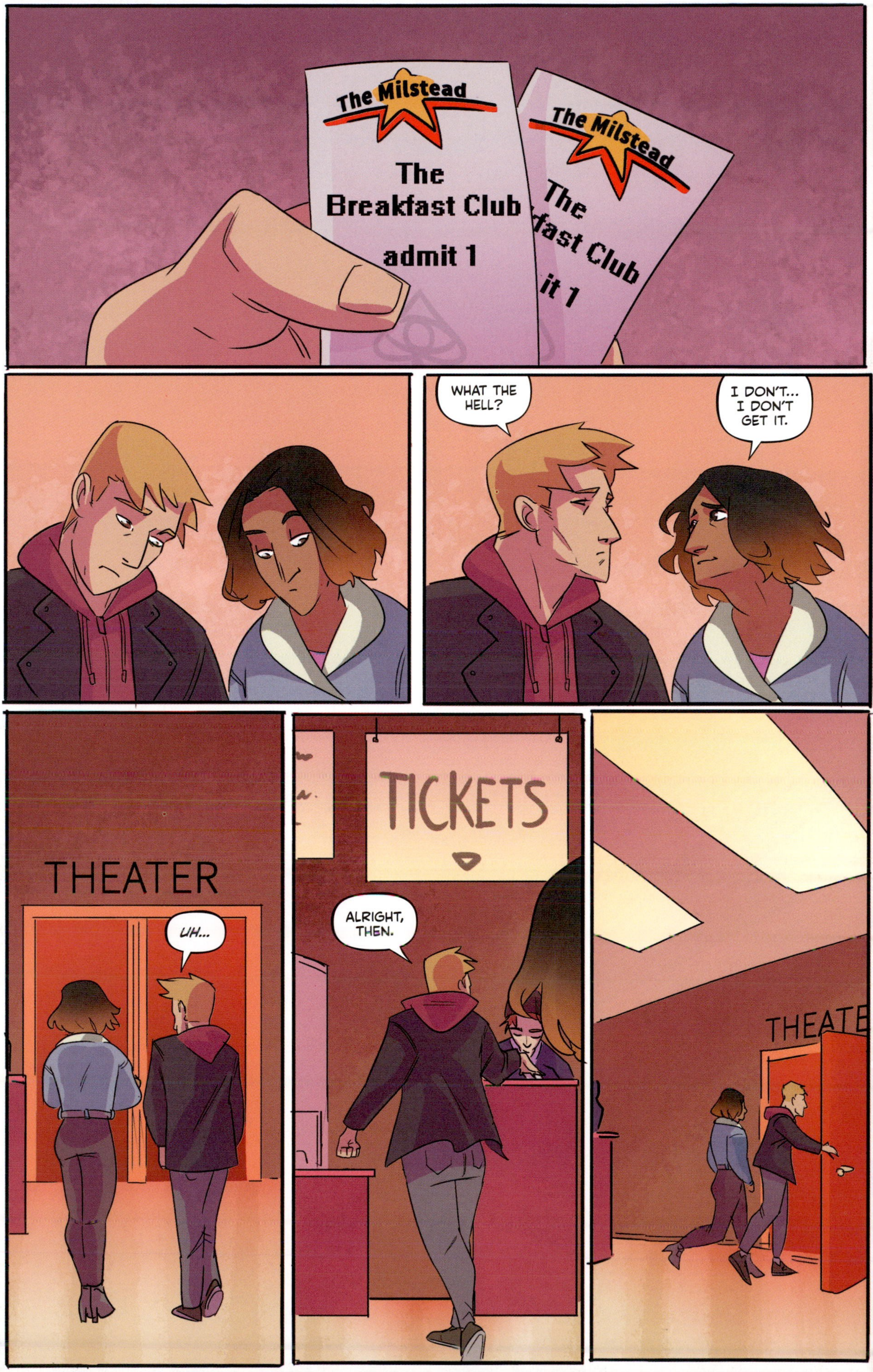
The Milstead
The Breakfast Club
admit 1
WHAT THE HELL?
I DON'T... I DON'T GET IT.
THEATER
UH...
TICKETS
ALRIGHT, THEN.

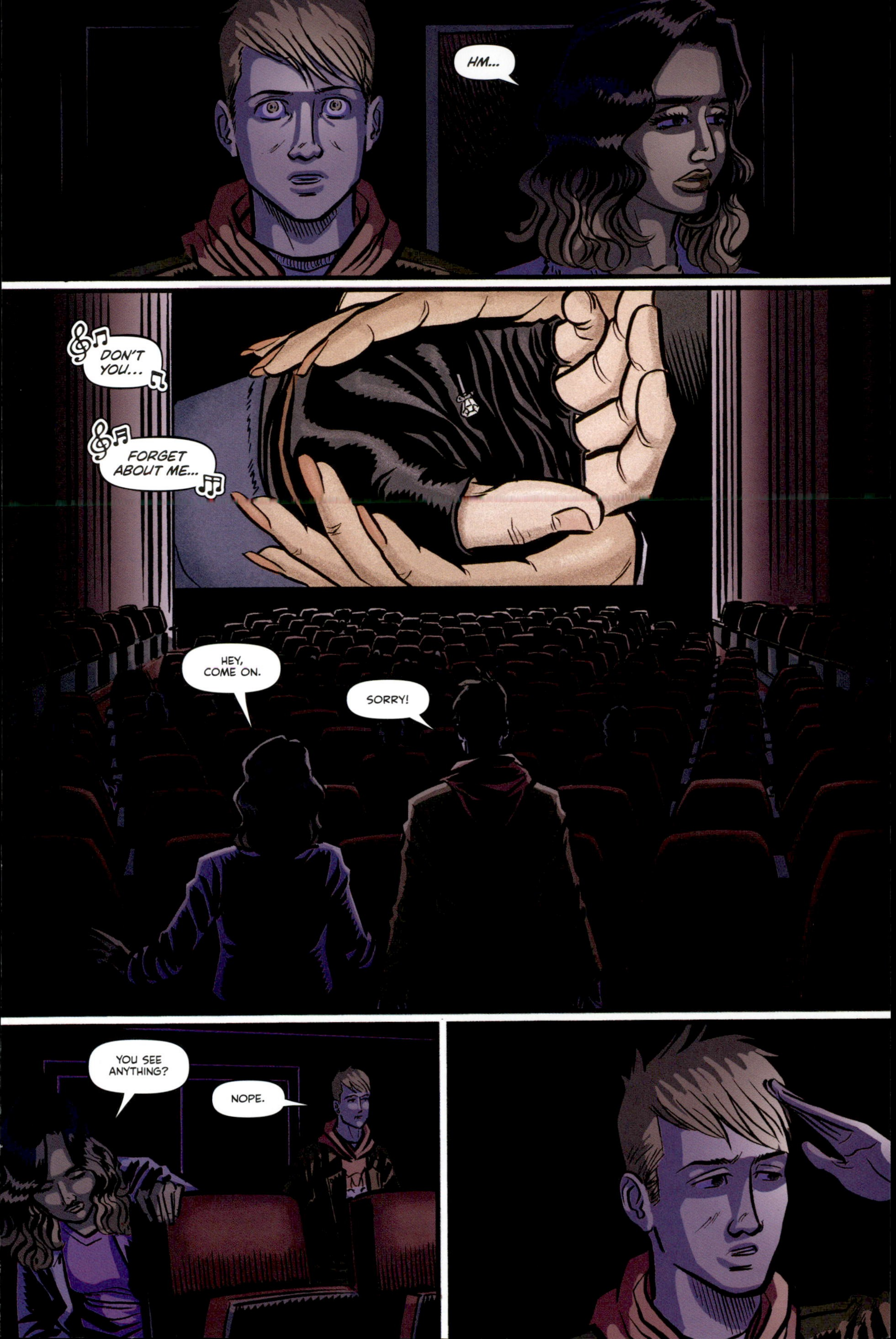
HM...
DON'T YOU...
FORGET ABOUT ME...
HEY, COME ON.
SORRY!
YOU SEE ANYTHING?
NOPE.

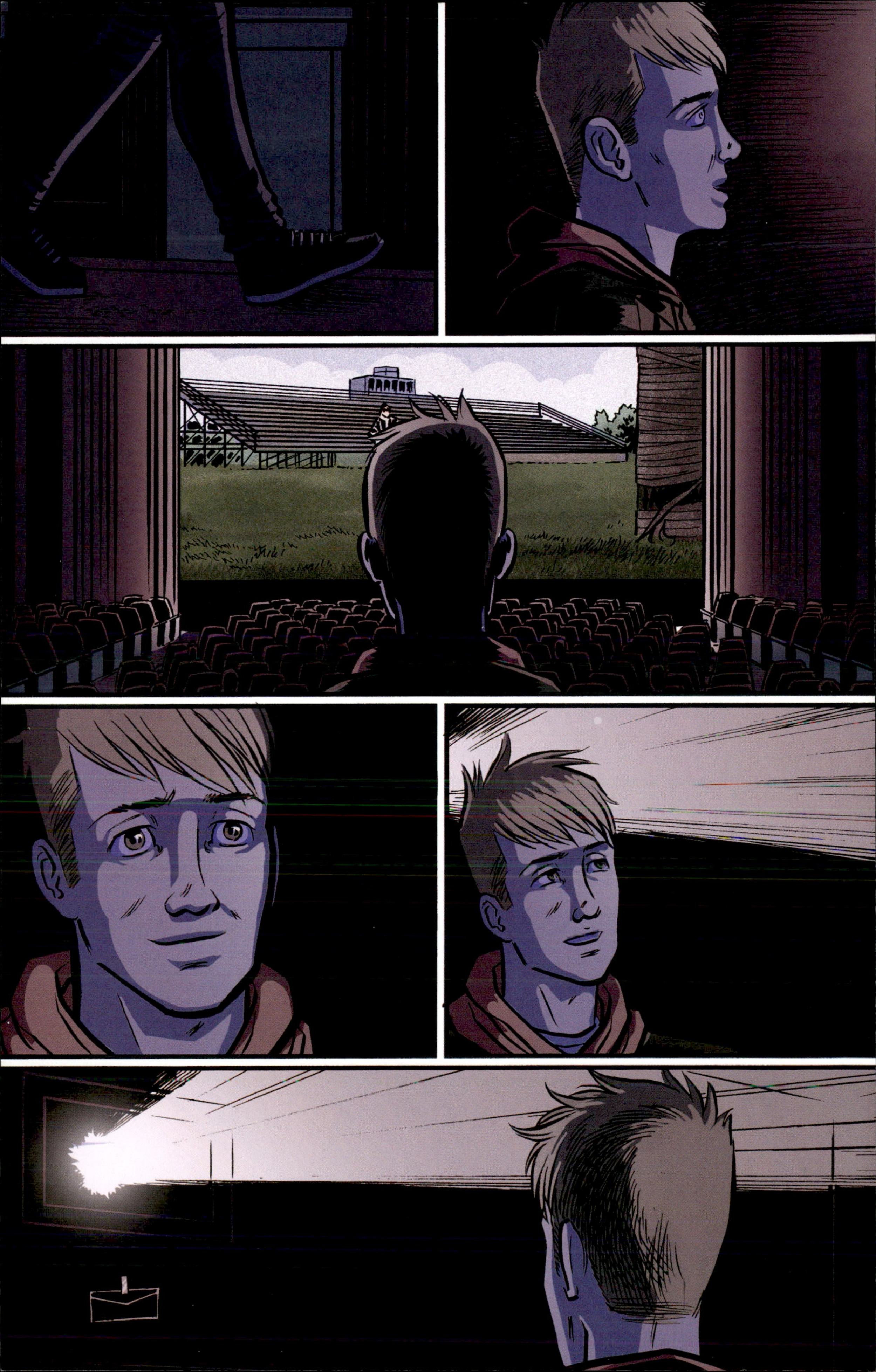

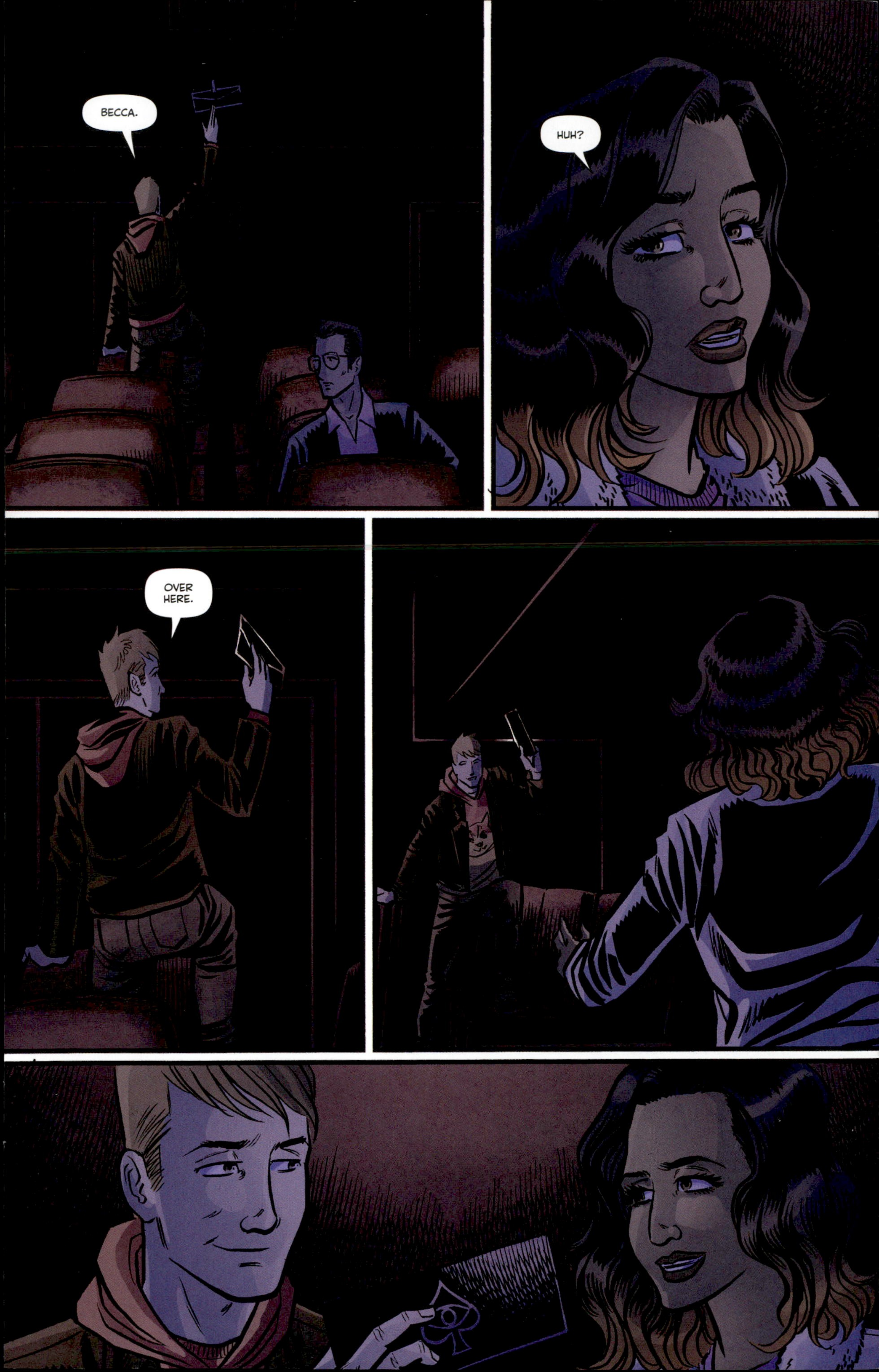
BECCA.
HUH?
OVER HERE.

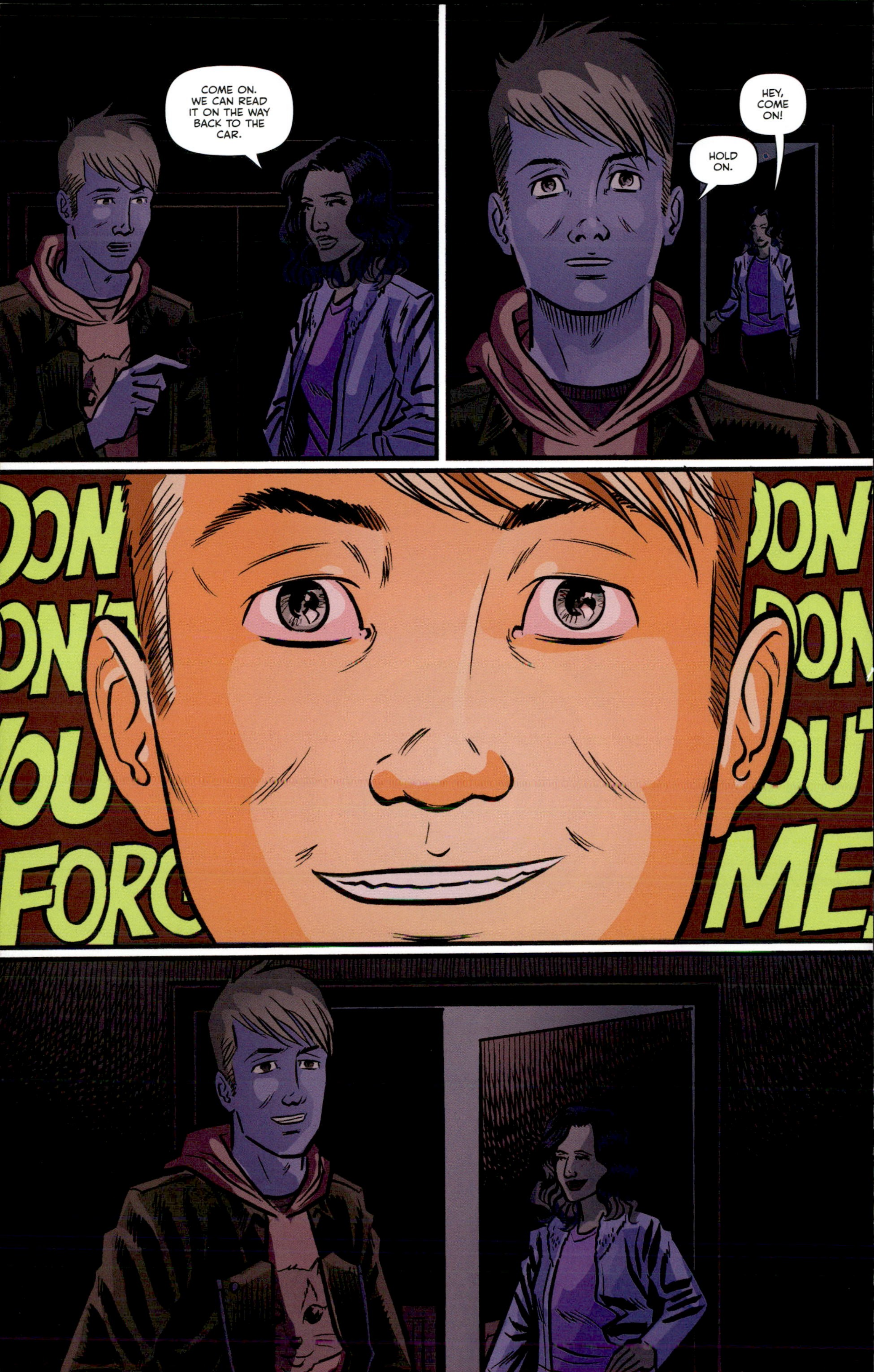
COME ON. WE CAN READ IT ON THE WAY BACK TO THE CAR.
HEY, COME ON!
HOLD ON.

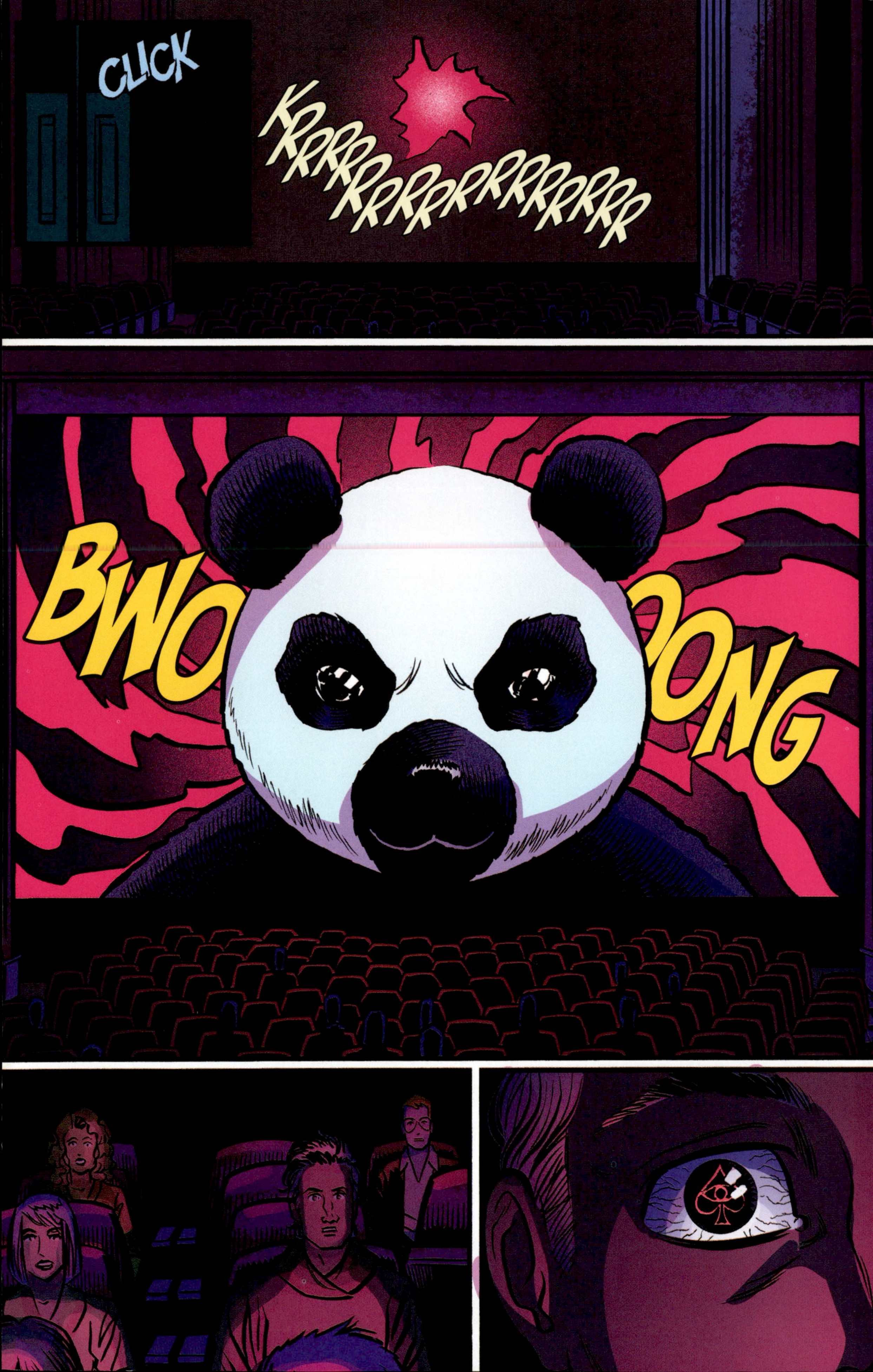
CLICK
KRRRRRRRRRRRRRRRR
BWOOONG

ALRIGHT, LET'S SEE IT.

OKAY, OKAY.

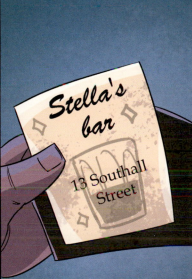

Stella's bar

13 Southall Street

SEEMS SIMPLE ENOUGH.

YEAH, BUT SOUTHALL STREET? THAT'S A WAYS OUT. AND IT'S ALREADY LIKE 10:30.

YEAH BUT COME ON, WE'VE MADE IT THIS FAR! SHOW'S AT MIDNIGHT. WE'VE GOT TIME.

I GUESS...

IT'LL BE WORTH IT.

TRUST ME.

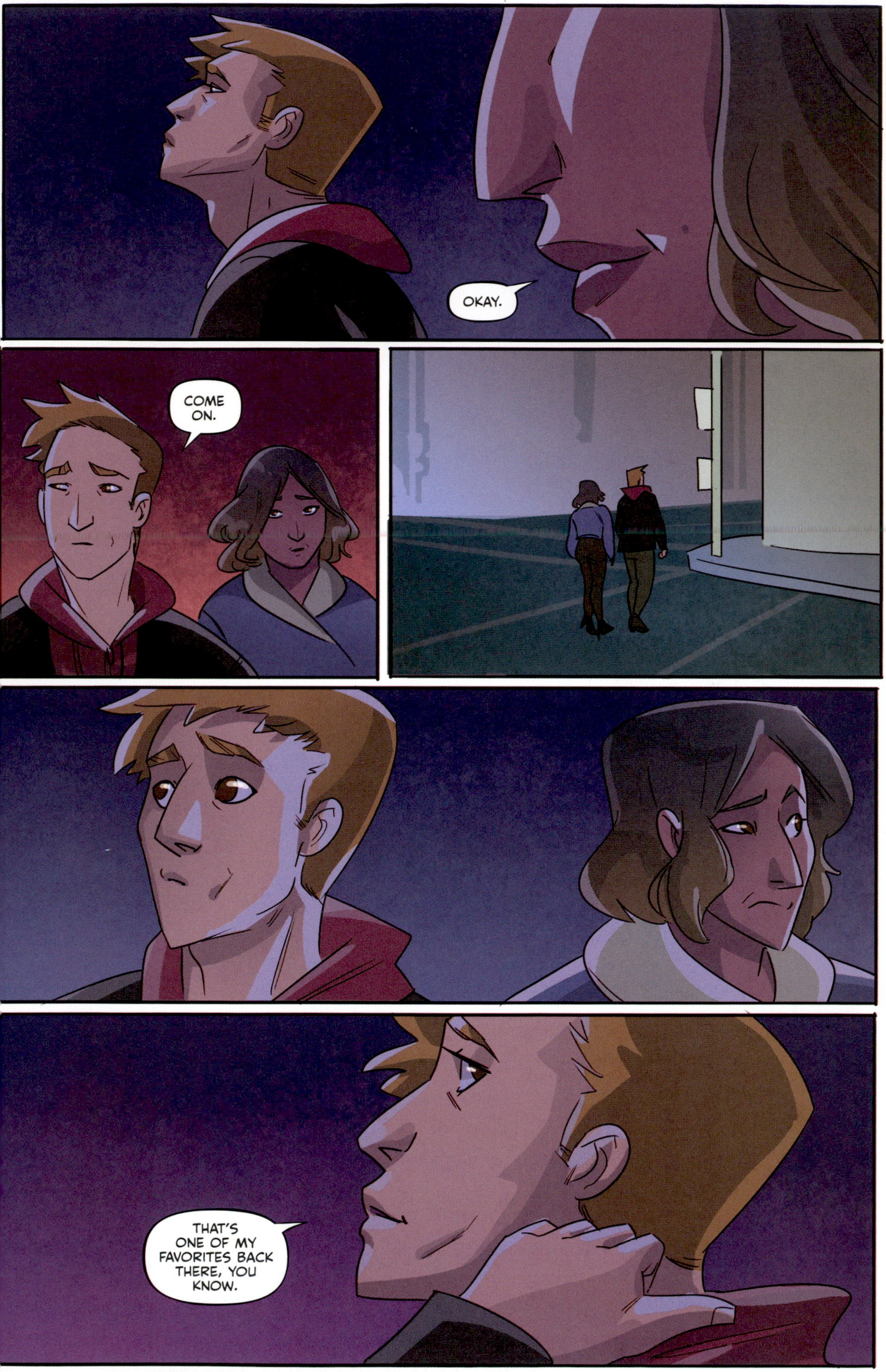
OKAY.
COME ON.
THAT'S ONE OF MY FAVORITES BACK THERE, YOU KNOW.

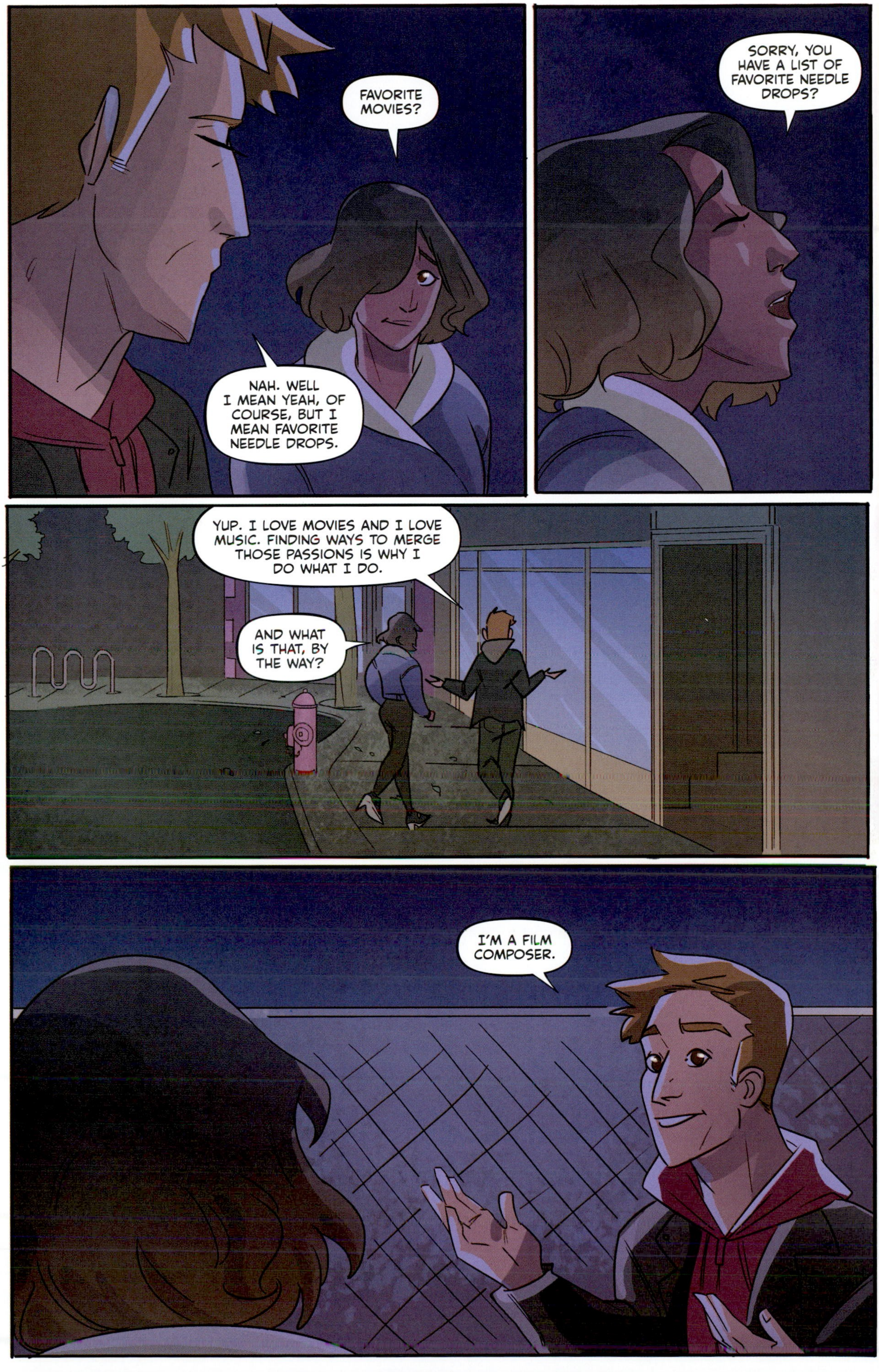
FAVORITE MOVIES?
NAH. WELL I MEAN YEAH, OF COURSE, BUT I MEAN FAVORITE NEEDLE DROPS.
SORRY, YOU HAVE A LIST OF FAVORITE NEEDLE DROPS?
YUP. I LOVE MOVIES AND I LOVE MUSIC. FINDING WAYS TO MERGE THOSE PASSIONS IS WHY I DO WHAT I DO.
AND WHAT IS THAT, BY THE WAY?
I'M A FILM COMPOSER.

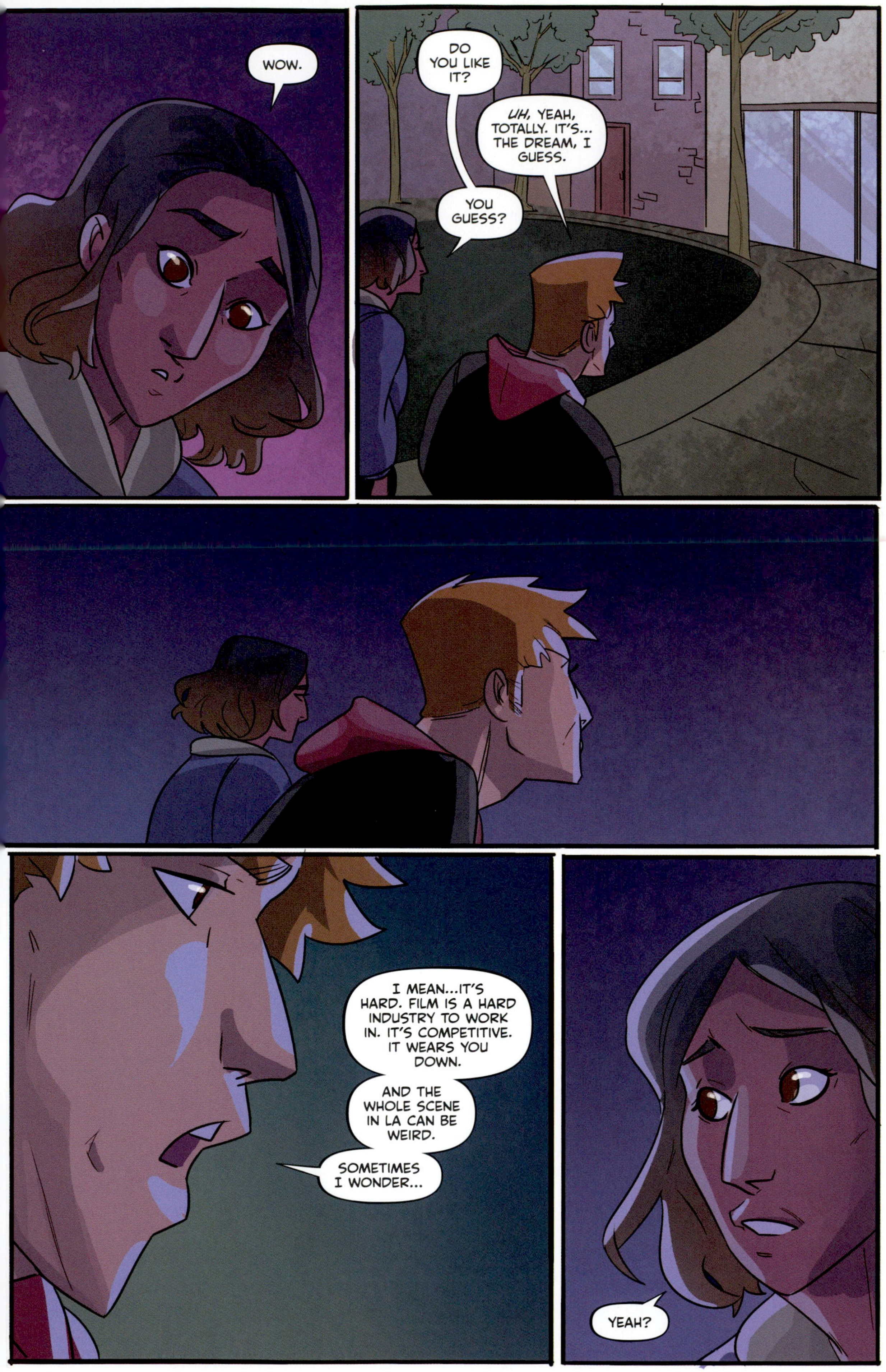
WOW.
DO YOU LIKE IT?
UH, YEAH, TOTALLY. IT'S... THE DREAM, I GUESS.
YOU GUESS?
I MEAN...IT'S HARD. FILM IS A HARD INDUSTRY TO WORK IN. IT'S COMPETITIVE. IT WEARS YOU DOWN.
AND THE WHOLE SCENE IN LA CAN BE WEIRD.
SOMETIMES I WONDER...
YEAH?

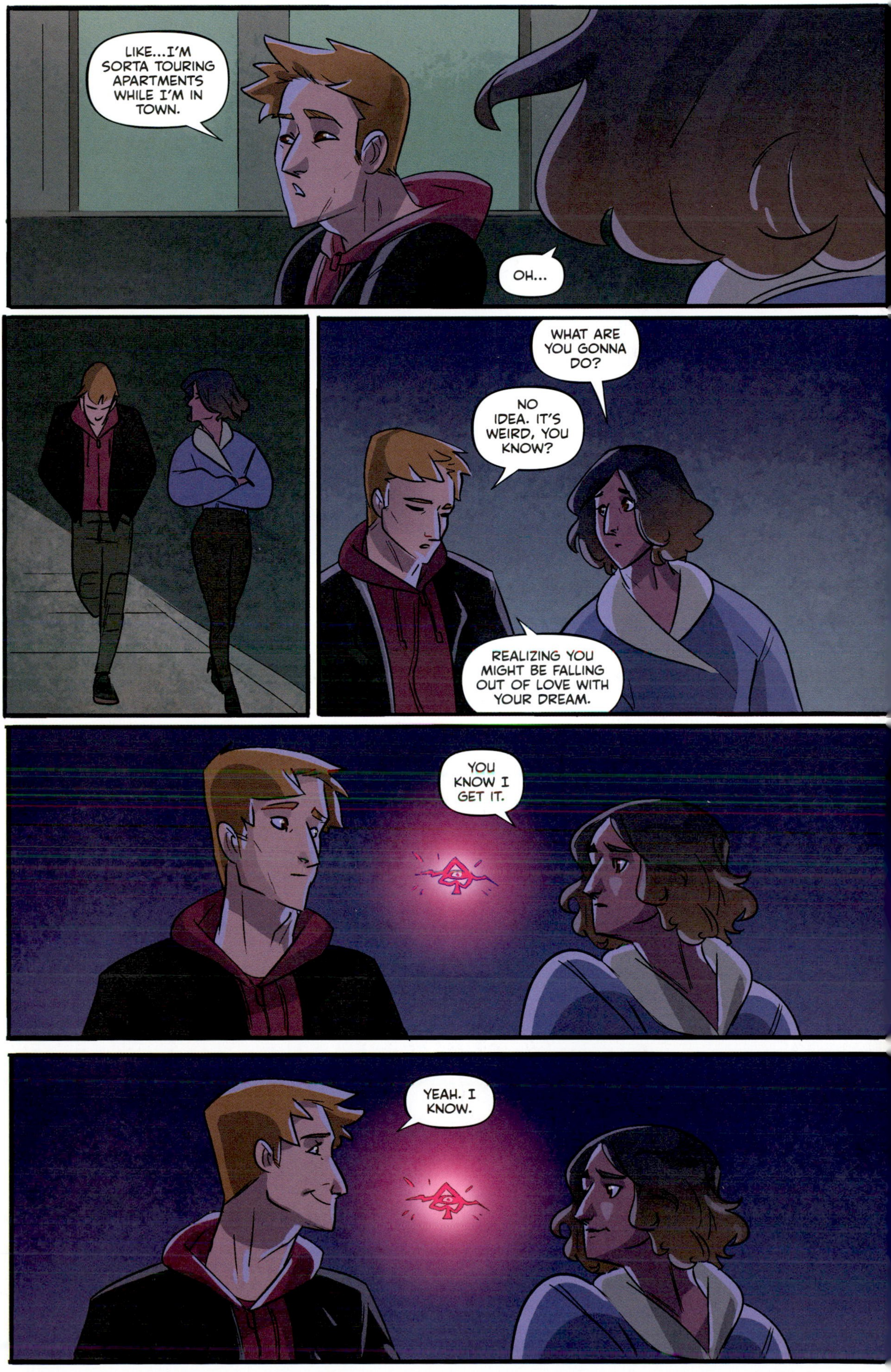
LIKE...I'M SORTA TOURING APARTMENTS WHILE I'M IN TOWN.
OH...
WHAT ARE YOU GONNA DO?
NO IDEA. IT'S WEIRD, YOU KNOW?
REALIZING YOU MIGHT BE FALLING OUT OF LOVE WITH YOUR DREAM.
YOU KNOW I GET IT.
YEAH. I KNOW.

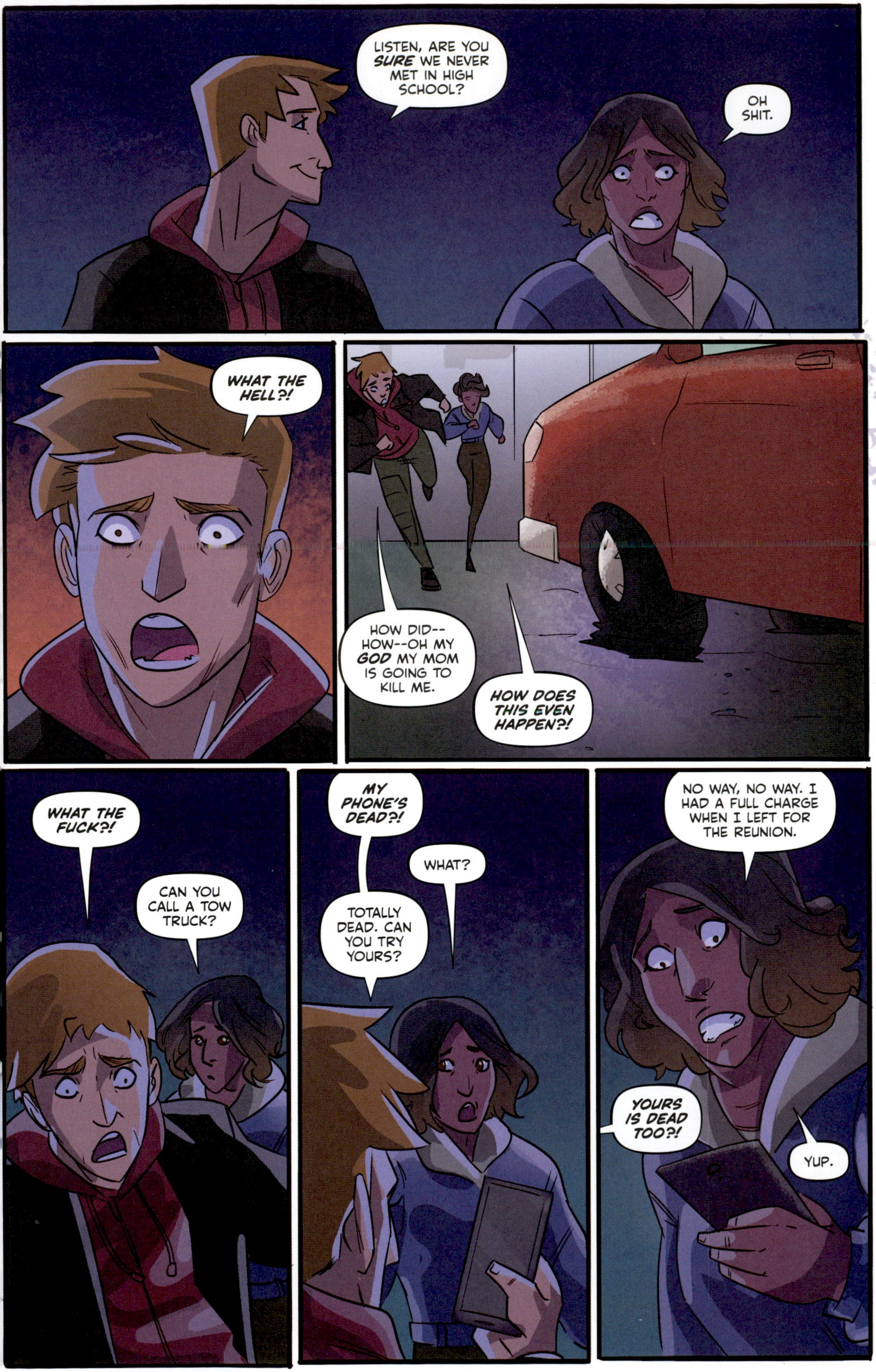

LISTEN, ARE YOU SURE WE NEVER MET IN HIGH SCHOOL?
OH SHIT.
WHAT THE HELL?!
HOW DID-- HOW--OH MY GOD MY MOM IS GOING TO KILL ME.
HOW DOES THIS EVEN HAPPEN?!
WHAT THE FUCK?!
CAN YOU CALL A TOW TRUCK?
MY PHONE'S DEAD?!
WHAT?
TOTALLY DEAD. CAN YOU TRY YOURS?
NO WAY, NO WAY. I HAD A FULL CHARGE WHEN I LEFT FOR THE REUNION.
YOURS IS DEAD TOO?!
YUP.

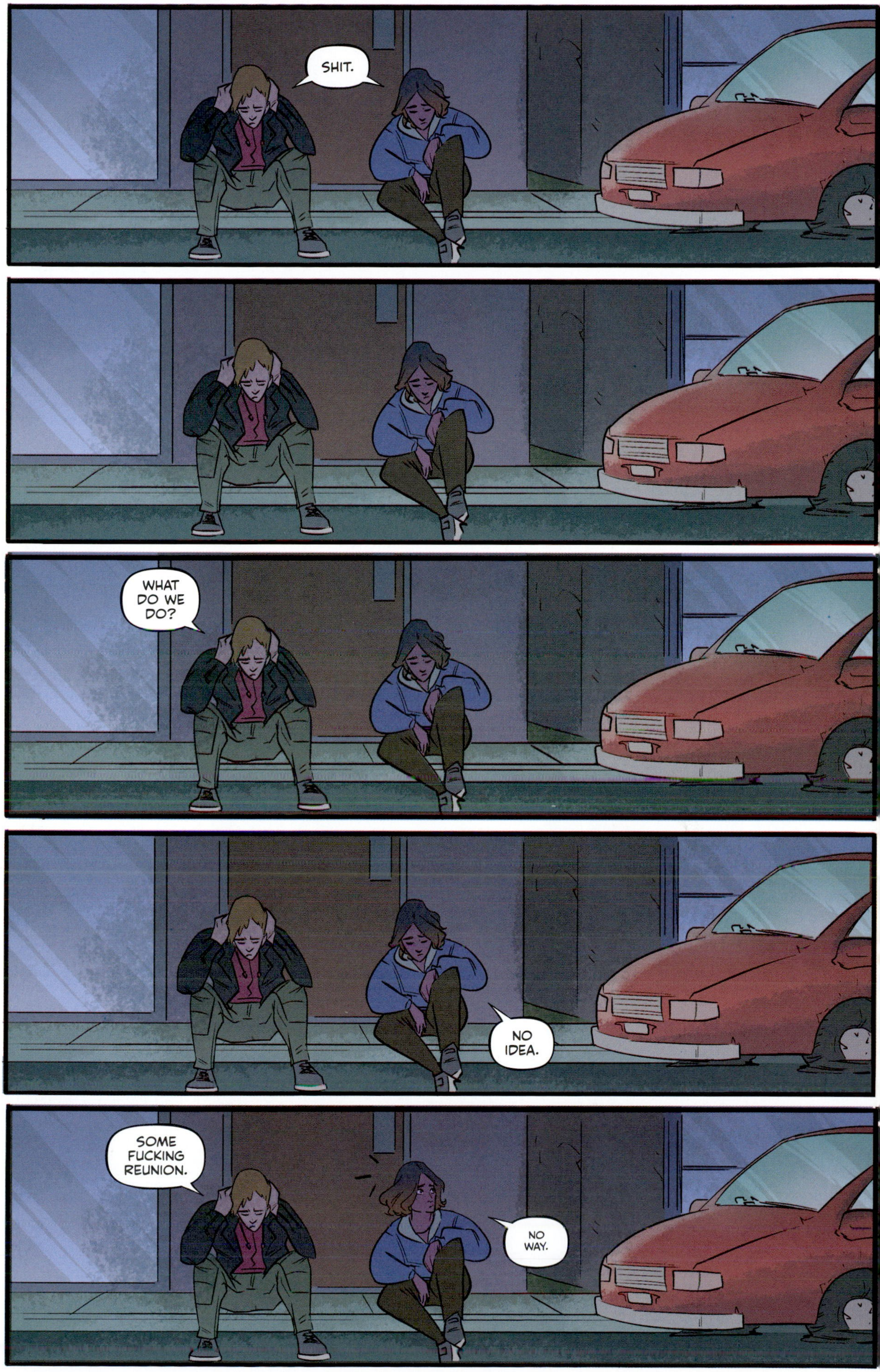
SHIT.
WHAT DO WE DO?
NO IDEA.
SOME FUCKING REUNION.
NO WAY.

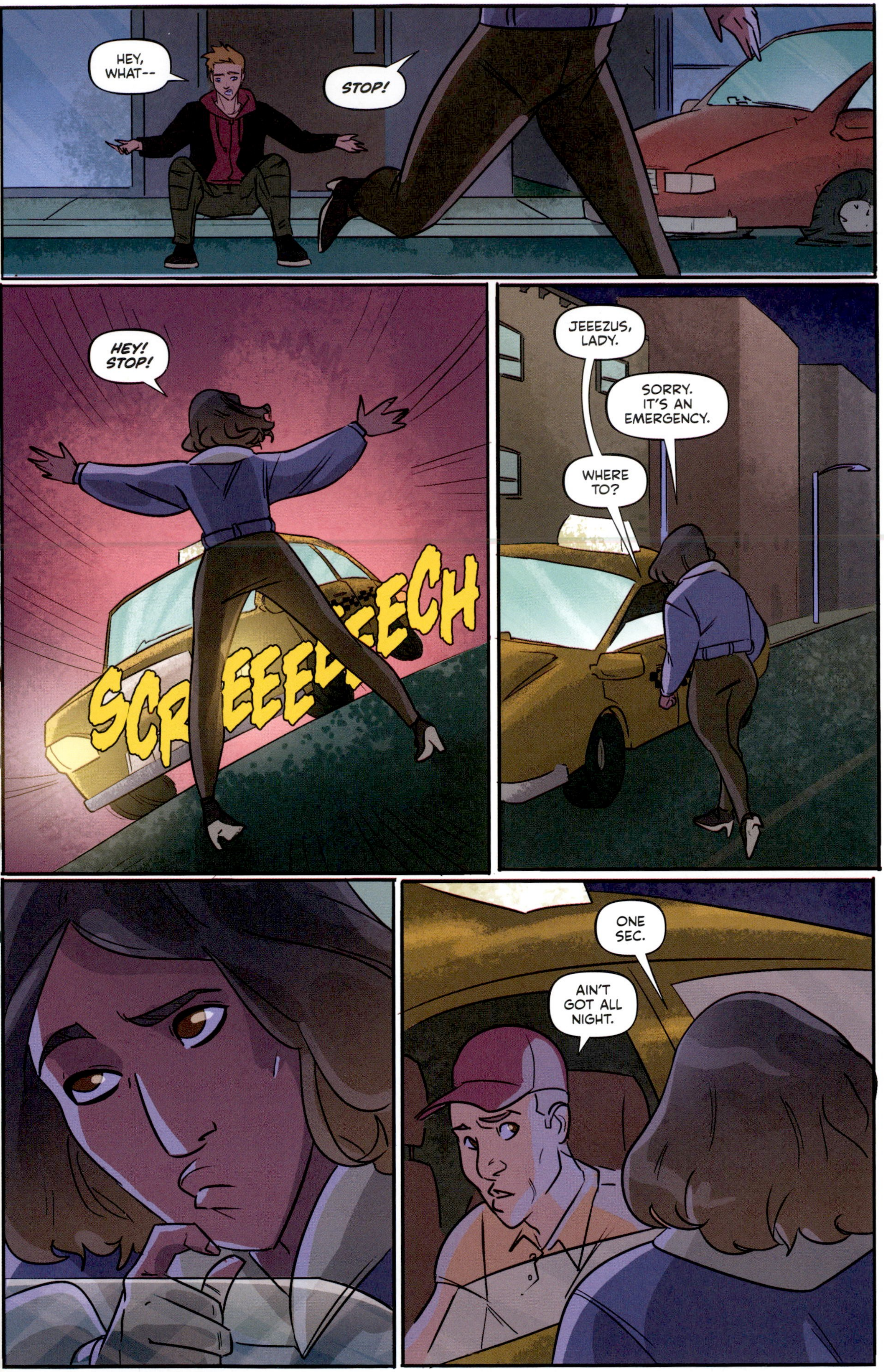
HEY, WHAT--
STOP!
HEY! STOP!
SCREEEEEEECH
JEEEZUS, LADY.
SORRY. IT'S AN EMERGENCY.
WHERE TO?
ONE SEC.
AIN'T GOT ALL NIGHT.

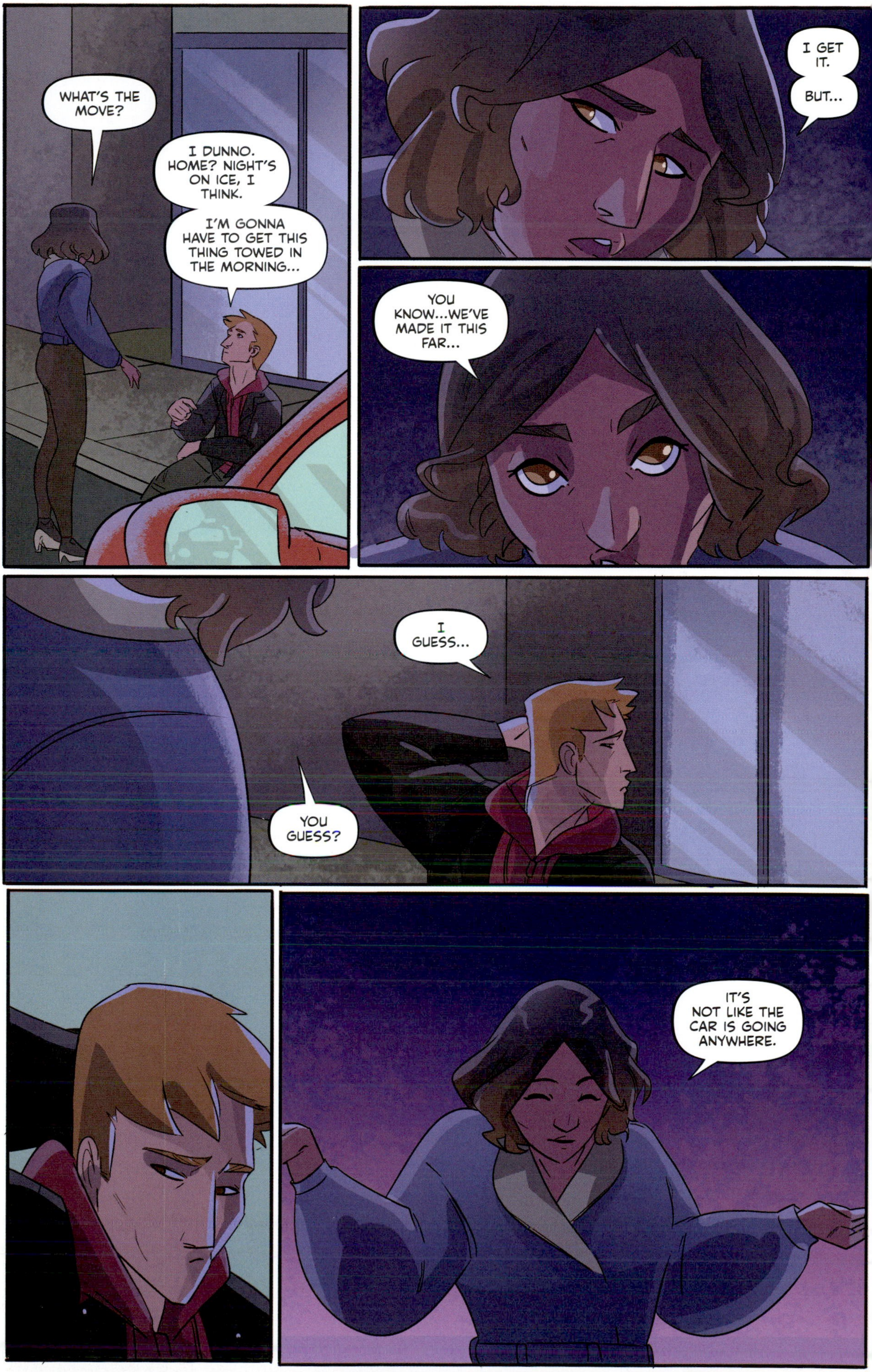
WHAT'S THE MOVE?
I DUNNO. HOME? NIGHT'S ON ICE, I THINK.
I'M GONNA HAVE TO GET THIS THING TOWED IN THE MORNING...
I GET IT.
BUT...
YOU KNOW...WE'VE MADE IT THIS FAR...
I GUESS...
YOU GUESS?
IT'S NOT LIKE THE CAR IS GOING ANYWHERE.

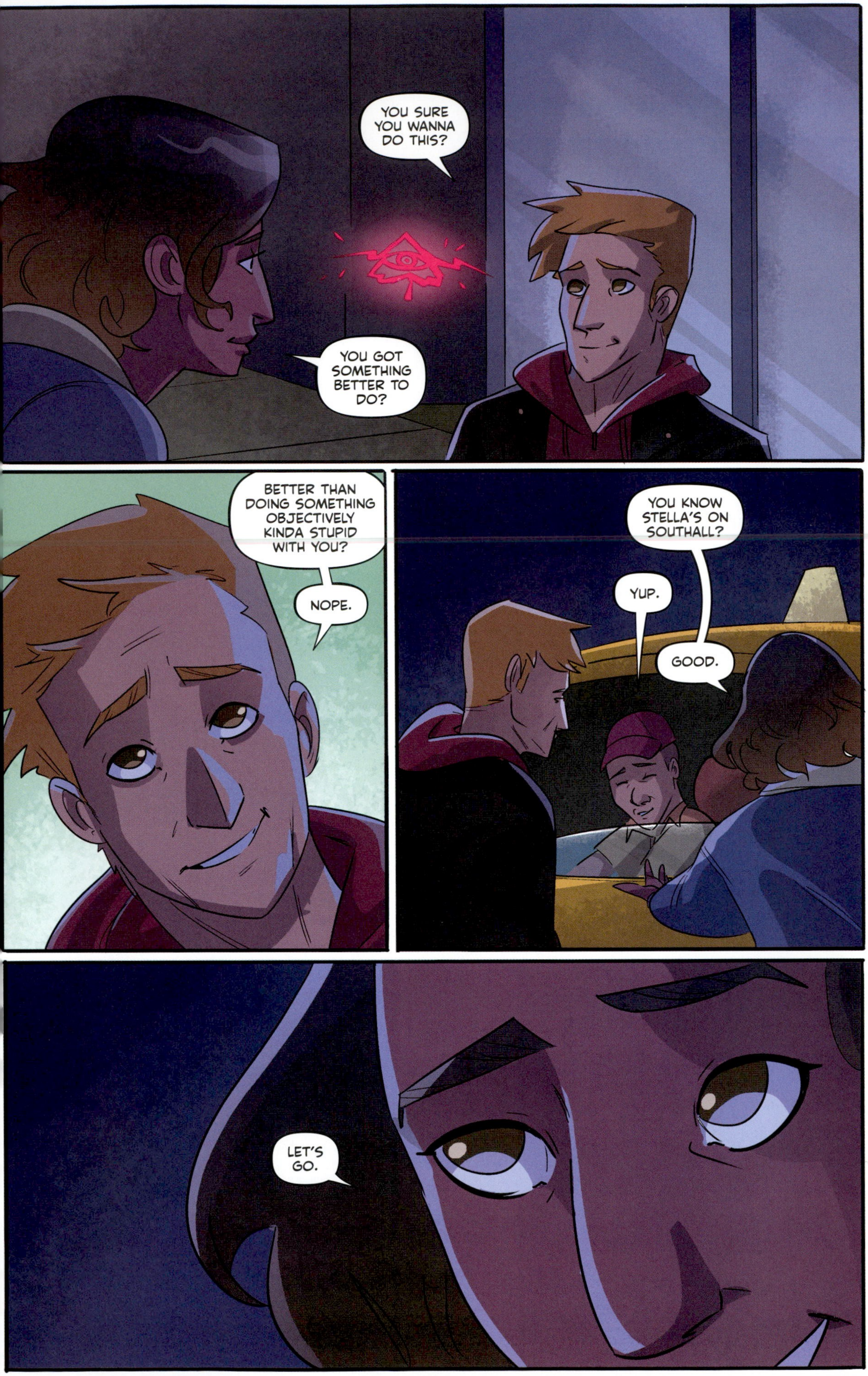
YOU SURE YOU WANNA DO THIS?
YOU GOT SOMETHING BETTER TO DO?
BETTER THAN DOING SOMETHING OBJECTIVELY KINDA STUPID WITH YOU?
NOPE.
YOU KNOW STELLA'S ON SOUTHALL?
YUP.
GOOD.
LET'S GO.

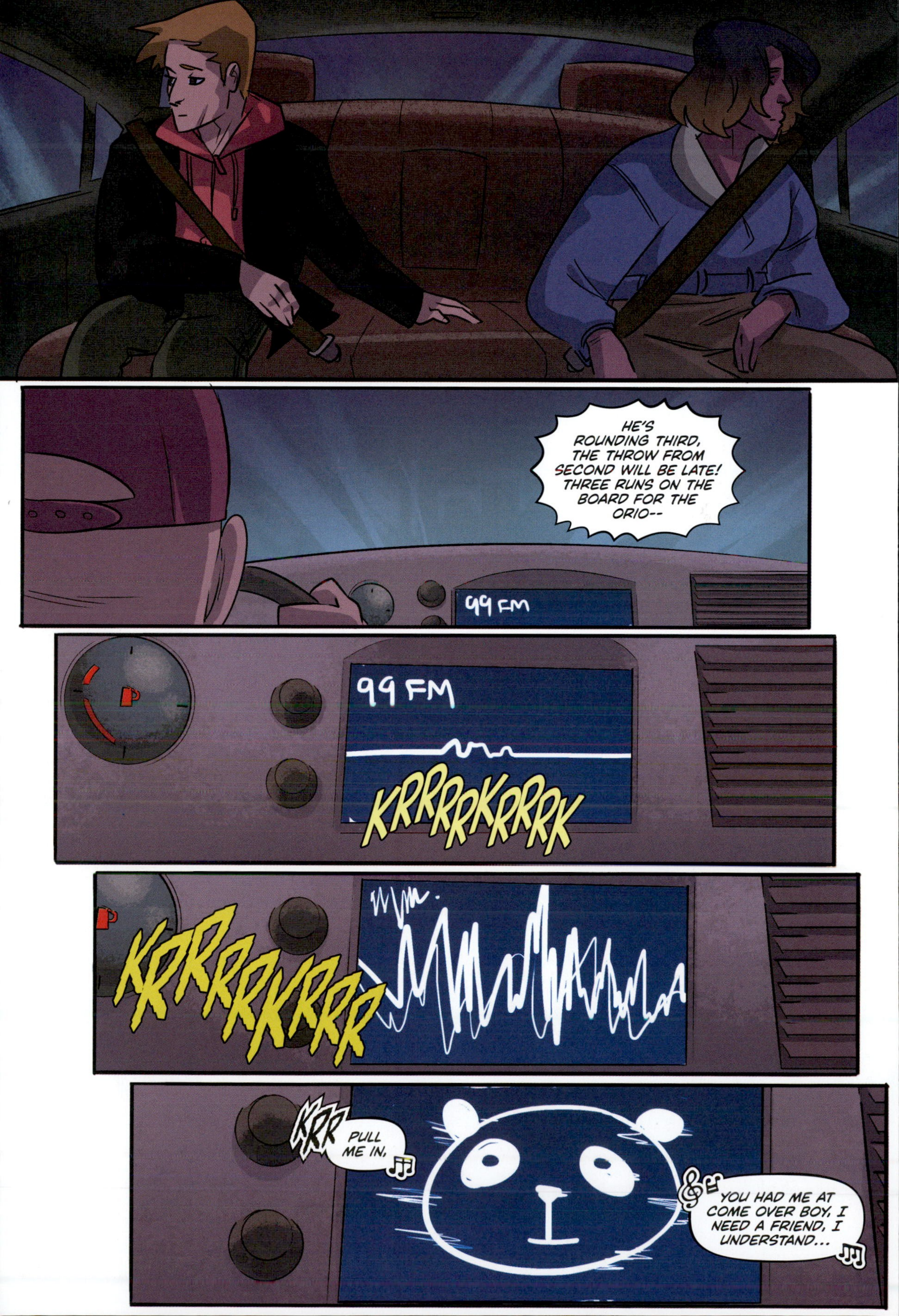
HE'S ROUNDING THIRD, THE THROW FROM SECOND WILL BE LATE! THREE RUNS ON THE BOARD FOR THE ORIO--
99 FM
99 FM
KRRRRKRRRK
KRRRRKRRR
KRR
PULL ME IN,
YOU HAD ME AT COME OVER BOY, I NEED A FRIEND, I UNDERSTAND...

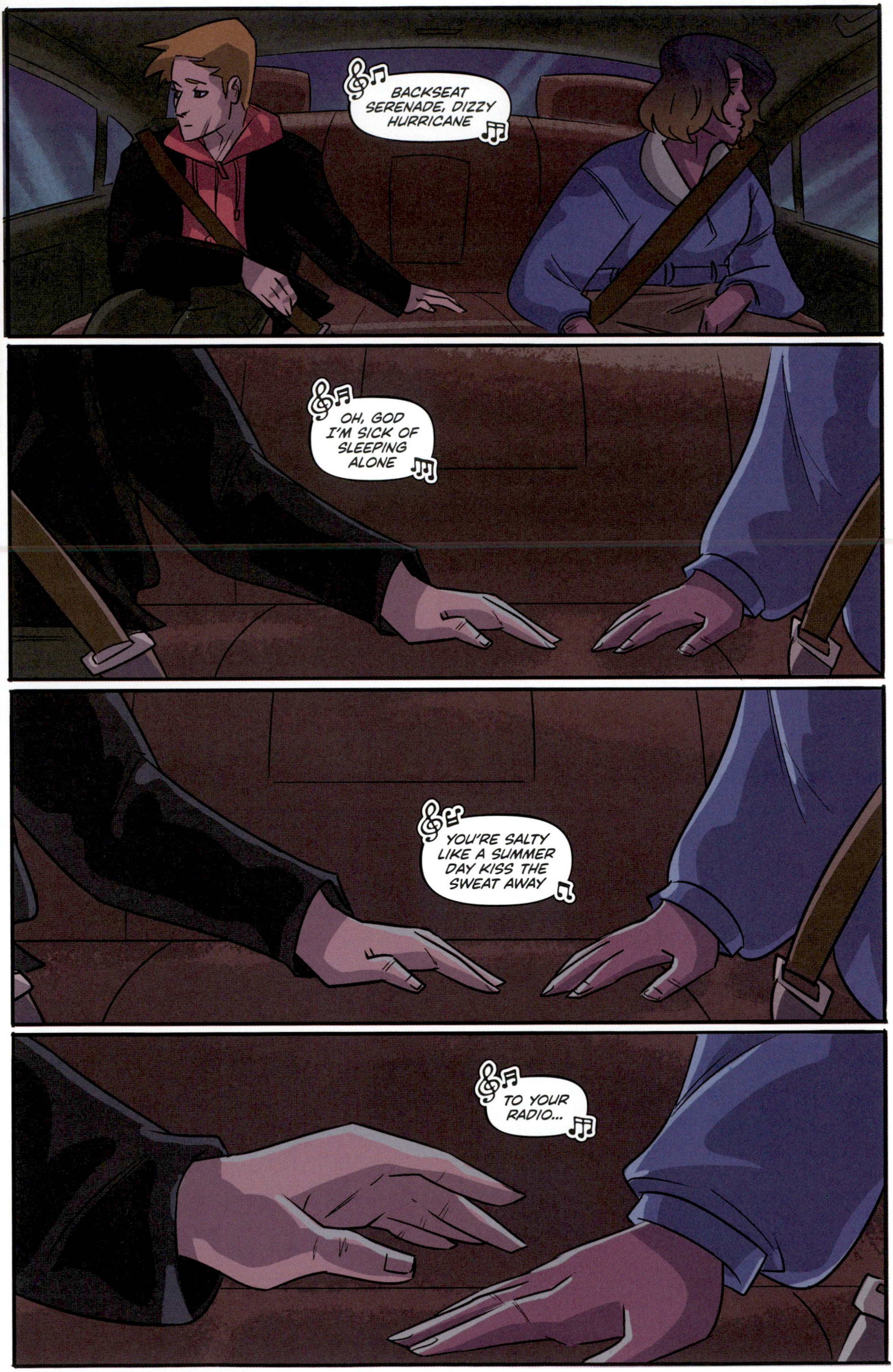
BACKSEAT SERENADE, DIZZY HURRICANE
OH, GOD I'M SICK OF SLEEPING ALONE
YOU'RE SALTY LIKE A SUMMER DAY KISS THE SWEAT AWAY
TO YOUR RADIO...

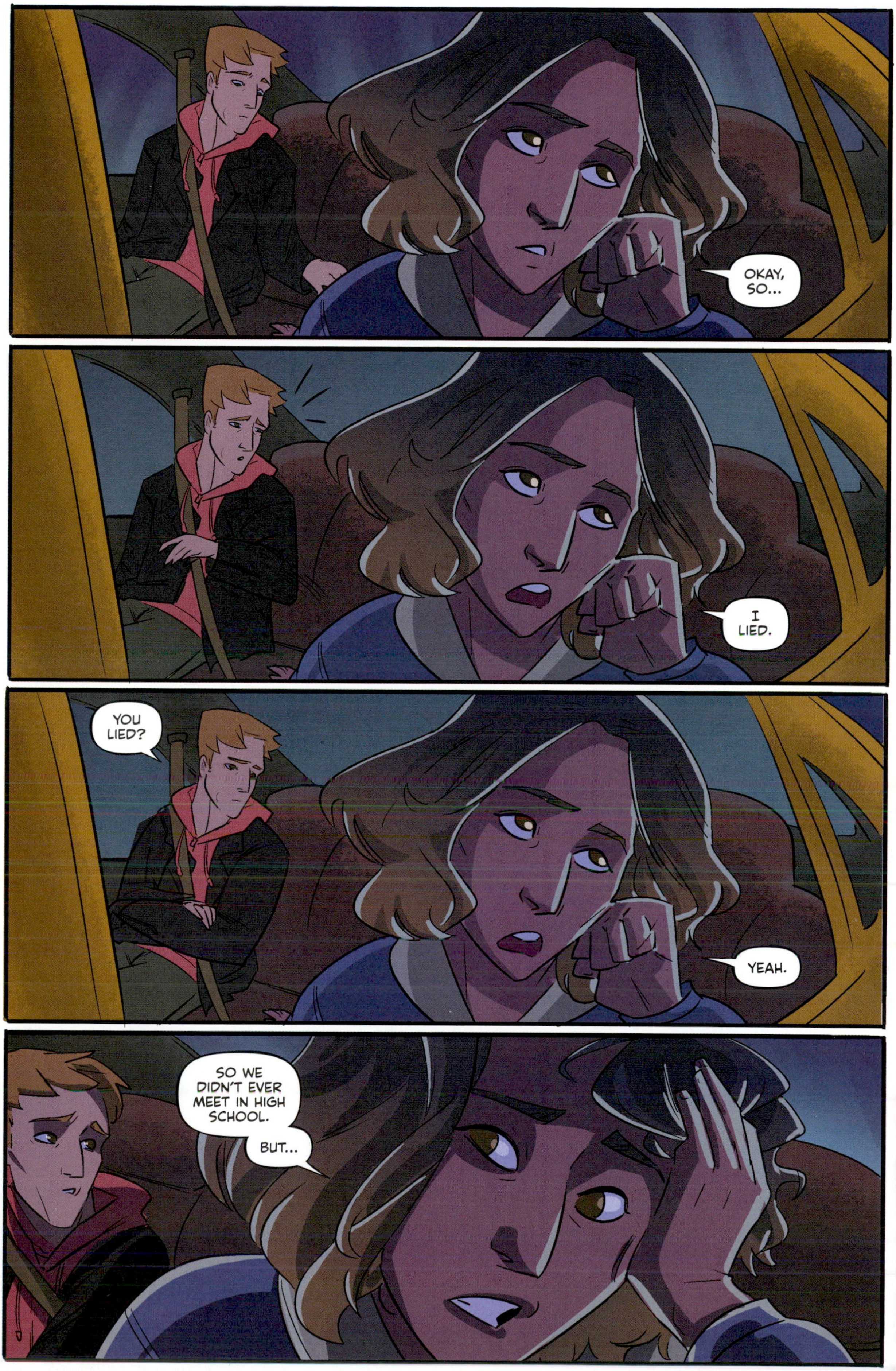
OKAY, SO...
I LIED.
YOU LIED?
YEAH.
SO WE DIDN'T EVER MEET IN HIGH SCHOOL.
BUT...

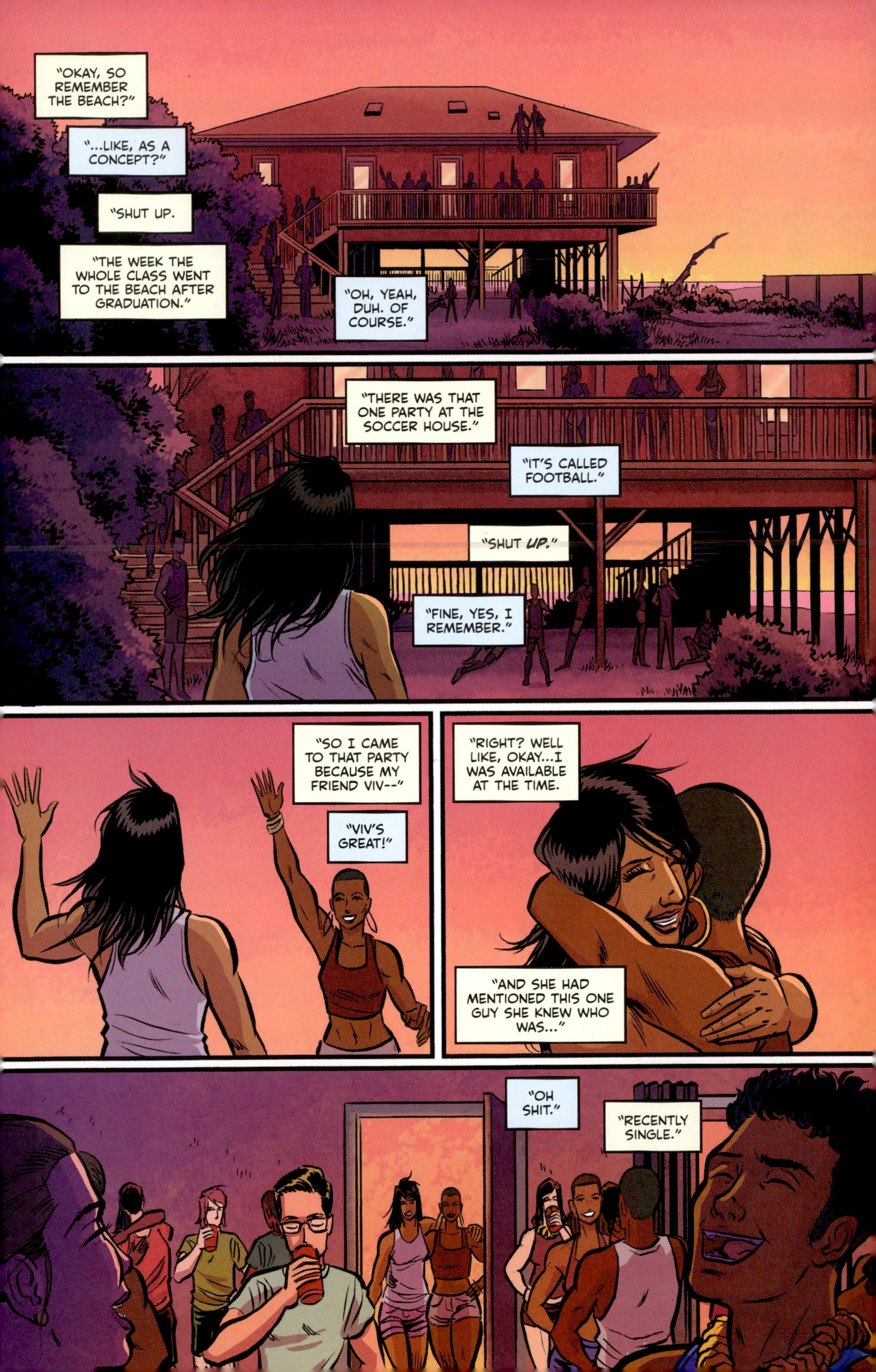
"OKAY, SO REMEMBER THE BEACH?"
"...LIKE, AS A CONCEPT?"
"SHUT UP.
"THE WEEK THE WHOLE CLASS WENT TO THE BEACH AFTER GRADUATION."
"OH, YEAH, DUH. OF COURSE."
"THERE WAS THAT ONE PARTY AT THE SOCCER HOUSE."
"IT'S CALLED FOOTBALL."
"SHUT *UP.*"
"FINE, YES, I REMEMBER."
"SO I CAME TO THAT PARTY BECAUSE MY FRIEND VIV--"
"VIV'S GREAT!"
"RIGHT? WELL LIKE, OKAY...I WAS AVAILABLE AT THE TIME.
"AND SHE HAD MENTIONED THIS ONE GUY SHE KNEW WHO WAS..."
"OH SHIT."
"RECENTLY SINGLE."

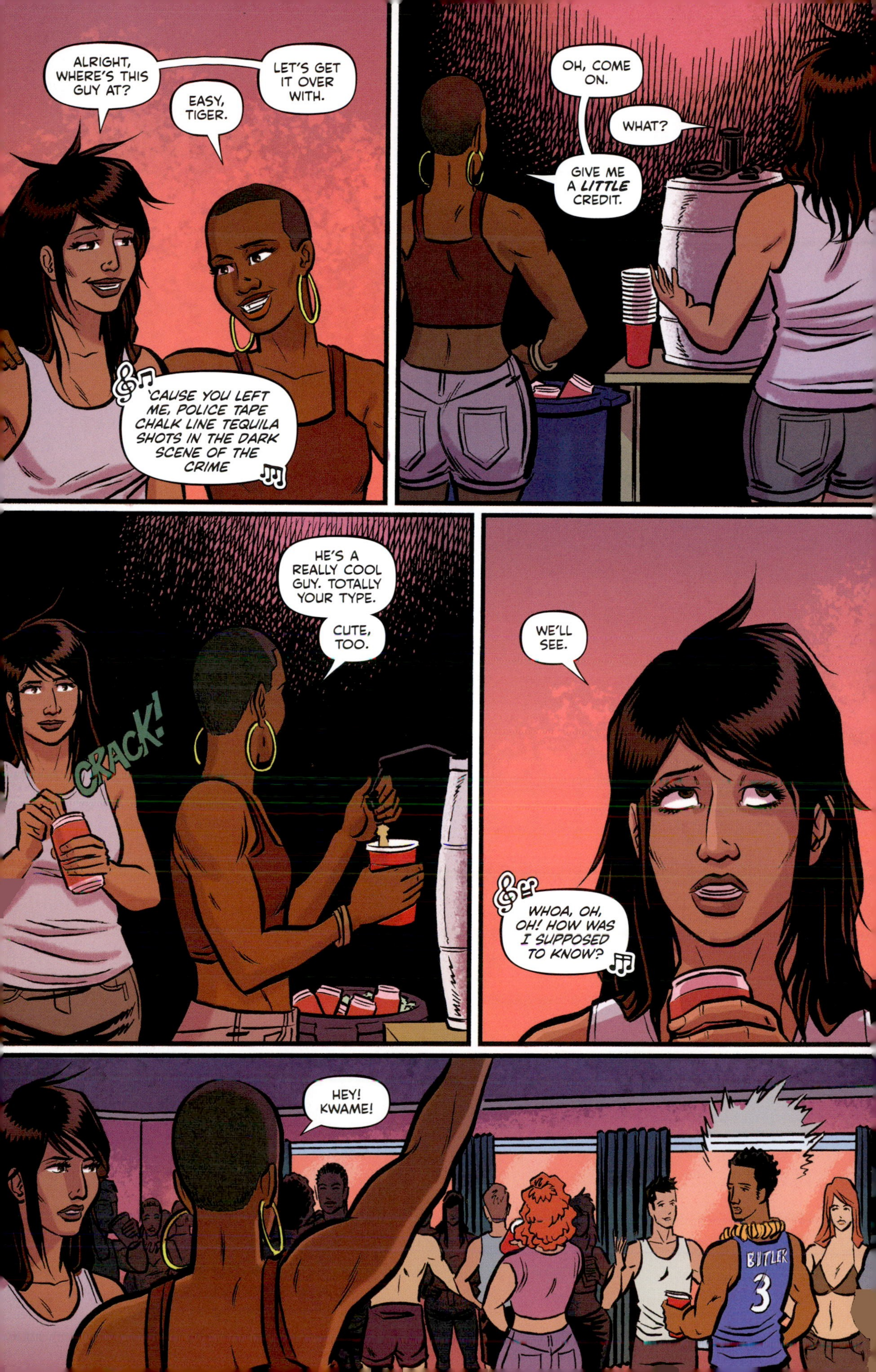
ALRIGHT, WHERE'S THIS GUY AT?
LET'S GET IT OVER WITH.
EASY, TIGER.
'CAUSE YOU LEFT ME, POLICE TAPE CHALK LINE TEQUILA SHOTS IN THE DARK SCENE OF THE CRIME
OH, COME ON.
WHAT?
GIVE ME A *LITTLE* CREDIT.
HE'S A REALLY COOL GUY. TOTALLY YOUR TYPE.
CUTE, TOO.
CRACK!
WE'LL SEE.
WHOA, OH, OH! HOW WAS I SUPPOSED TO KNOW?
HEY! KWAME!
BUTLER
3

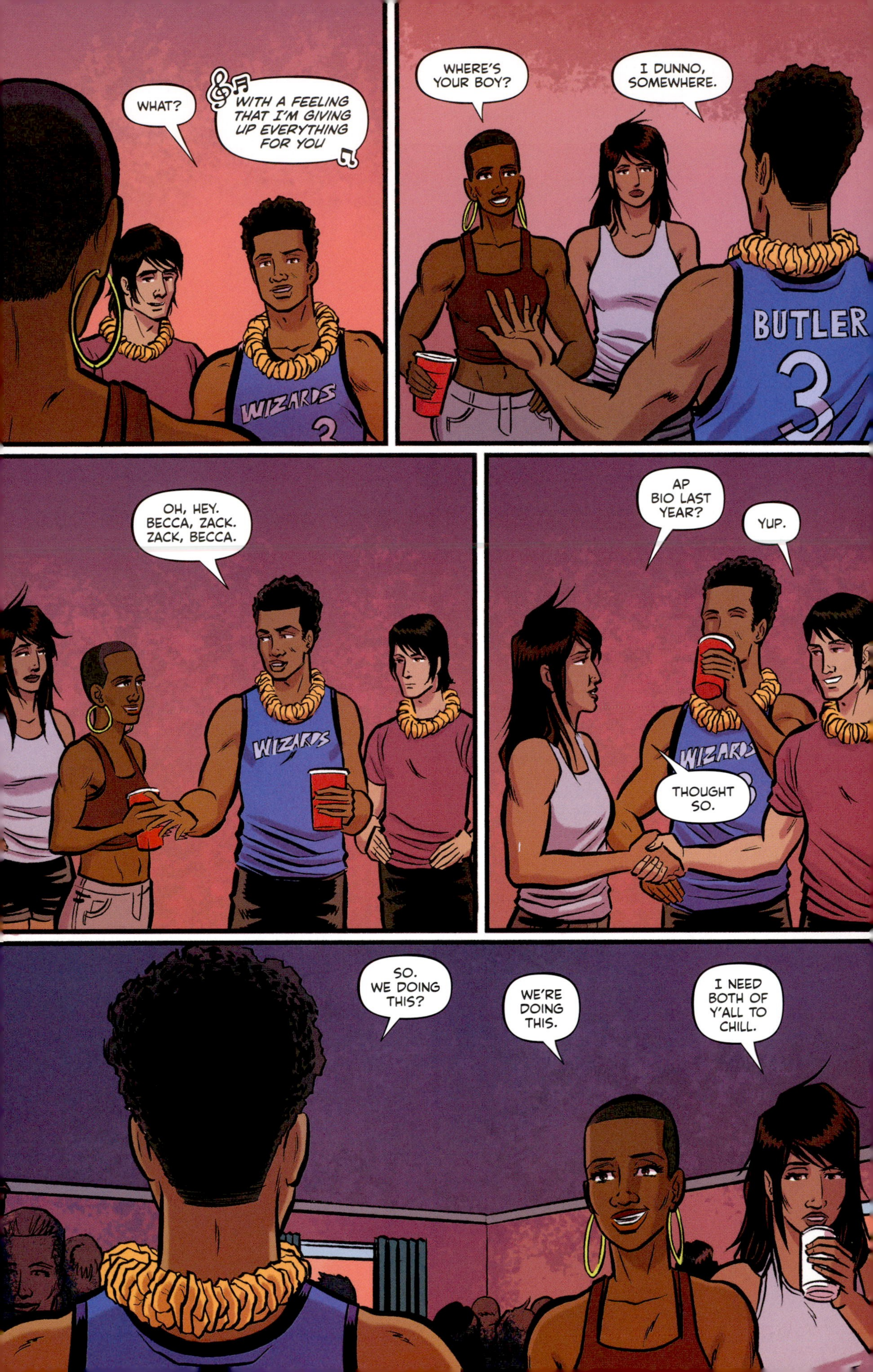
WHAT?
WITH A FEELING THAT I'M GIVING UP EVERYTHING FOR YOU
WHERE'S YOUR BOY?
I DUNNO, SOMEWHERE.
BUTLER 3
OH, HEY. BECCA, ZACK. ZACK, BECCA.
WIZARDS
AP BIO LAST YEAR?
YUP.
THOUGHT SO.
SO. WE DOING THIS?
WE'RE DOING THIS.
I NEED BOTH OF Y'ALL TO CHILL.

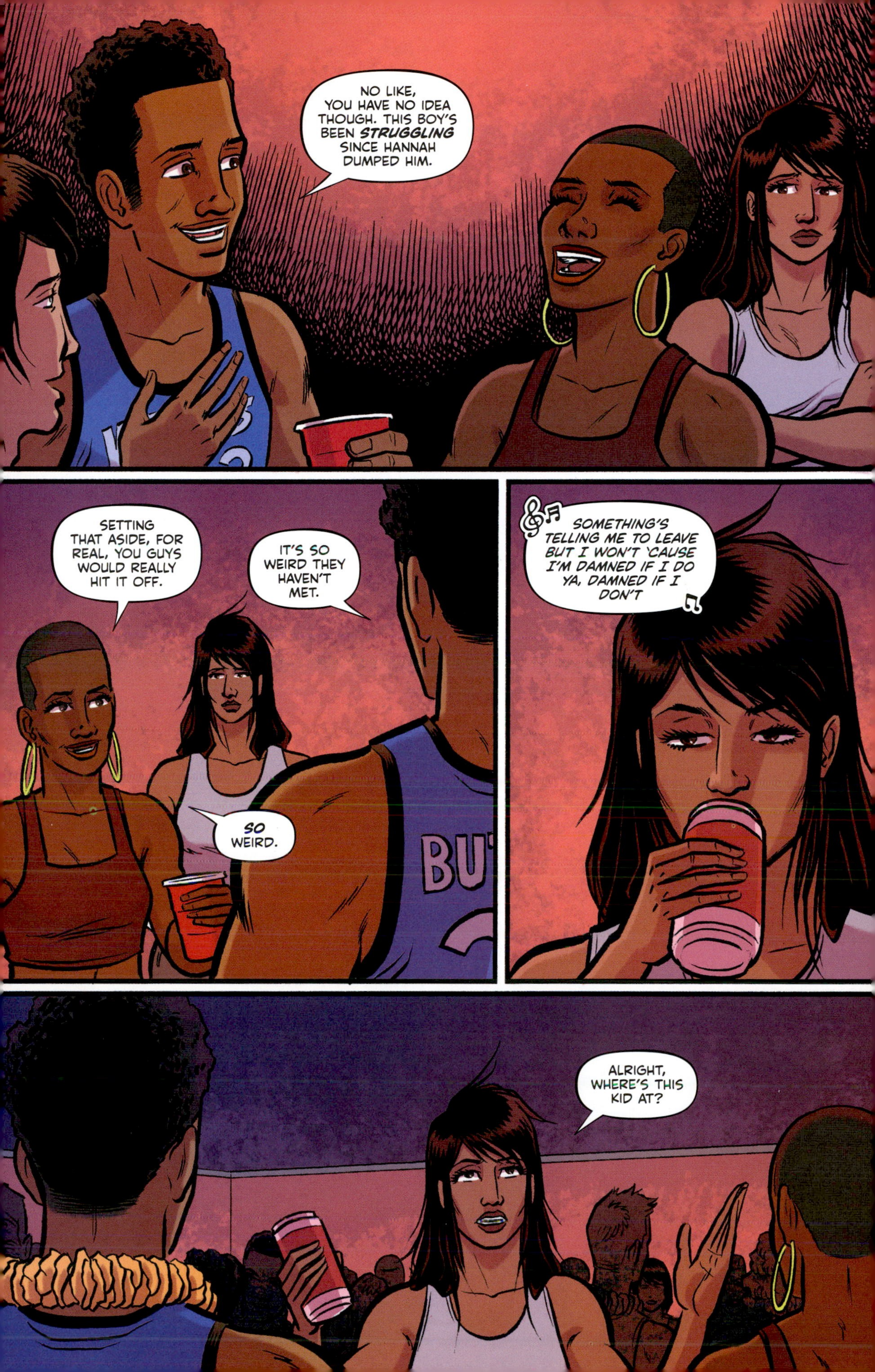
NO LIKE, YOU HAVE NO IDEA THOUGH. THIS BOY'S BEEN **STRUGGLING** SINCE HANNAH DUMPED HIM.
SETTING THAT ASIDE, FOR REAL, YOU GUYS WOULD REALLY HIT IT OFF.
IT'S SO WEIRD THEY HAVEN'T MET.
SO WEIRD.
BU
SOMETHING'S TELLING ME TO LEAVE BUT I WON'T 'CAUSE I'M DAMNED IF I DO YA, DAMNED IF I DON'T
ALRIGHT, WHERE'S THIS KID AT?

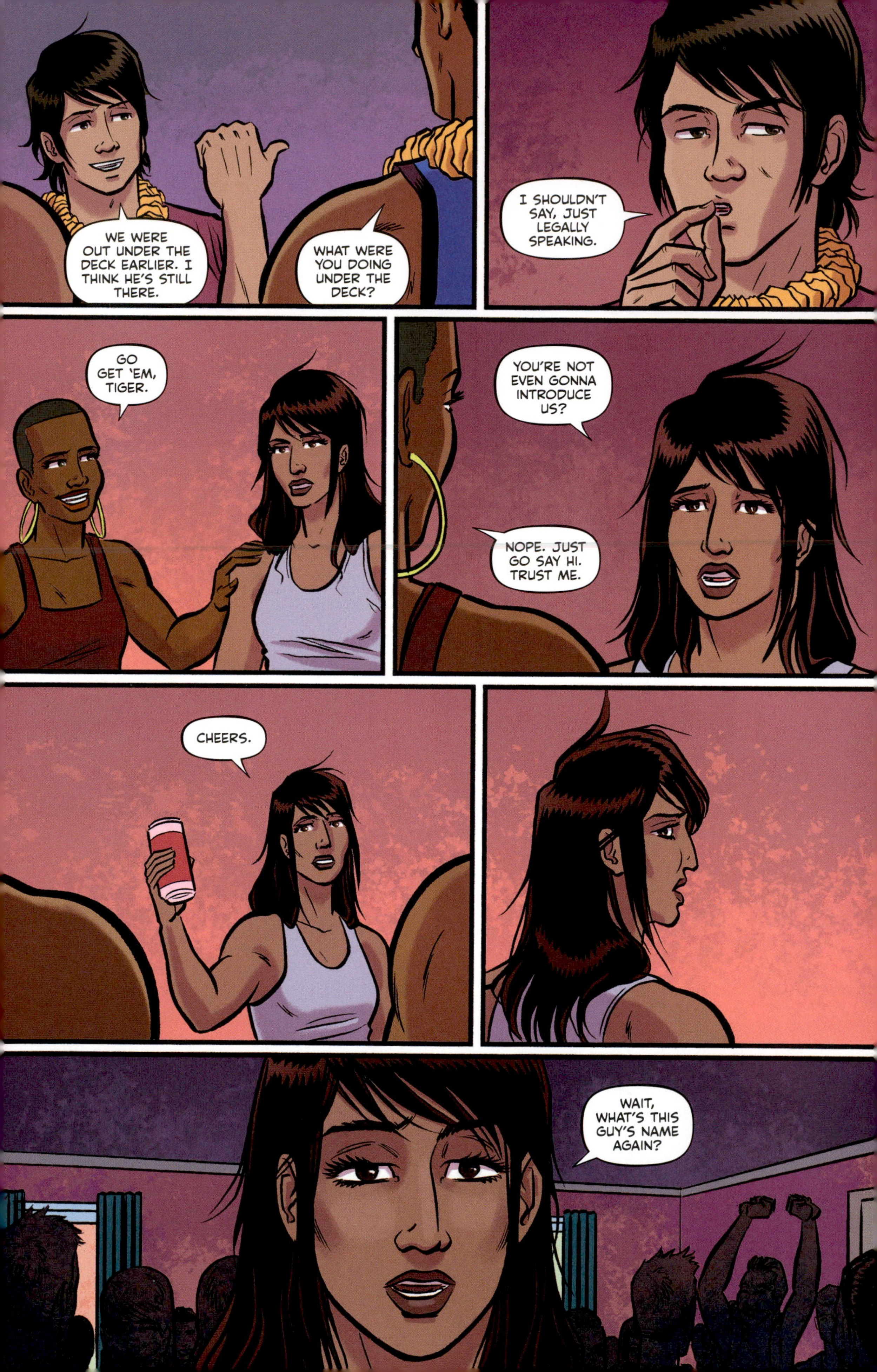
WE WERE OUT UNDER THE DECK EARLIER. I THINK HE'S STILL THERE.
WHAT WERE YOU DOING UNDER THE DECK?
I SHOULDN'T SAY, JUST LEGALLY SPEAKING.
GO GET 'EM, TIGER.
YOU'RE NOT EVEN GONNA INTRODUCE US?
NOPE. JUST GO SAY HI. TRUST ME.
CHEERS.
WAIT, WHAT'S THIS GUY'S NAME AGAIN?

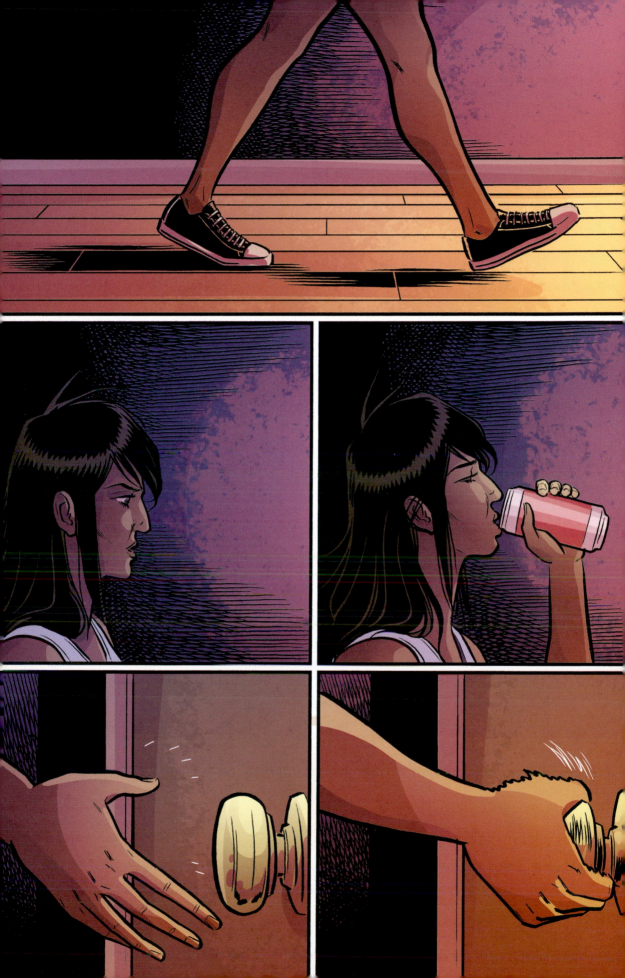

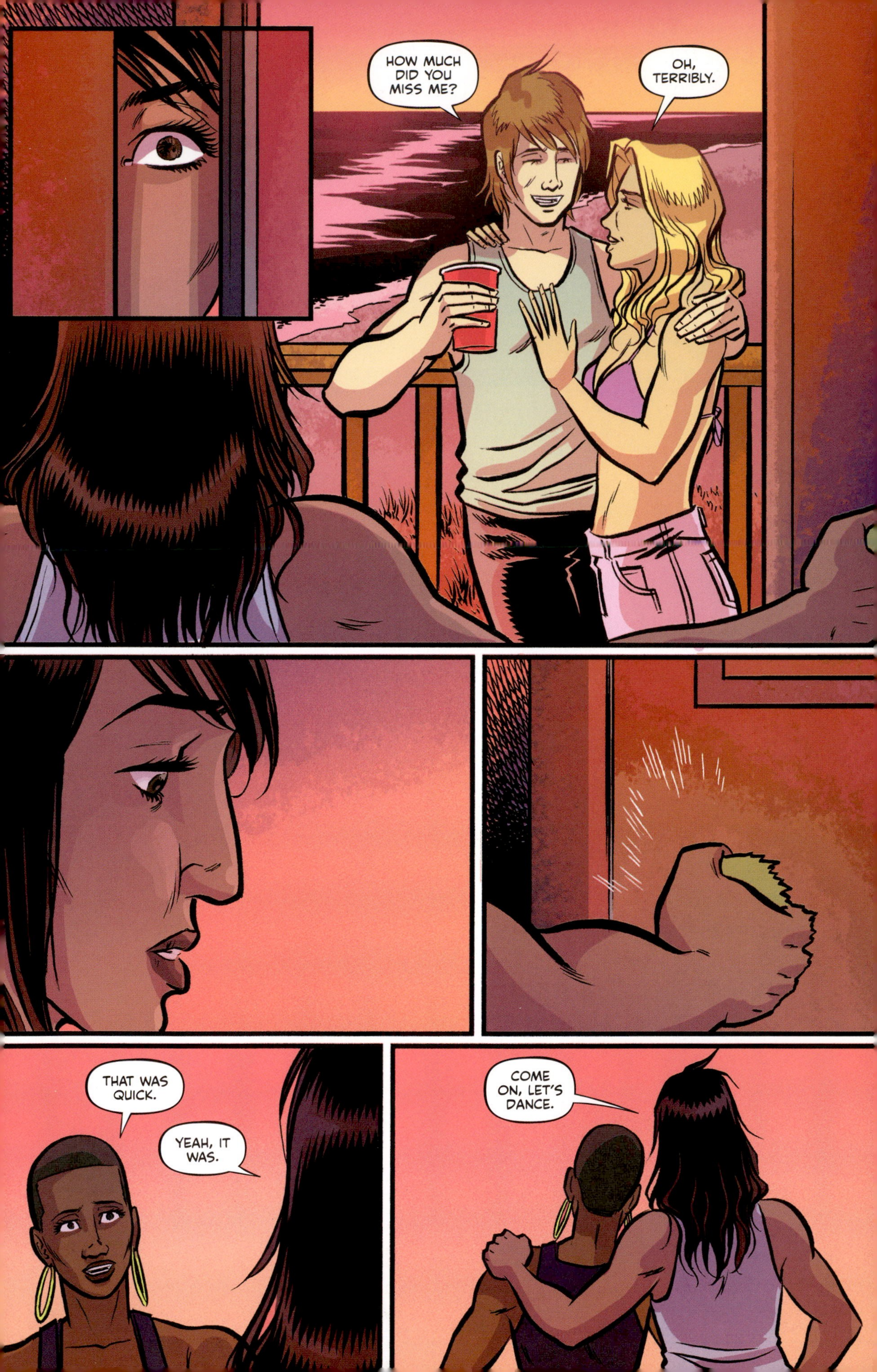
HOW MUCH DID YOU MISS ME?
OH, TERRIBLY.
THAT WAS QUICK.
YEAH, IT WAS.
COME ON, LET'S DANCE.

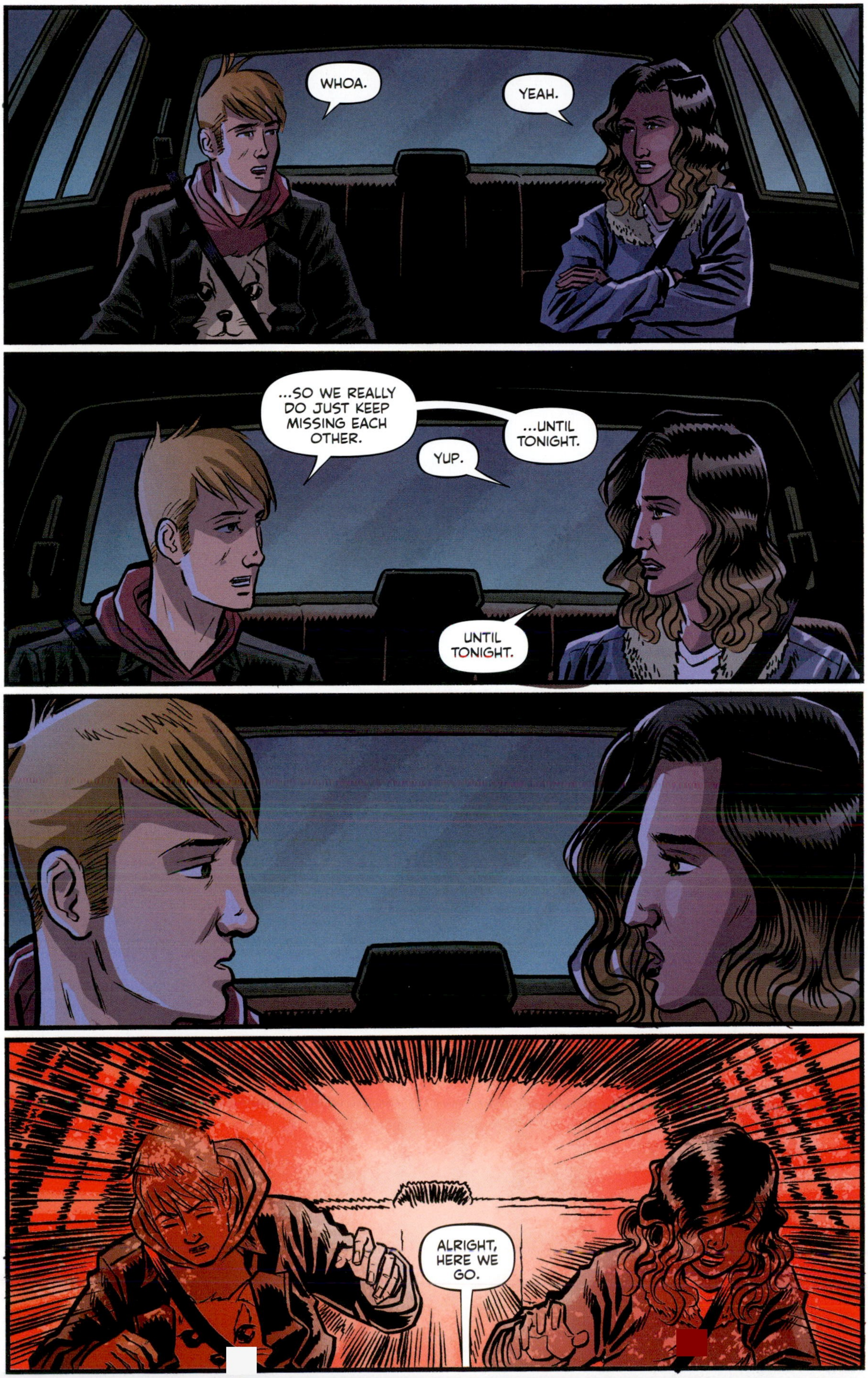
WHOA.
YEAH.
...SO WE REALLY DO JUST KEEP MISSING EACH OTHER.
YUP.
...UNTIL TONIGHT.
UNTIL TONIGHT.
ALRIGHT, HERE WE GO.

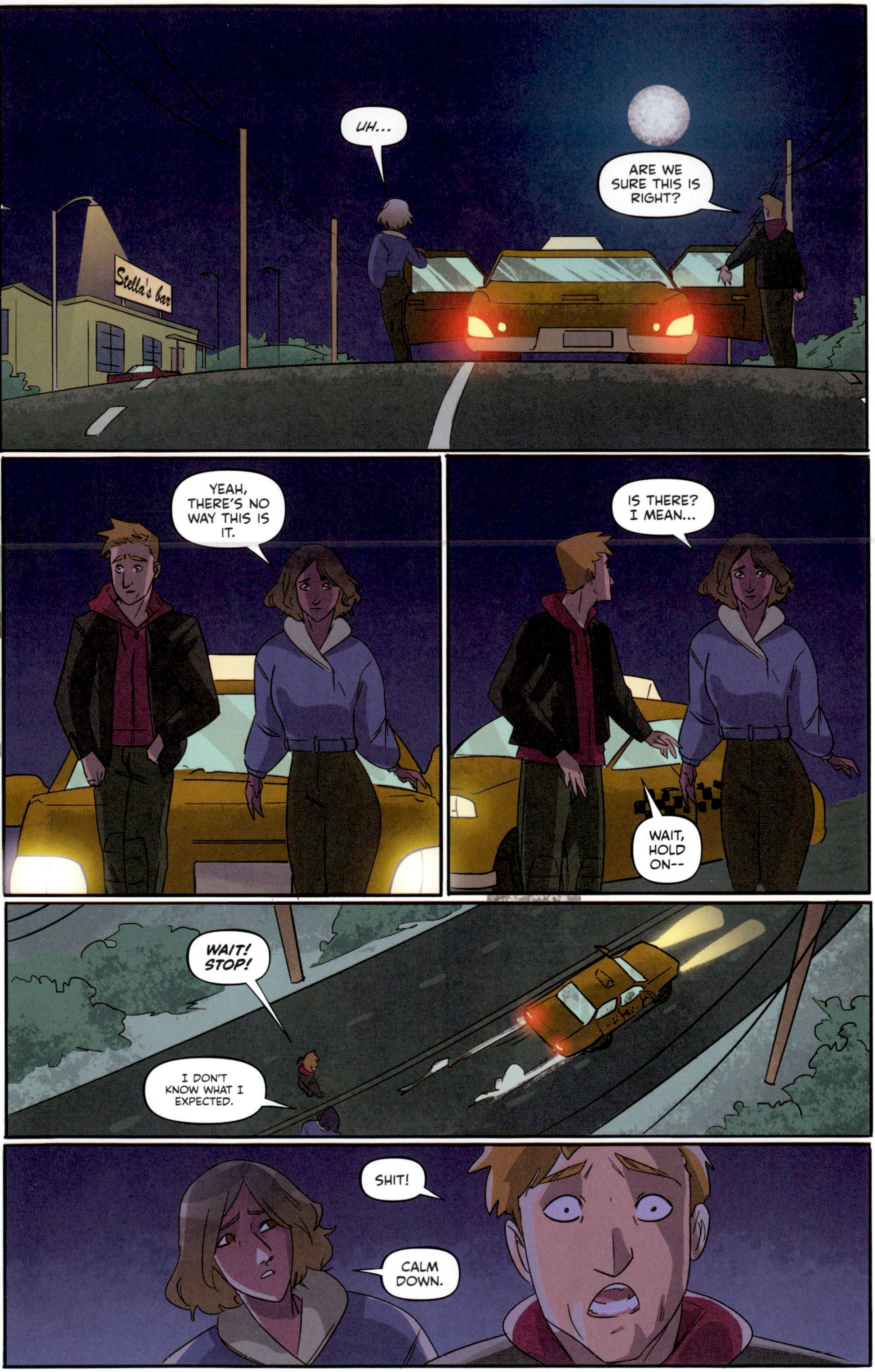
Stella's bar
UH...
ARE WE SURE THIS IS RIGHT?
YEAH, THERE'S NO WAY THIS IS IT.
IS THERE? I MEAN...
WAIT, HOLD ON--
WAIT! STOP!
I DON'T KNOW WHAT I EXPECTED.
SHIT!
CALM DOWN.

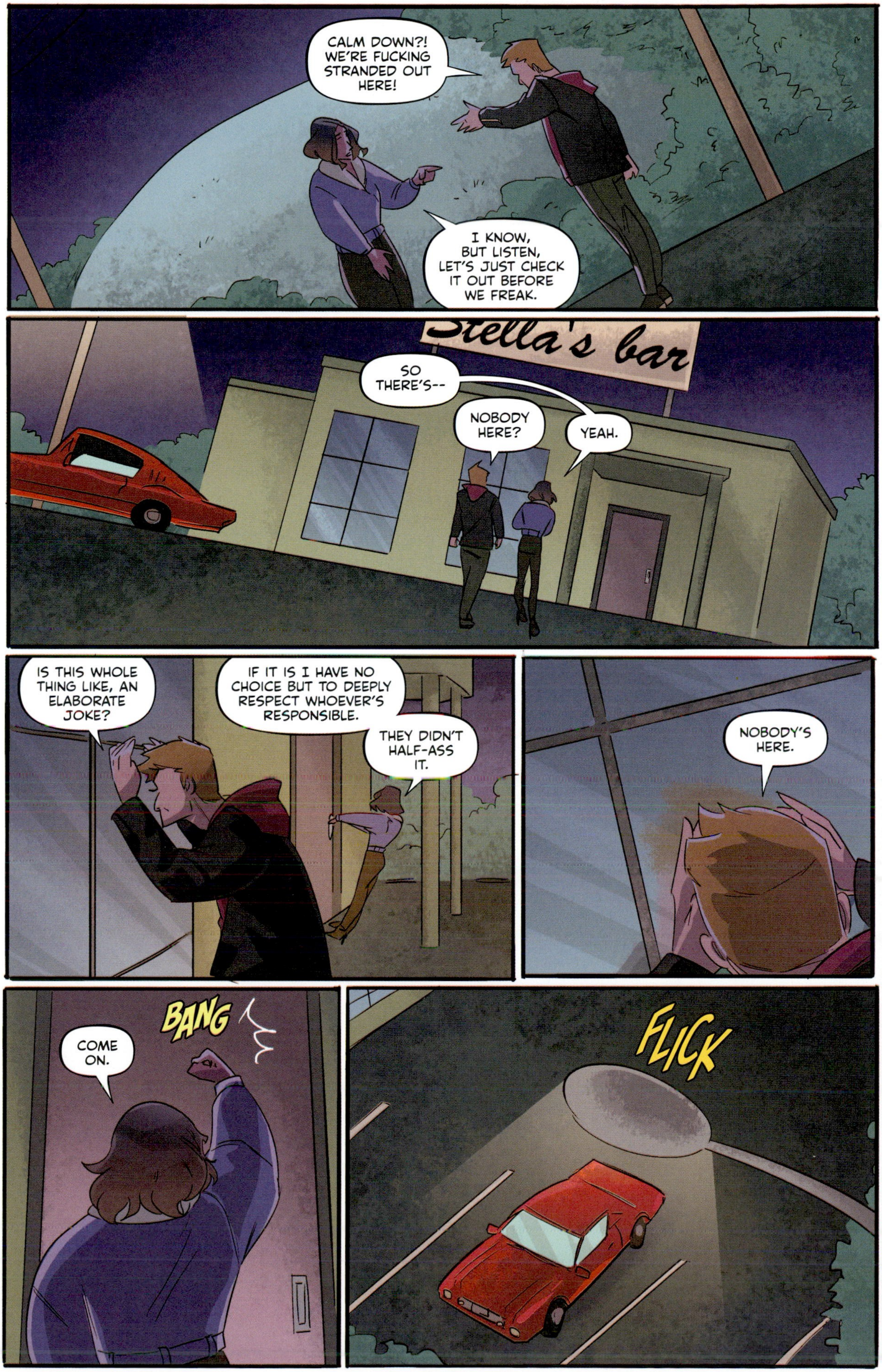
CALM DOWN?! WE'RE FUCKING STRANDED OUT HERE!
I KNOW, BUT LISTEN, LET'S JUST CHECK IT OUT BEFORE WE FREAK.
Stella's bar
SO THERE'S--
NOBODY HERE?
YEAH.
IS THIS WHOLE THING LIKE, AN ELABORATE JOKE?
IF IT IS I HAVE NO CHOICE BUT TO DEEPLY RESPECT WHOEVER'S RESPONSIBLE.
THEY DIDN'T HALF-ASS IT.
NOBODY'S HERE.
BANG
COME ON.
FLICK

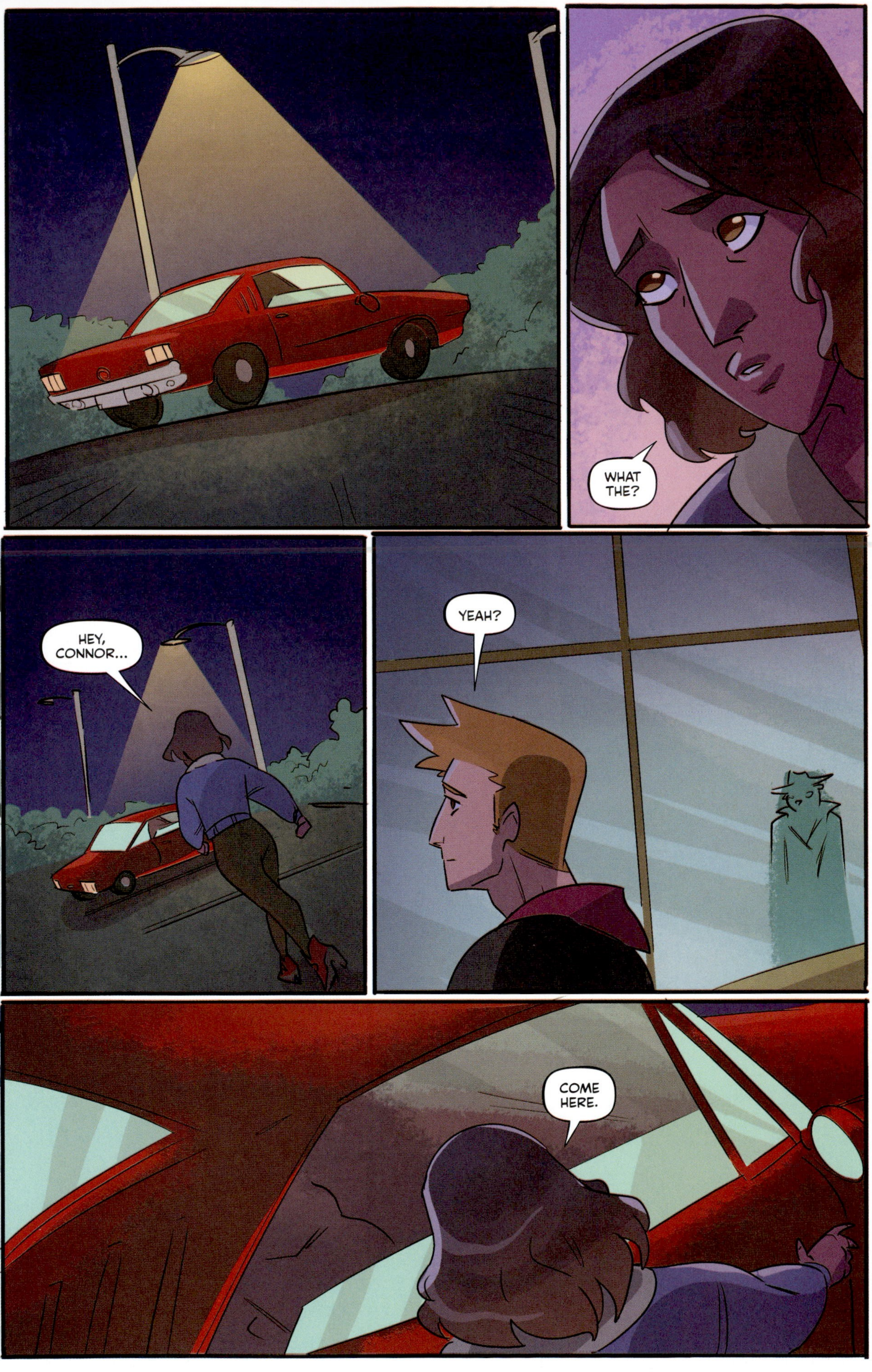
WHAT THE?
HEY, CONNOR...
YEAH?
COME HERE.

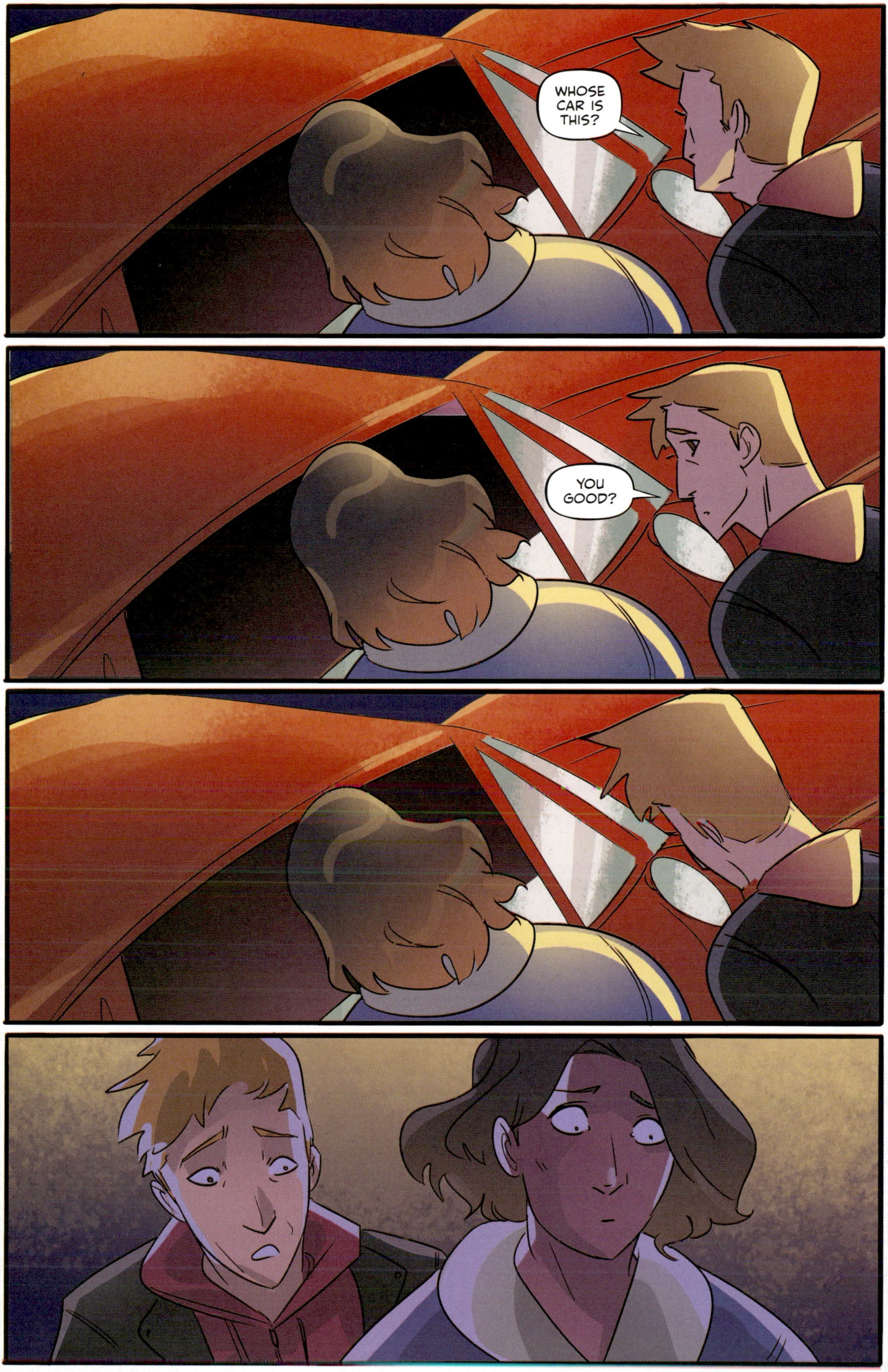
WHOSE CAR IS THIS?
YOU GOOD?

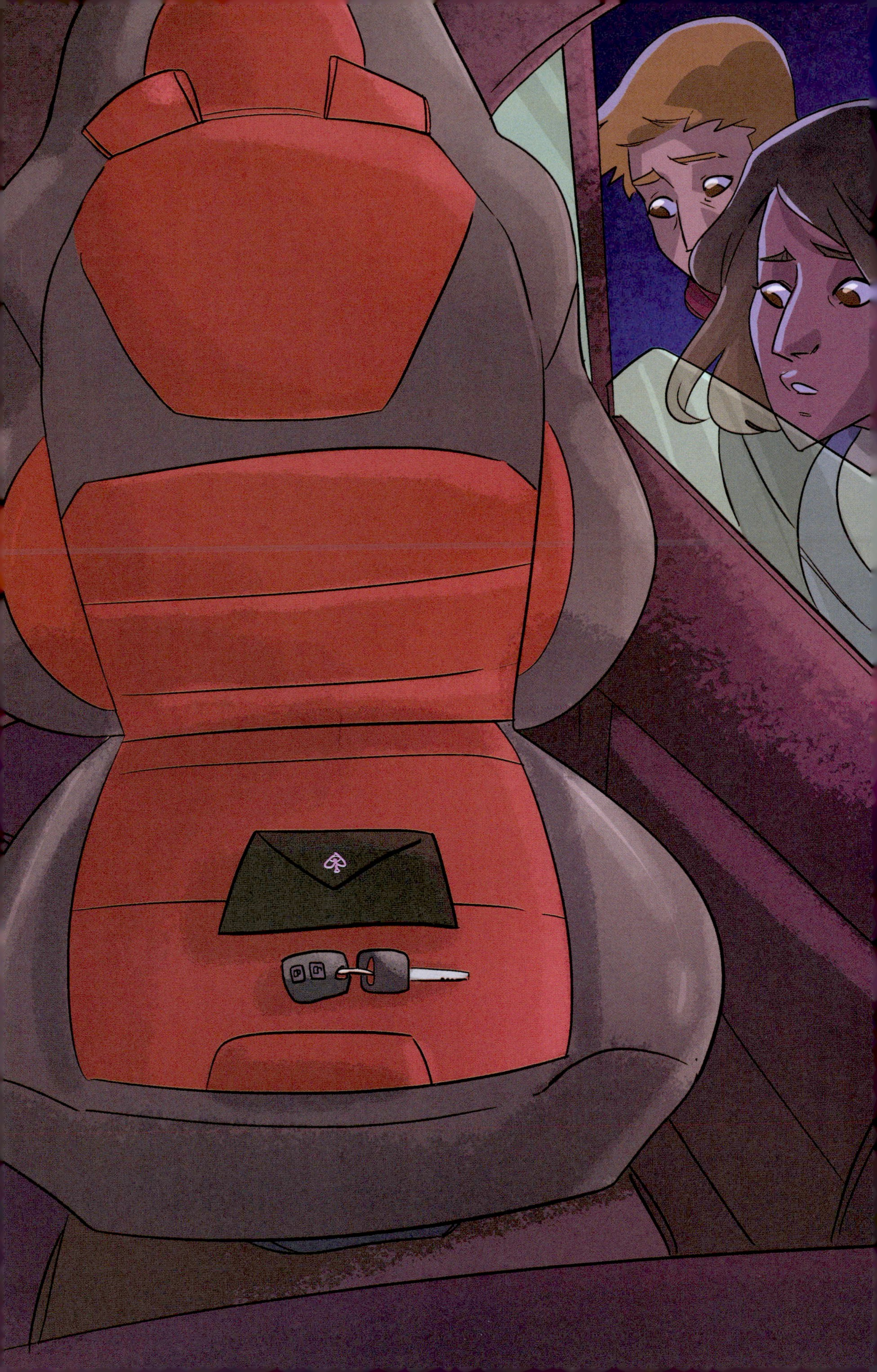

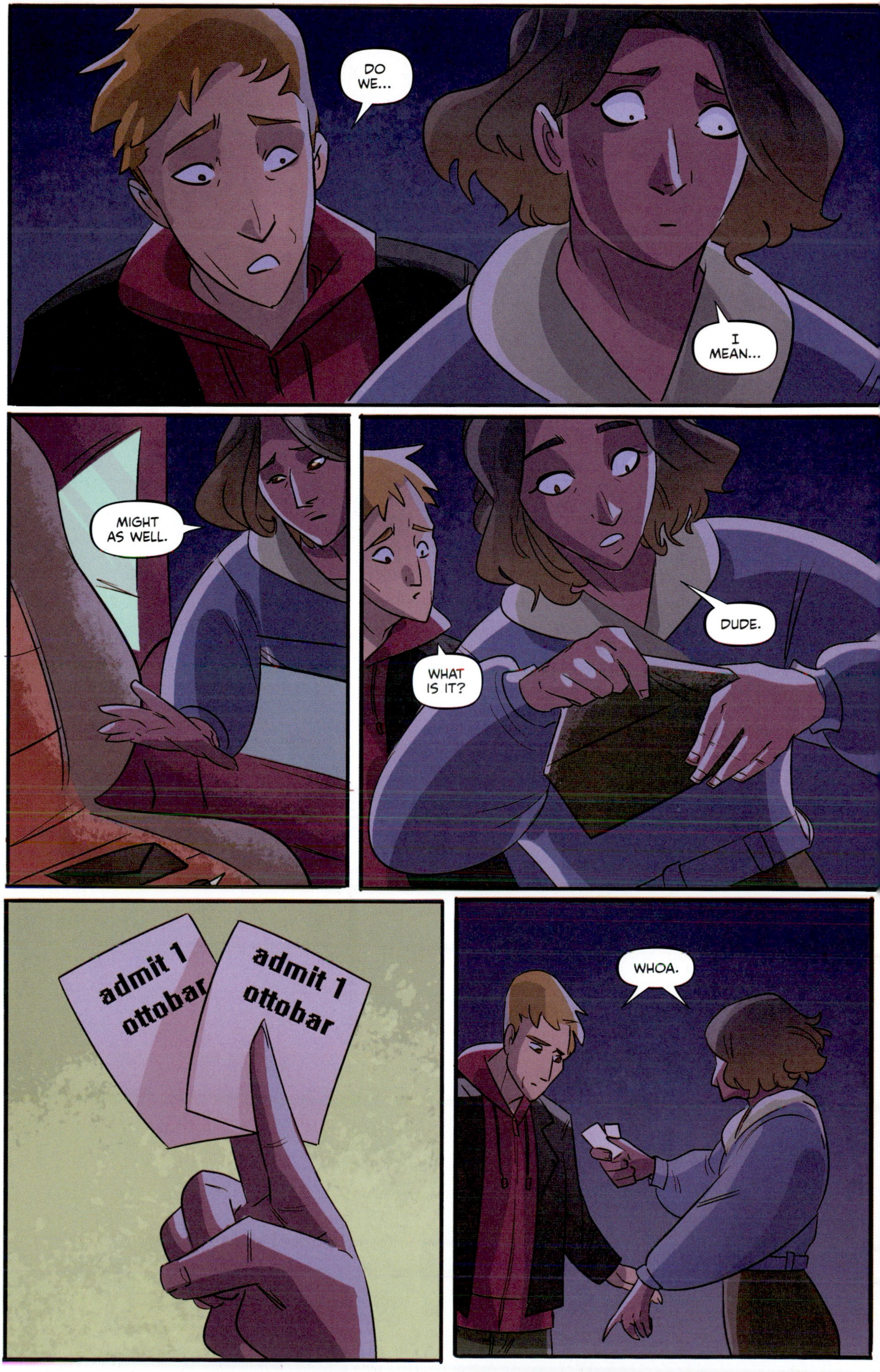
DO WE...
I MEAN...
MIGHT AS WELL.
DUDE.
WHAT IS IT?
admit 1 ottobar
admit 1 ottobar
WHOA.

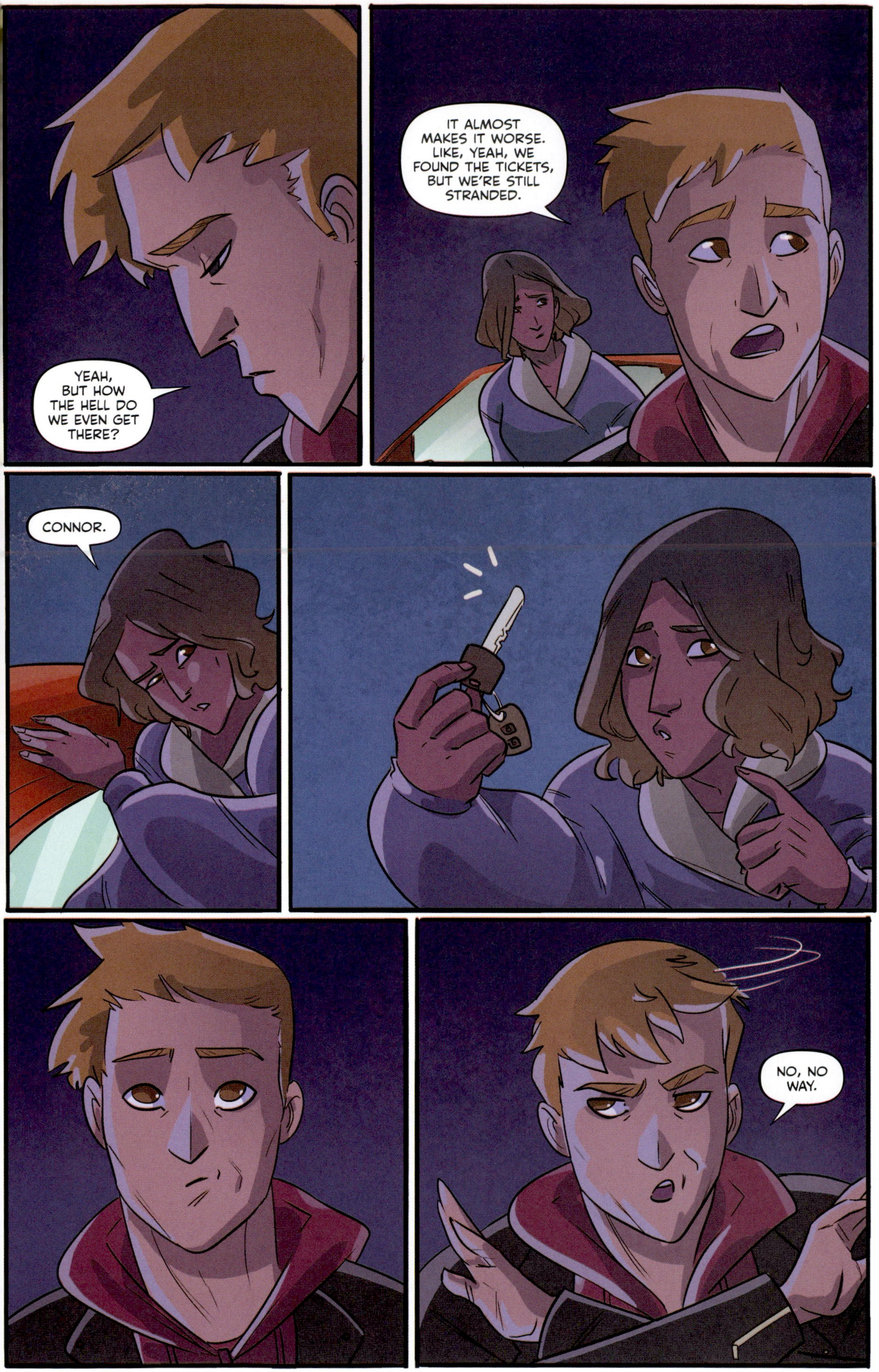
YEAH, BUT HOW THE HELL DO WE EVEN GET THERE?
IT ALMOST MAKES IT WORSE. LIKE, YEAH, WE FOUND THE TICKETS, BUT WE'RE STILL STRANDED.
CONNOR.
NO, NO WAY.

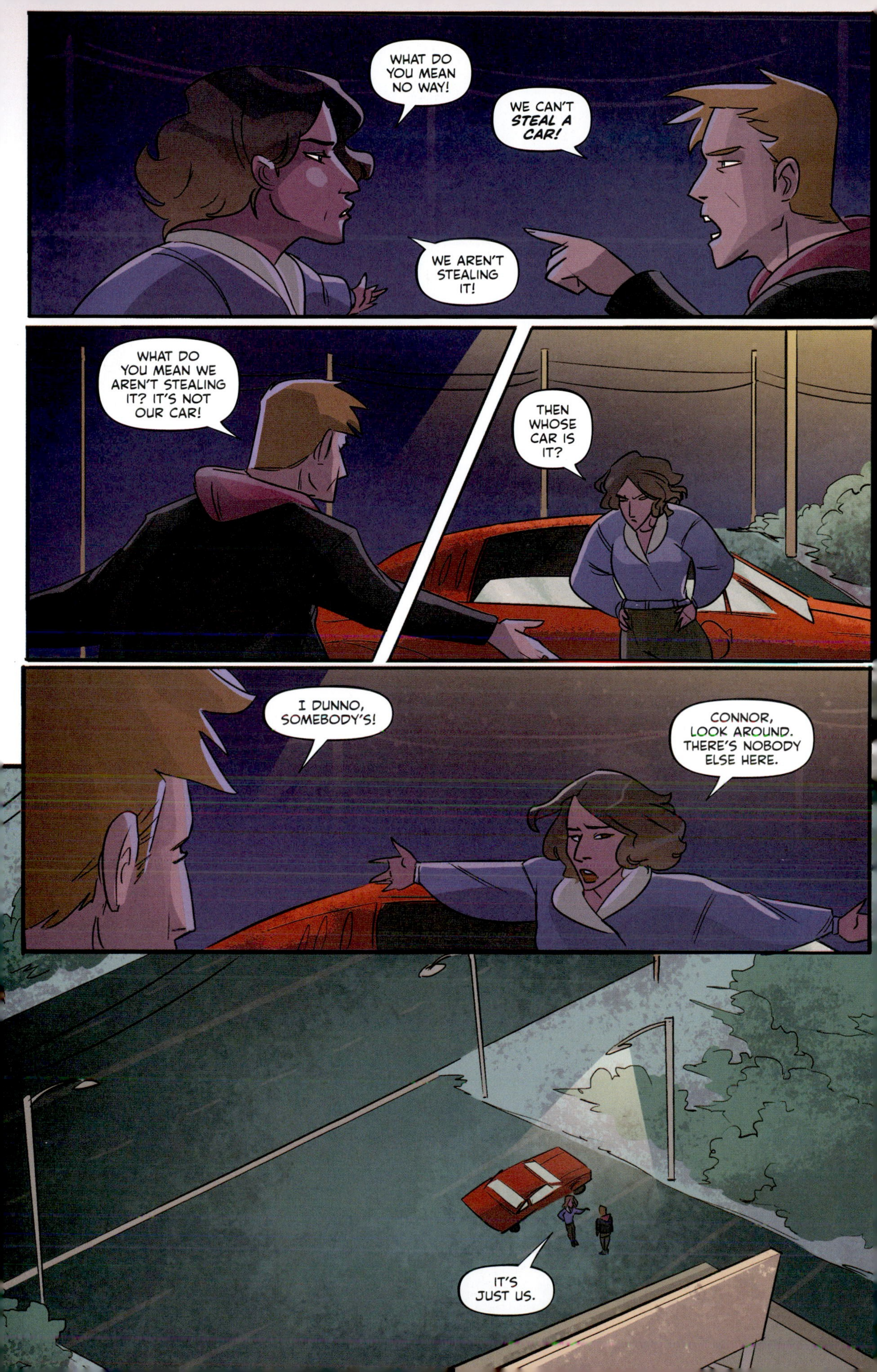
WHAT DO YOU MEAN NO WAY!
WE CAN'T STEAL A CAR!
WE AREN'T STEALING IT!
WHAT DO YOU MEAN WE AREN'T STEALING IT? IT'S NOT OUR CAR!
THEN WHOSE CAR IS IT?
I DUNNO, SOMEBODY'S!
CONNOR, LOOK AROUND. THERE'S NOBODY ELSE HERE.
IT'S JUST US.

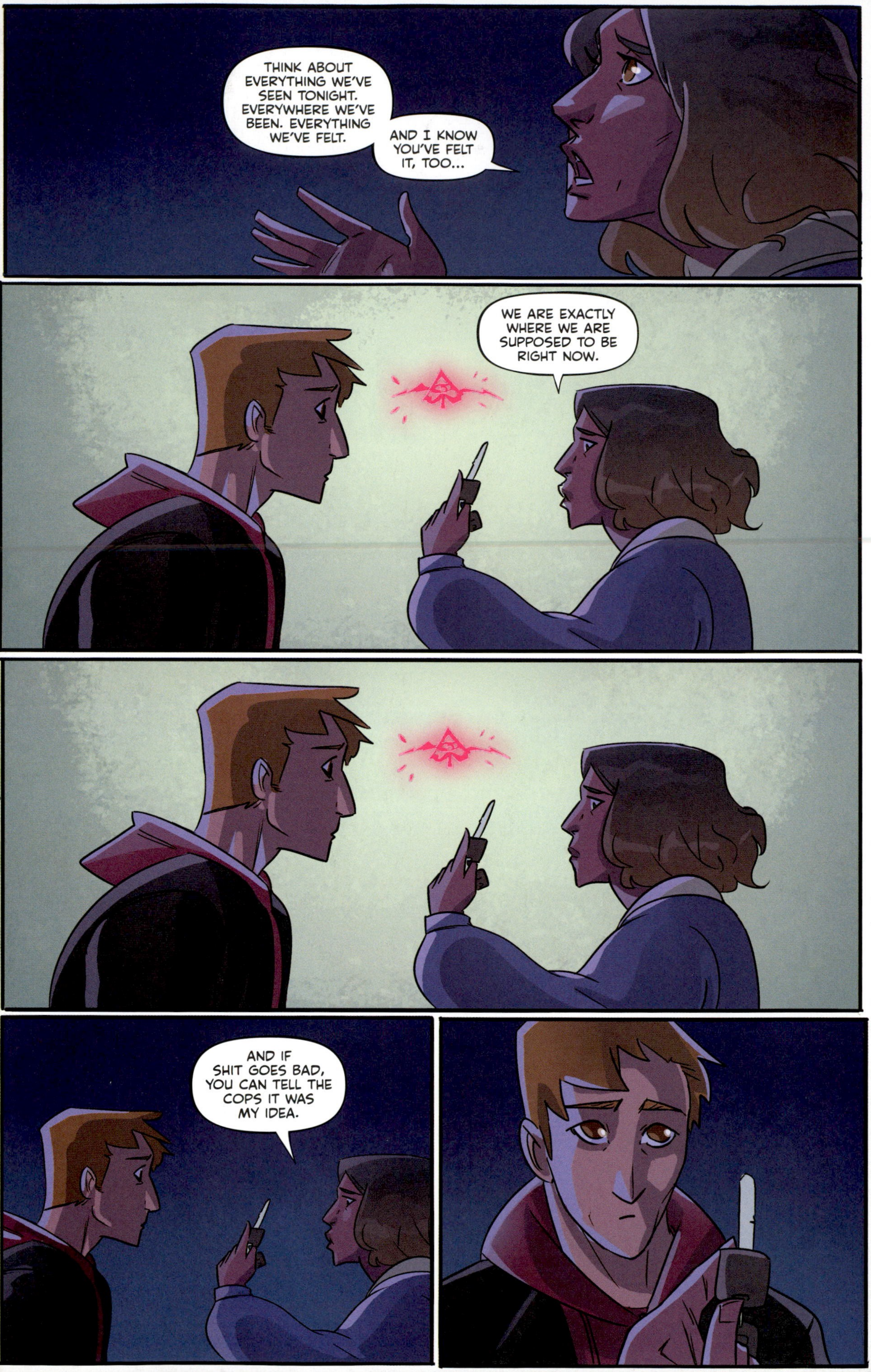
THINK ABOUT EVERYTHING WE'VE SEEN TONIGHT. EVERYWHERE WE'VE BEEN. EVERYTHING WE'VE FELT.
AND I KNOW YOU'VE FELT IT, TOO...
WE ARE EXACTLY WHERE WE ARE SUPPOSED TO BE RIGHT NOW.
AND IF SHIT GOES BAD, YOU CAN TELL THE COPS IT WAS MY IDEA.

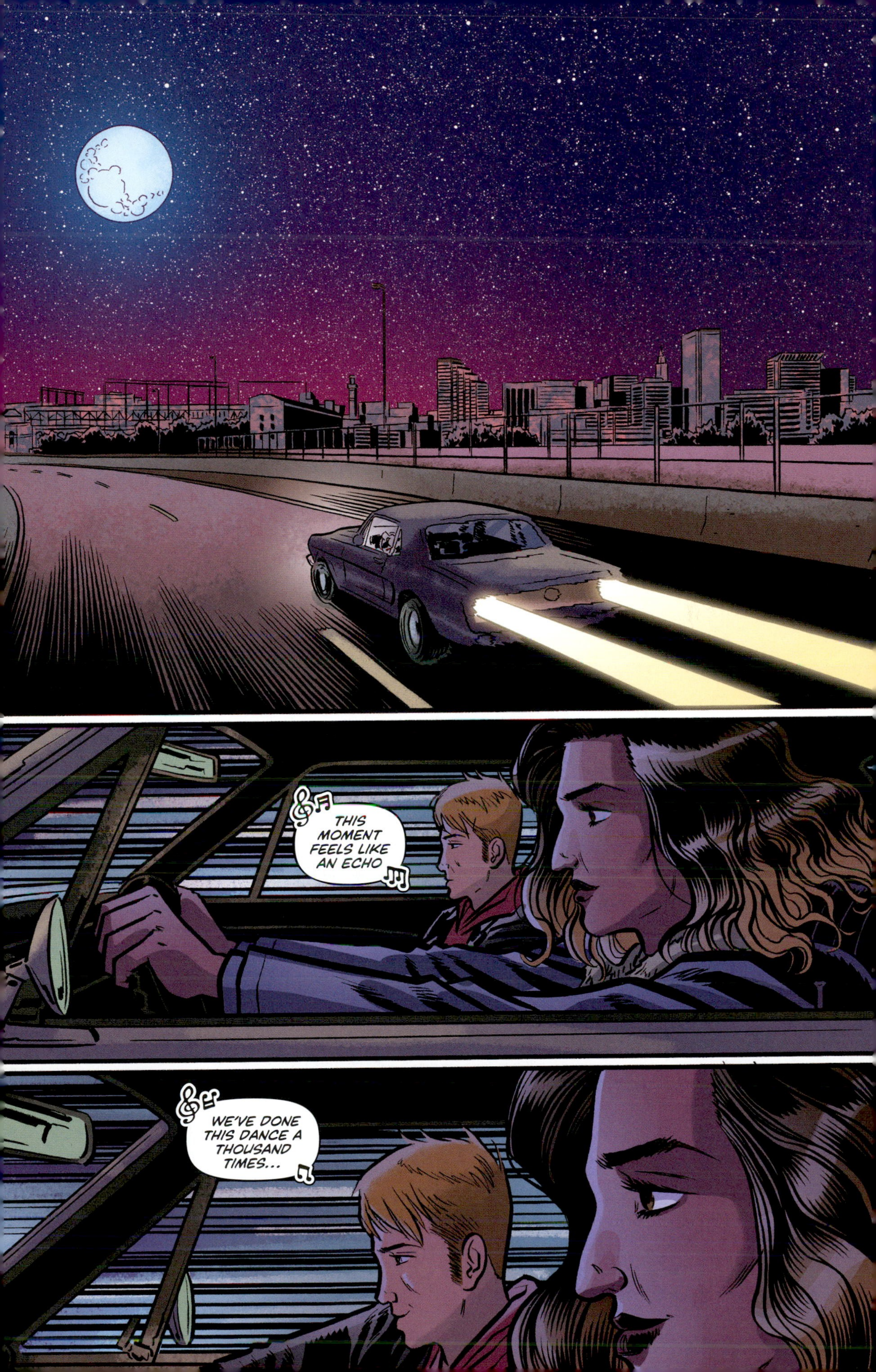
THIS MOMENT FEELS LIKE AN ECHO
WE'VE DONE THIS DANCE A THOUSAND TIMES...

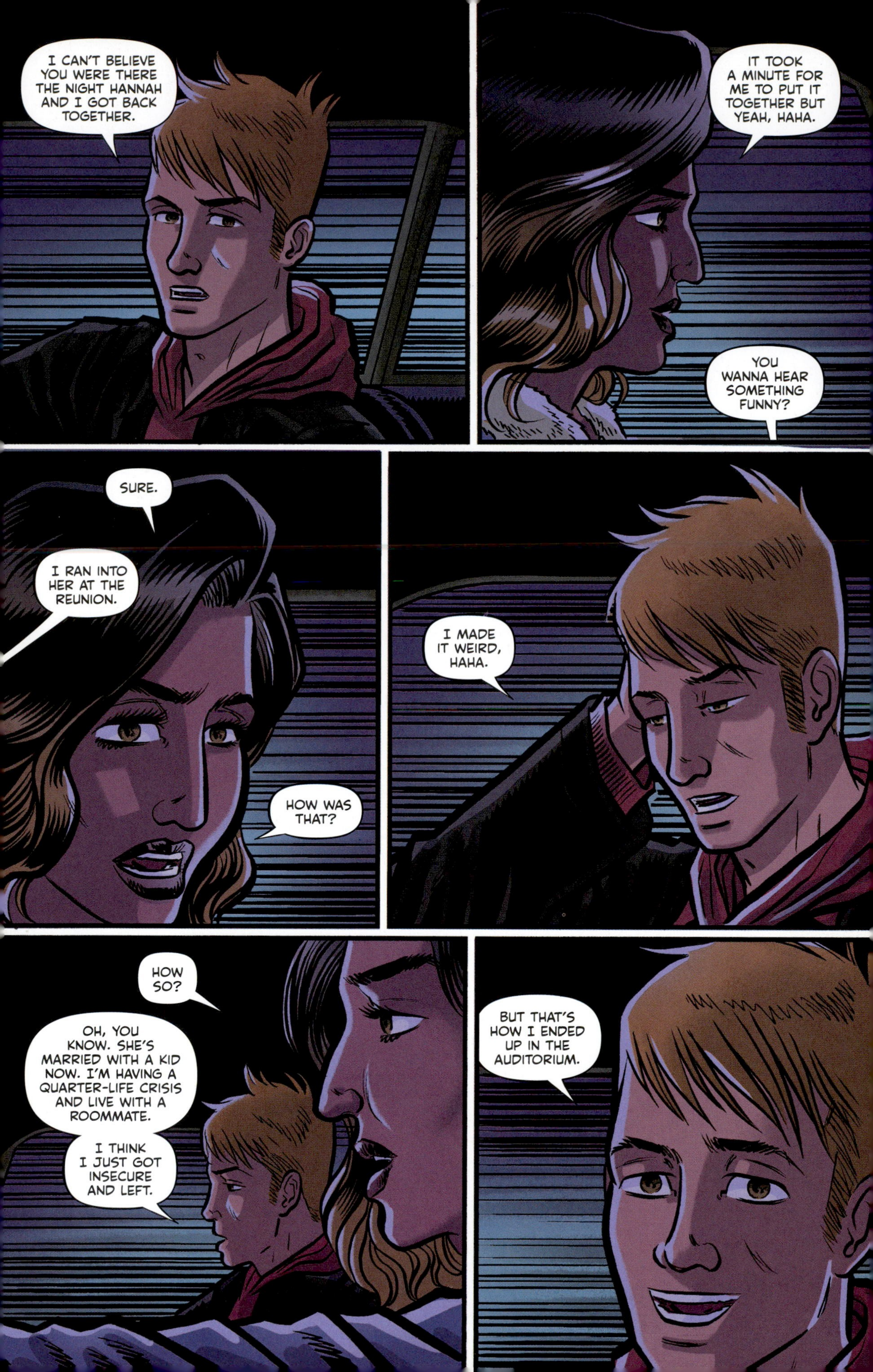
I CAN'T BELIEVE YOU WERE THERE THE NIGHT HANNAH AND I GOT BACK TOGETHER.
IT TOOK A MINUTE FOR ME TO PUT IT TOGETHER BUT YEAH, HAHA.
YOU WANNA HEAR SOMETHING FUNNY?
SURE.
I RAN INTO HER AT THE REUNION.
HOW WAS THAT?
I MADE IT WEIRD, HAHA.
HOW SO?
OH, YOU KNOW. SHE'S MARRIED WITH A KID NOW. I'M HAVING A QUARTER-LIFE CRISIS AND LIVE WITH A ROOMMATE.
I THINK I JUST GOT INSECURE AND LEFT.
BUT THAT'S HOW I ENDED UP IN THE AUDITORIUM.

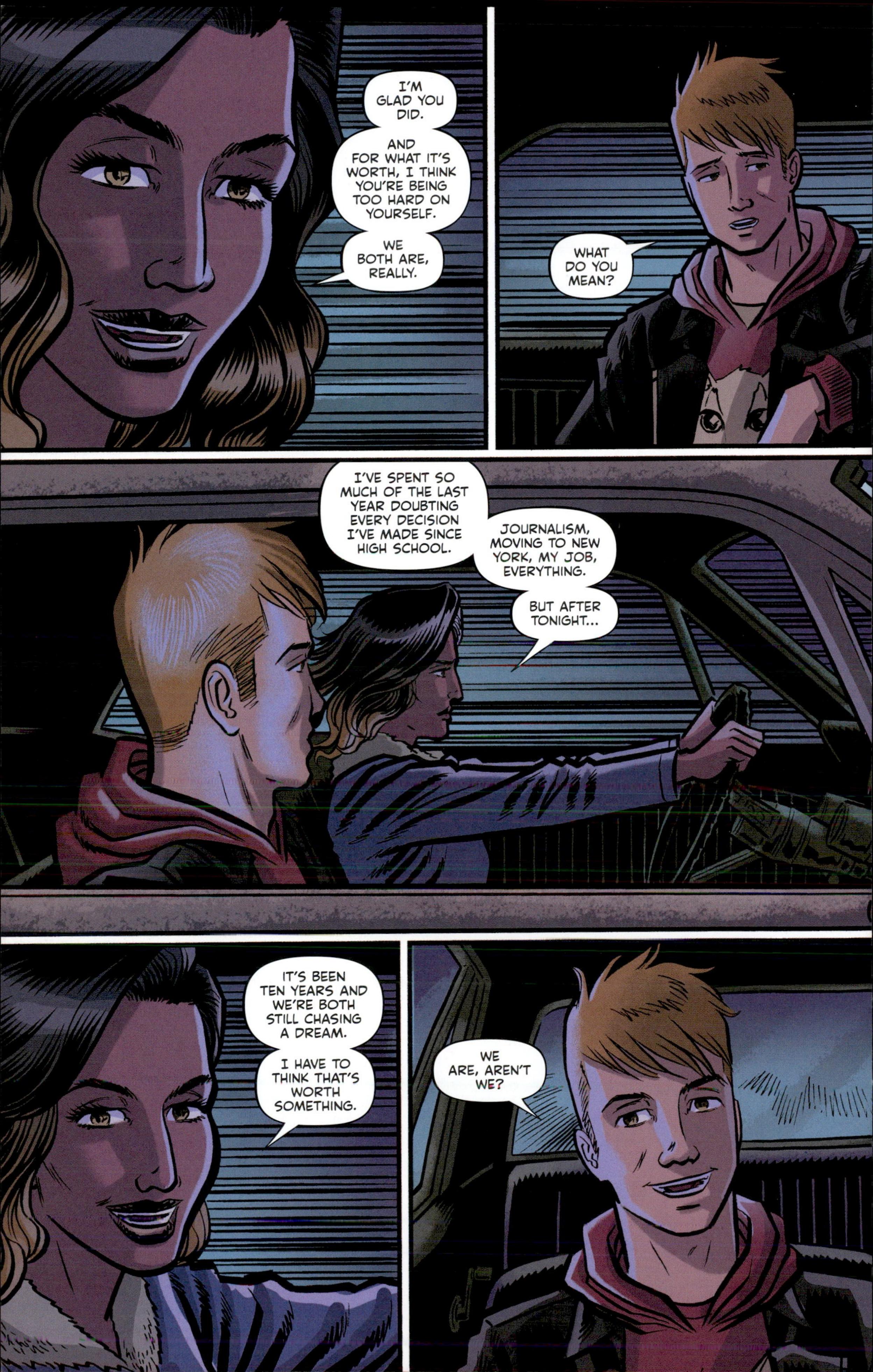
I'M GLAD YOU DID.
AND FOR WHAT IT'S WORTH, I THINK YOU'RE BEING TOO HARD ON YOURSELF.
WE BOTH ARE, REALLY.
WHAT DO YOU MEAN?
I'VE SPENT SO MUCH OF THE LAST YEAR DOUBTING EVERY DECISION I'VE MADE SINCE HIGH SCHOOL.
JOURNALISM, MOVING TO NEW YORK, MY JOB, EVERYTHING.
BUT AFTER TONIGHT...
IT'S BEEN TEN YEARS AND WE'RE BOTH STILL CHASING A DREAM.
I HAVE TO THINK THAT'S WORTH SOMETHING.
WE ARE, AREN'T WE?

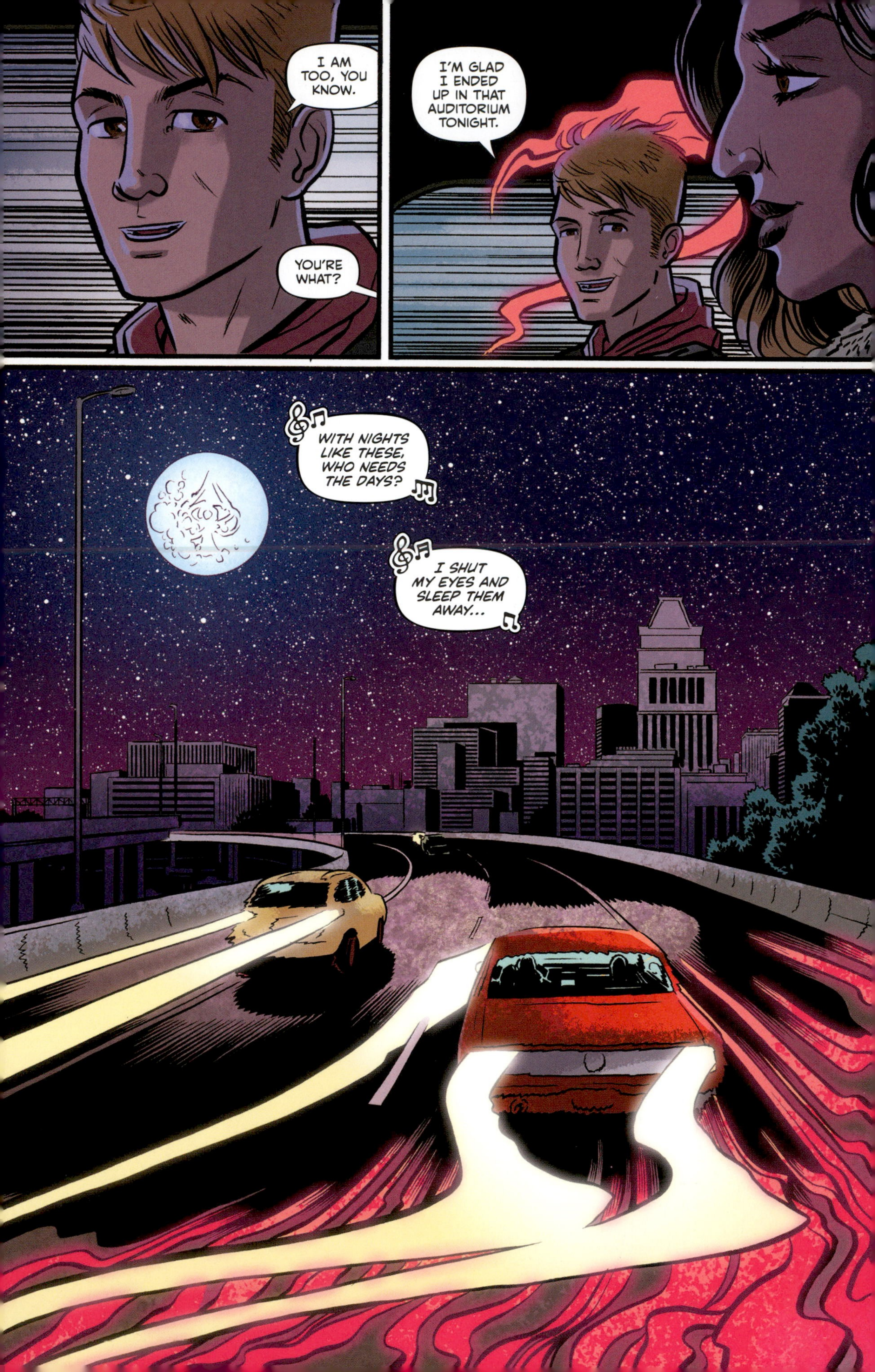
I AM TOO, YOU KNOW.
YOU'RE WHAT?
I'M GLAD I ENDED UP IN THAT AUDITORIUM TONIGHT.
WITH NIGHTS LIKE THESE, WHO NEEDS THE DAYS?
I SHUT MY EYES AND SLEEP THEM AWAY...

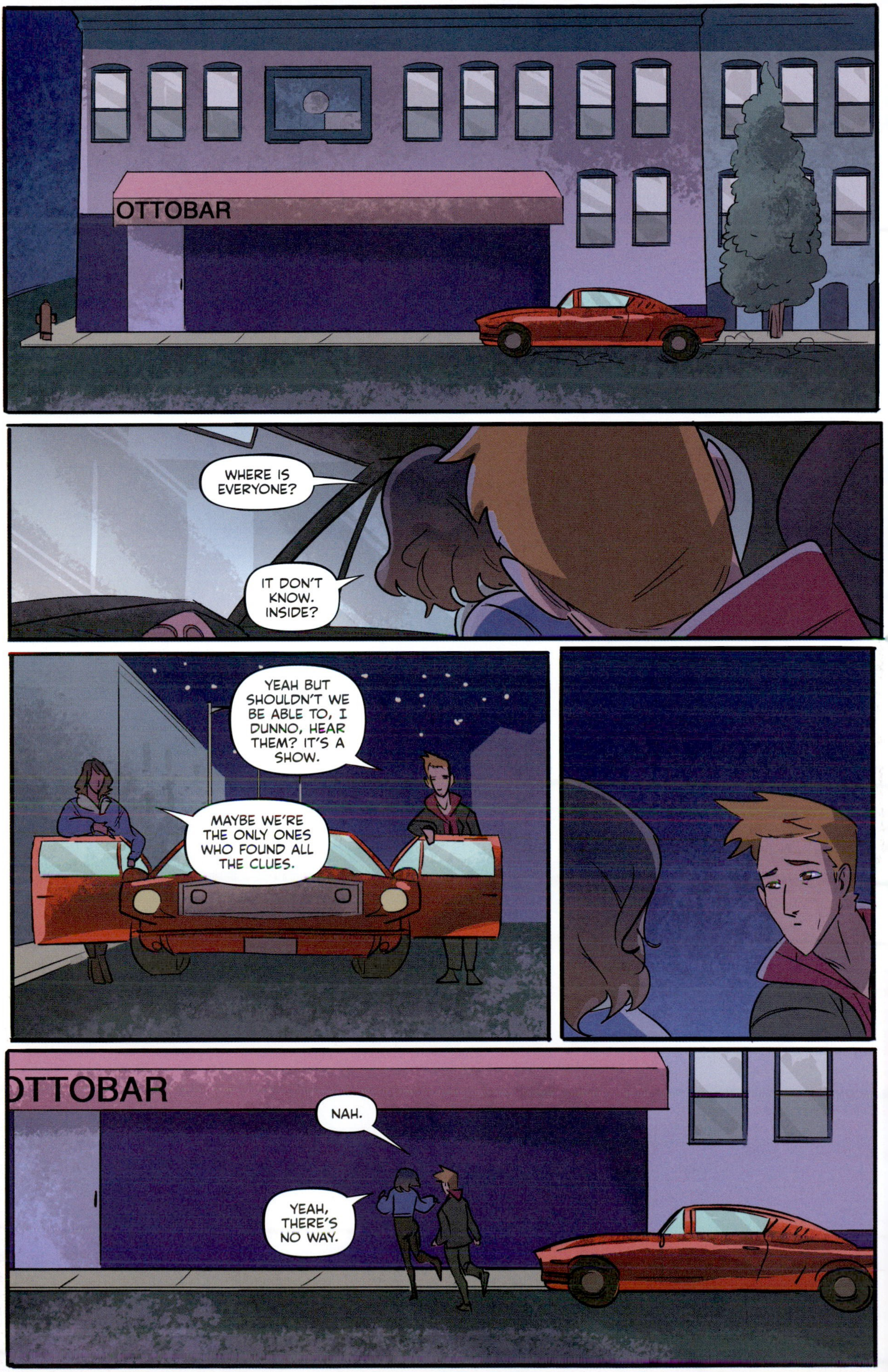
OTTOBAR
WHERE IS EVERYONE?
I DON'T KNOW. INSIDE?
YEAH BUT SHOULDN'T WE BE ABLE TO, I DUNNO, HEAR THEM? IT'S A SHOW.
MAYBE WE'RE THE ONLY ONES WHO FOUND ALL THE CLUES.
OTTOBAR
NAH.
YEAH, THERE'S NO WAY.

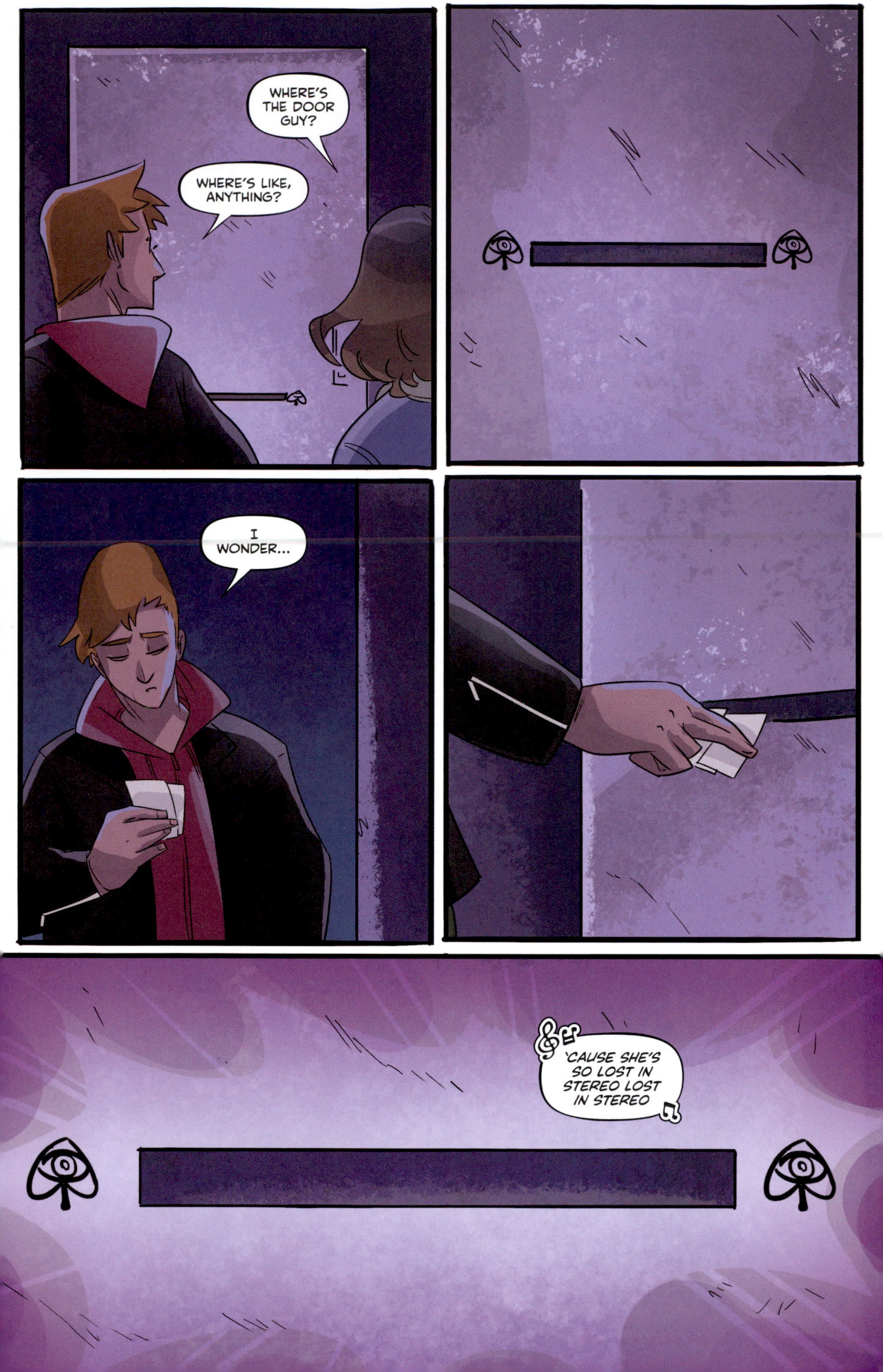
WHERE'S THE DOOR GUY?
WHERE'S LIKE, ANYTHING?
I WONDER...
'CAUSE SHE'S SO LOST IN STEREO LOST IN STEREO

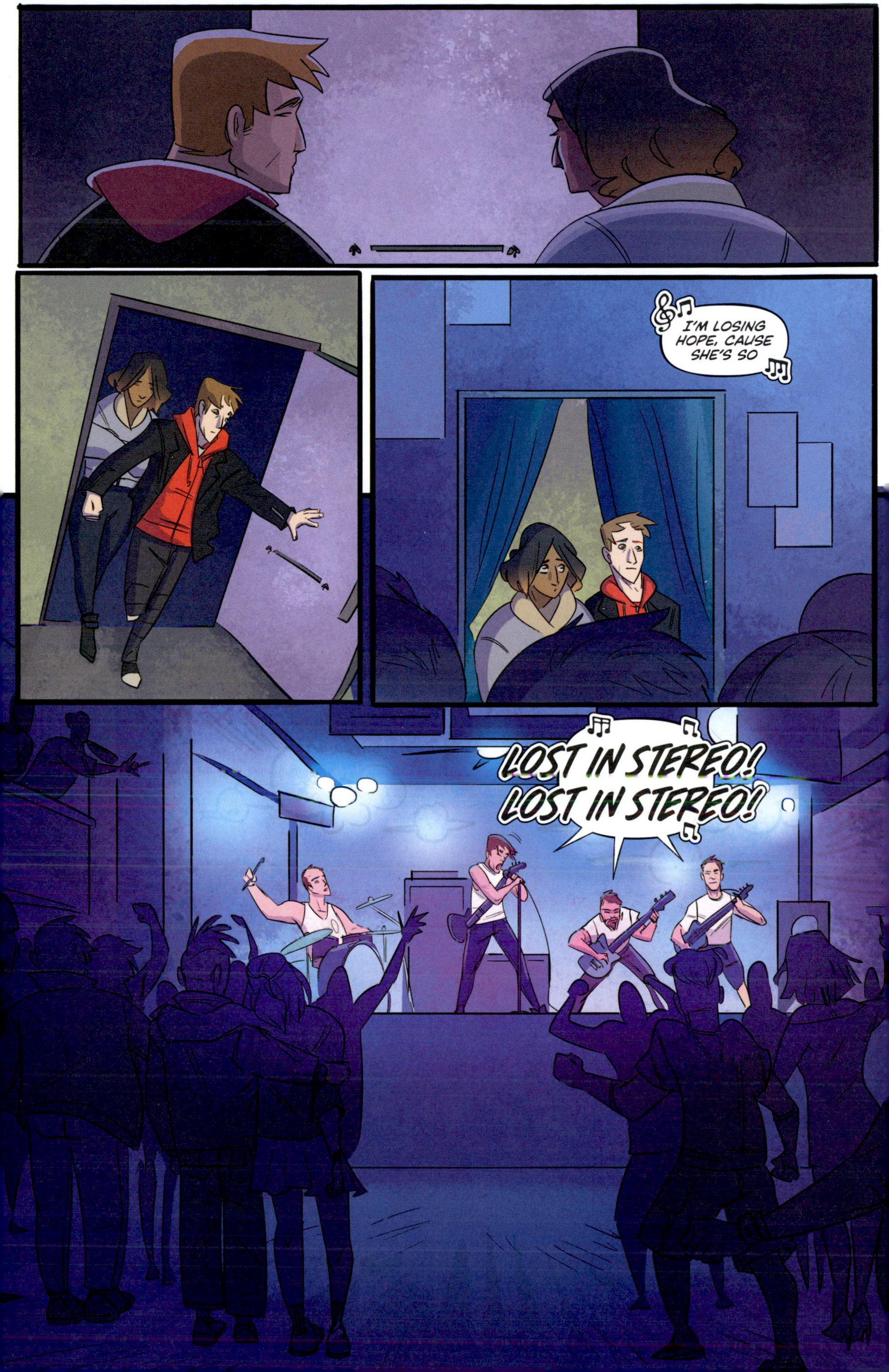
I'M LOSING HOPE, CAUSE SHE'S SO
LOST IN STEREO! LOST IN STEREO!

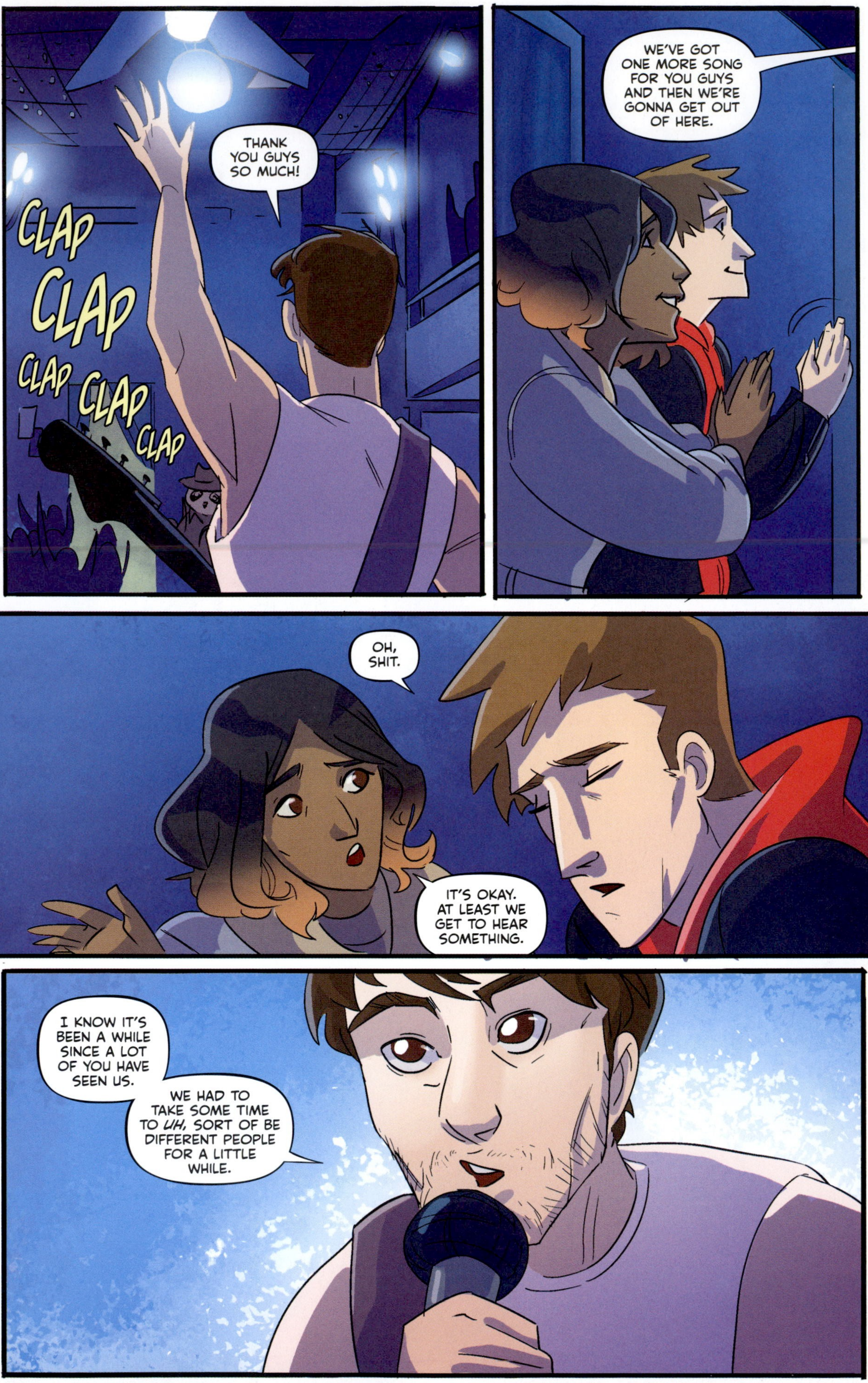
THANK YOU GUYS SO MUCH!
CLAP
CLAP
CLAP
CLAP
CLAP
WE'VE GOT ONE MORE SONG FOR YOU GUYS AND THEN WE'RE GONNA GET OUT OF HERE.
OH, SHIT.
IT'S OKAY. AT LEAST WE GET TO HEAR SOMETHING.
I KNOW IT'S BEEN A WHILE SINCE A LOT OF YOU HAVE SEEN US.
WE HAD TO TAKE SOME TIME TO *UH*, SORT OF BE DIFFERENT PEOPLE FOR A LITTLE WHILE.

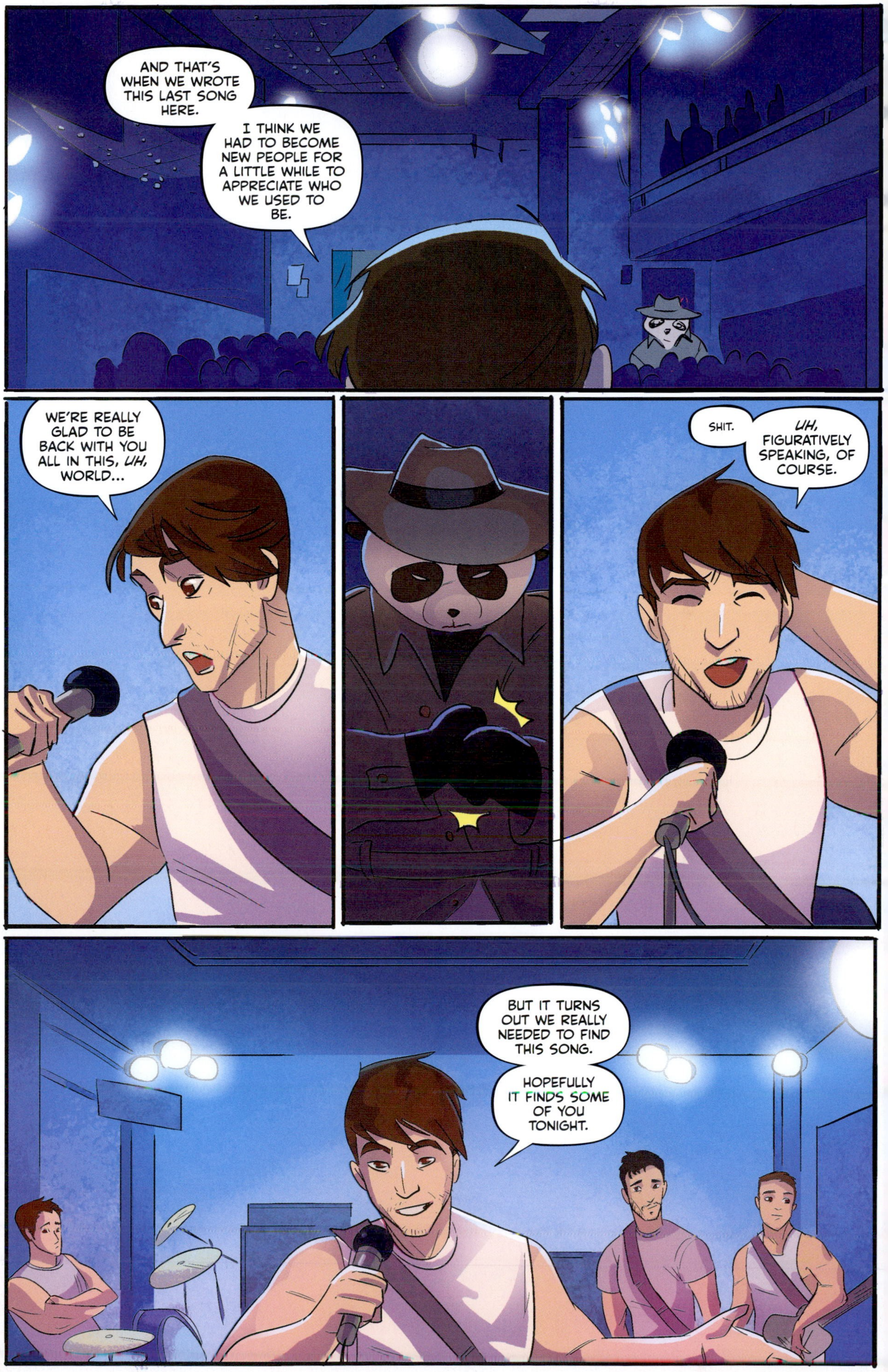
AND THAT'S WHEN WE WROTE THIS LAST SONG HERE.
I THINK WE HAD TO BECOME NEW PEOPLE FOR A LITTLE WHILE TO APPRECIATE WHO WE USED TO BE.
WE'RE REALLY GLAD TO BE BACK WITH YOU ALL IN THIS, *UH,* WORLD...
SHIT.
UH, FIGURATIVELY SPEAKING, OF COURSE.
BUT IT TURNS OUT WE REALLY NEEDED TO FIND THIS SONG.
HOPEFULLY IT FINDS SOME OF YOU TONIGHT.

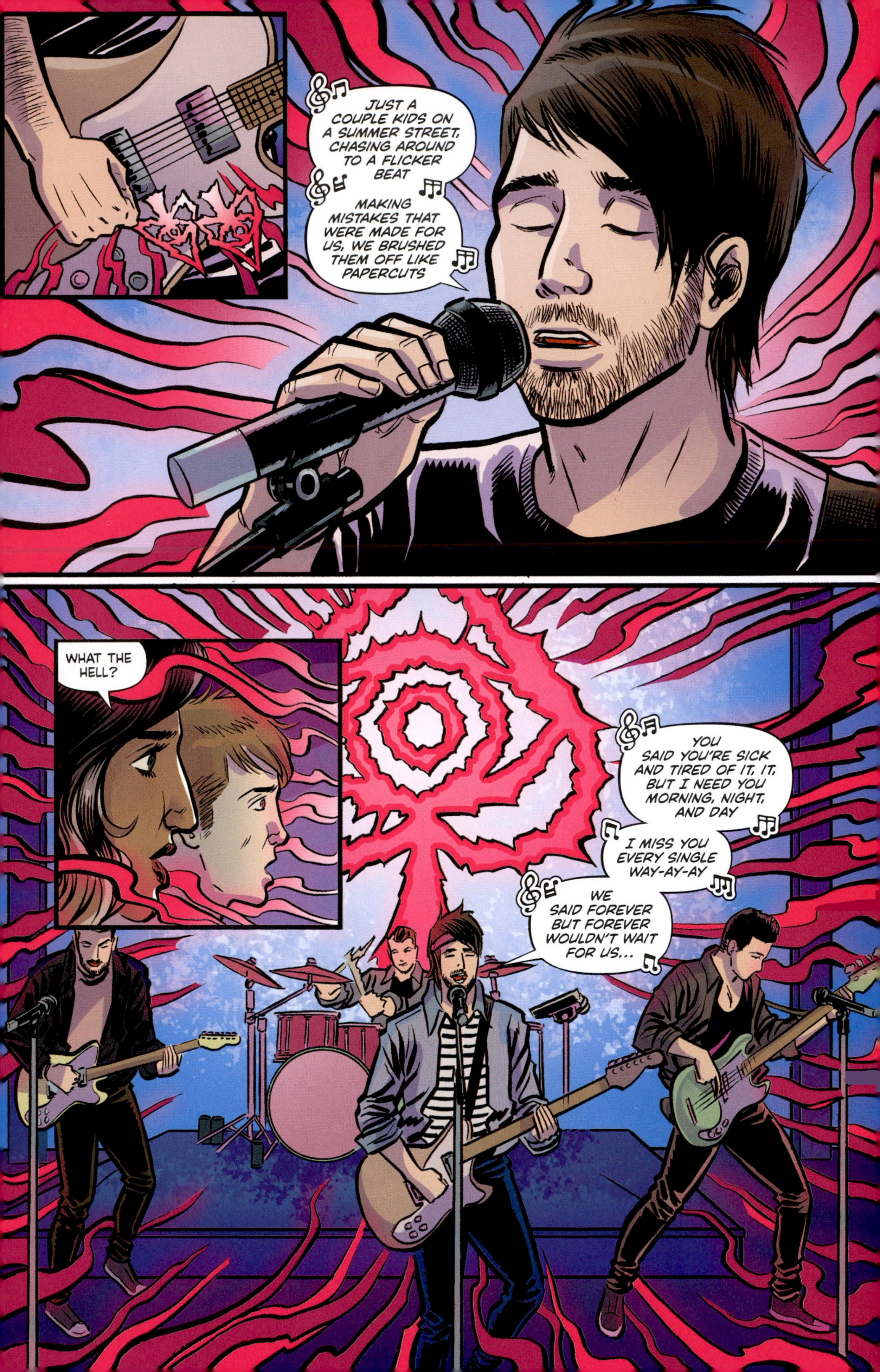
JUST A COUPLE KIDS ON A SUMMER STREET, CHASING AROUND TO A FLICKER BEAT
MAKING MISTAKES THAT WERE MADE FOR US, WE BRUSHED THEM OFF LIKE PAPERCUTS
WHAT THE HELL?
YOU SAID YOU'RE SICK AND TIRED OF IT, IT, BUT I NEED YOU MORNING, NIGHT, AND DAY
I MISS YOU EVERY SINGLE WAY-AY-AY
WE SAID FOREVER BUT FOREVER WOULDN'T WAIT FOR US...

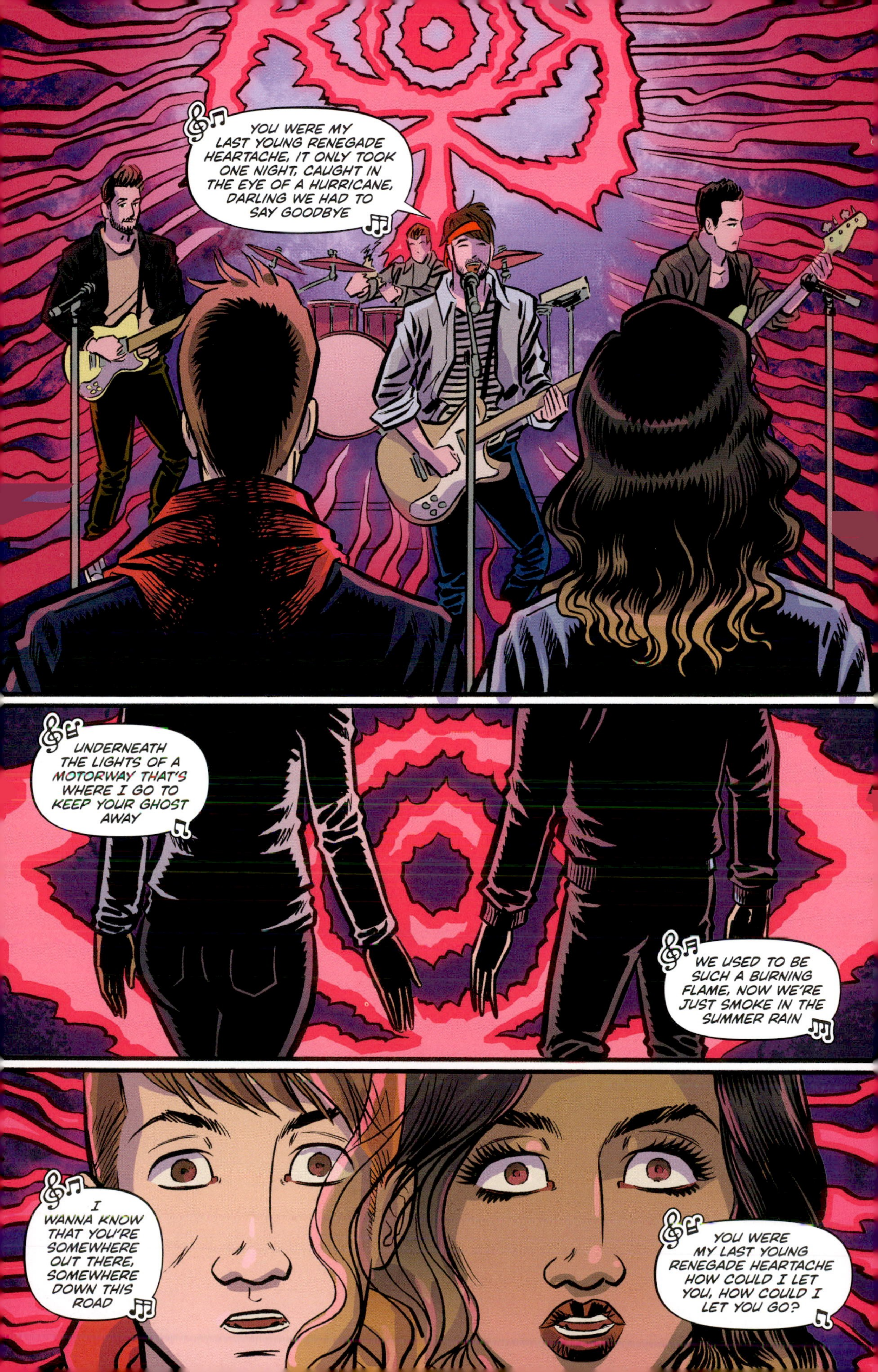
YOU WERE MY LAST YOUNG RENEGADE HEARTACHE, IT ONLY TOOK ONE NIGHT, CAUGHT IN THE EYE OF A HURRICANE, DARLING WE HAD TO SAY GOODBYE
UNDERNEATH THE LIGHTS OF A MOTORWAY THAT'S WHERE I GO TO KEEP YOUR GHOST AWAY
WE USED TO BE SUCH A BURNING FLAME, NOW WE'RE JUST SMOKE IN THE SUMMER RAIN
I WANNA KNOW THAT YOU'RE SOMEWHERE OUT THERE, SOMEWHERE DOWN THIS ROAD
YOU WERE MY LAST YOUNG RENEGADE HEARTACHE HOW COULD I LET YOU, HOW COULD I LET YOU GO?

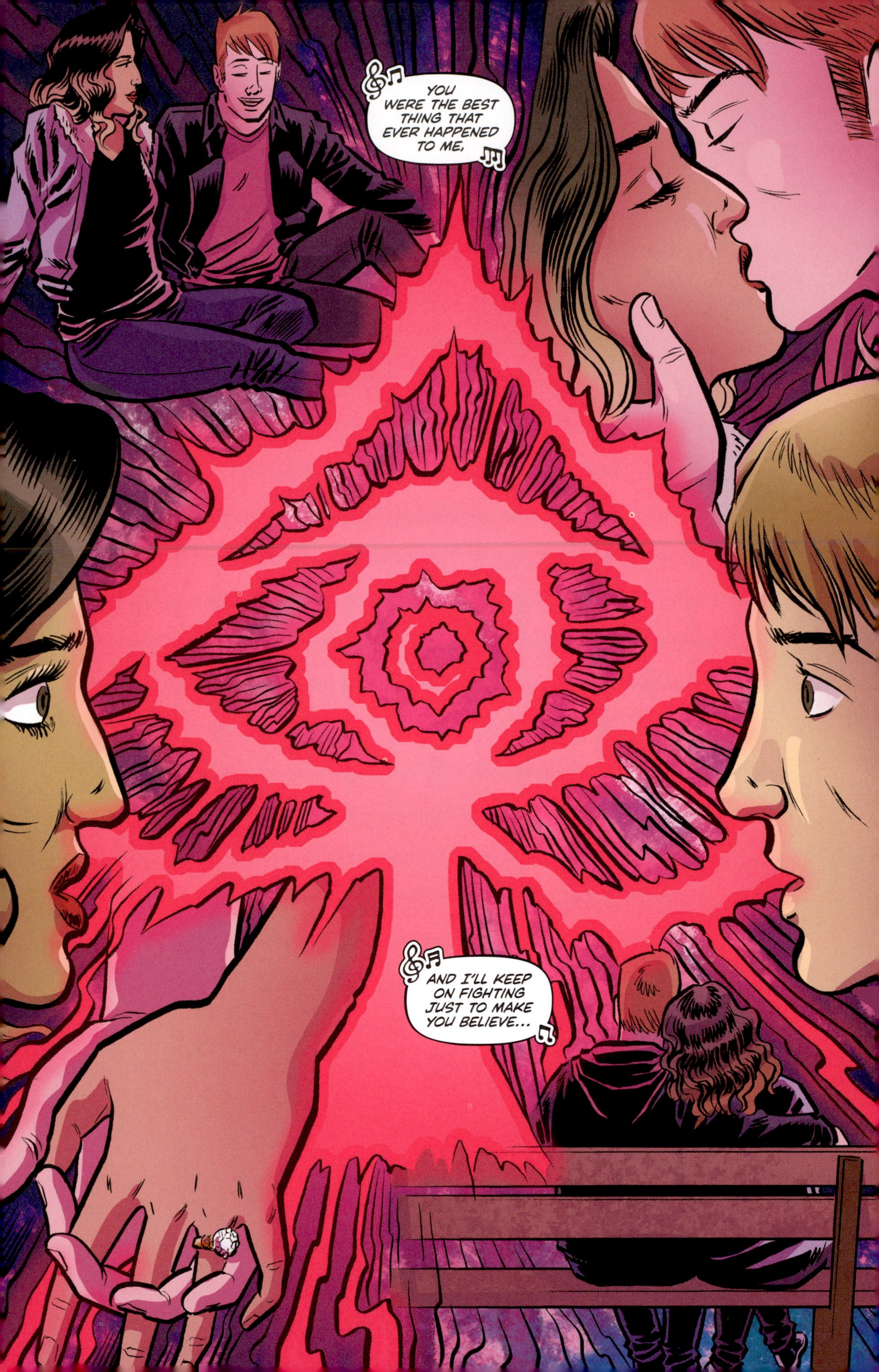
YOU WERE THE BEST THING THAT EVER HAPPENED TO ME,
AND I'LL KEEP ON FIGHTING JUST TO MAKE YOU BELIEVE...

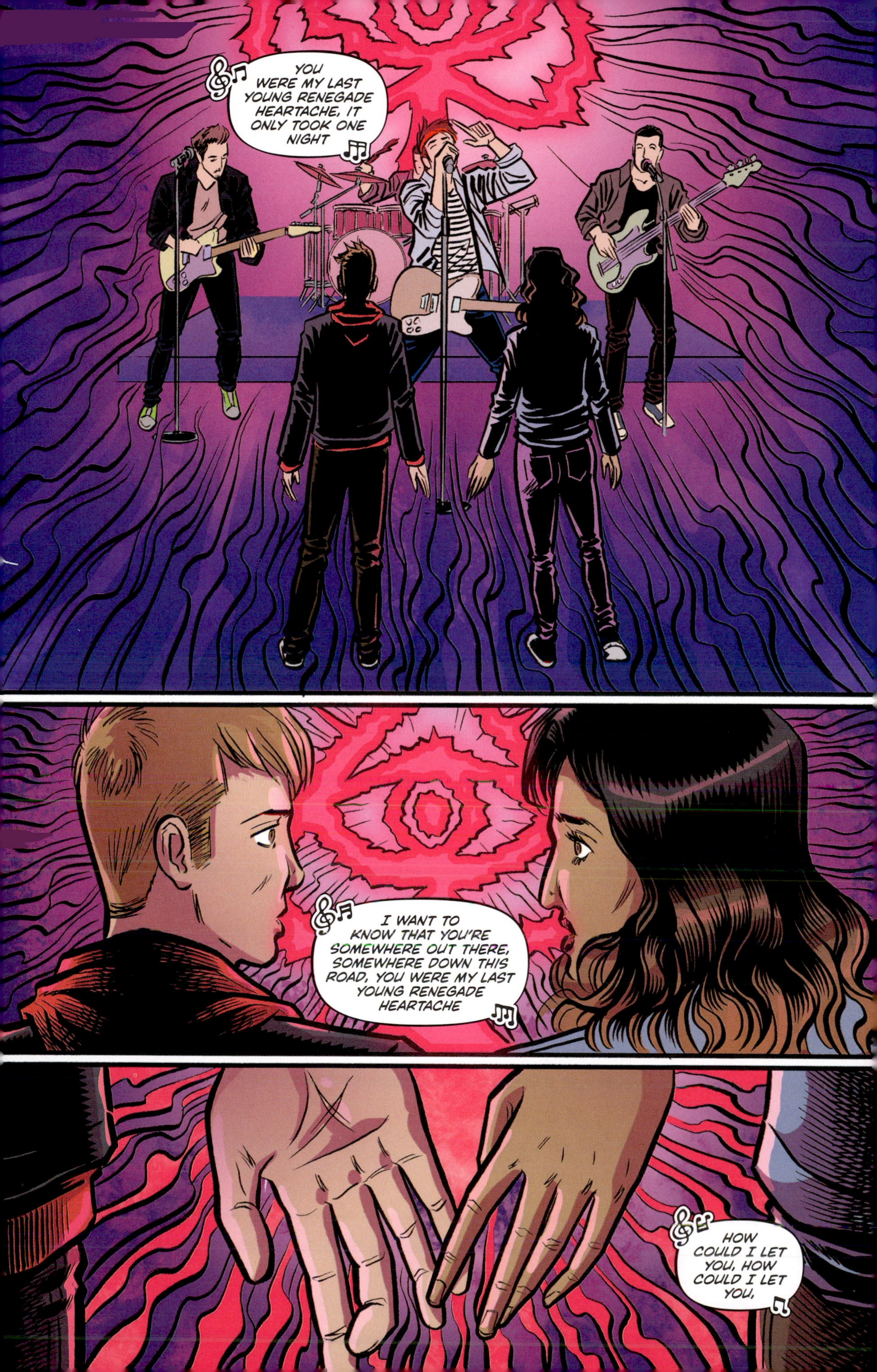
YOU WERE MY LAST YOUNG RENEGADE HEARTACHE, IT ONLY TOOK ONE NIGHT
I WANT TO KNOW THAT YOU'RE SOMEWHERE OUT THERE, SOMEWHERE DOWN THIS ROAD, YOU WERE MY LAST YOUNG RENEGADE HEARTACHE
HOW COULD I LET YOU, HOW COULD I LET YOU,

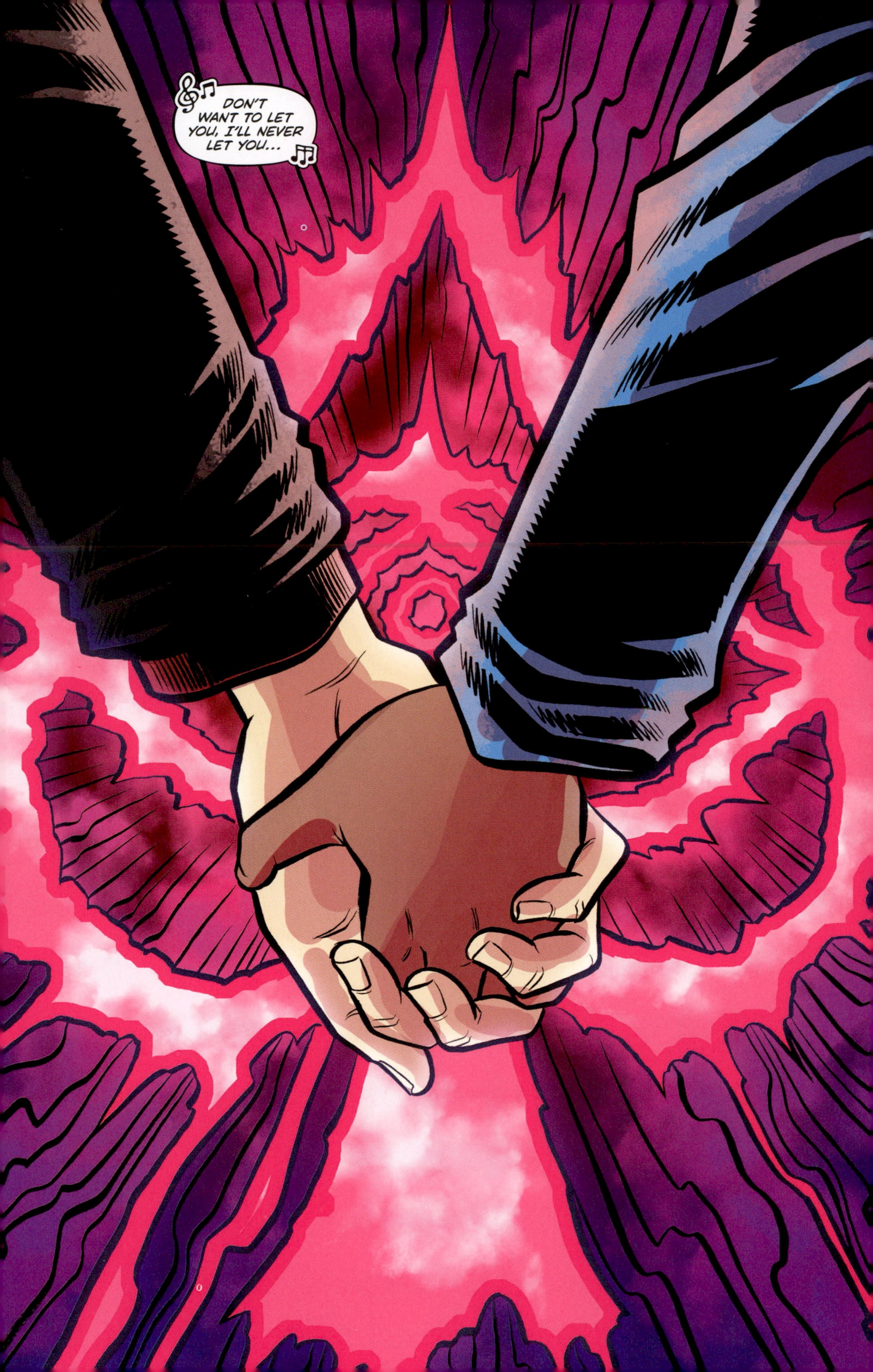
DON'T WANT TO LET YOU, I'LL NEVER LET YOU...

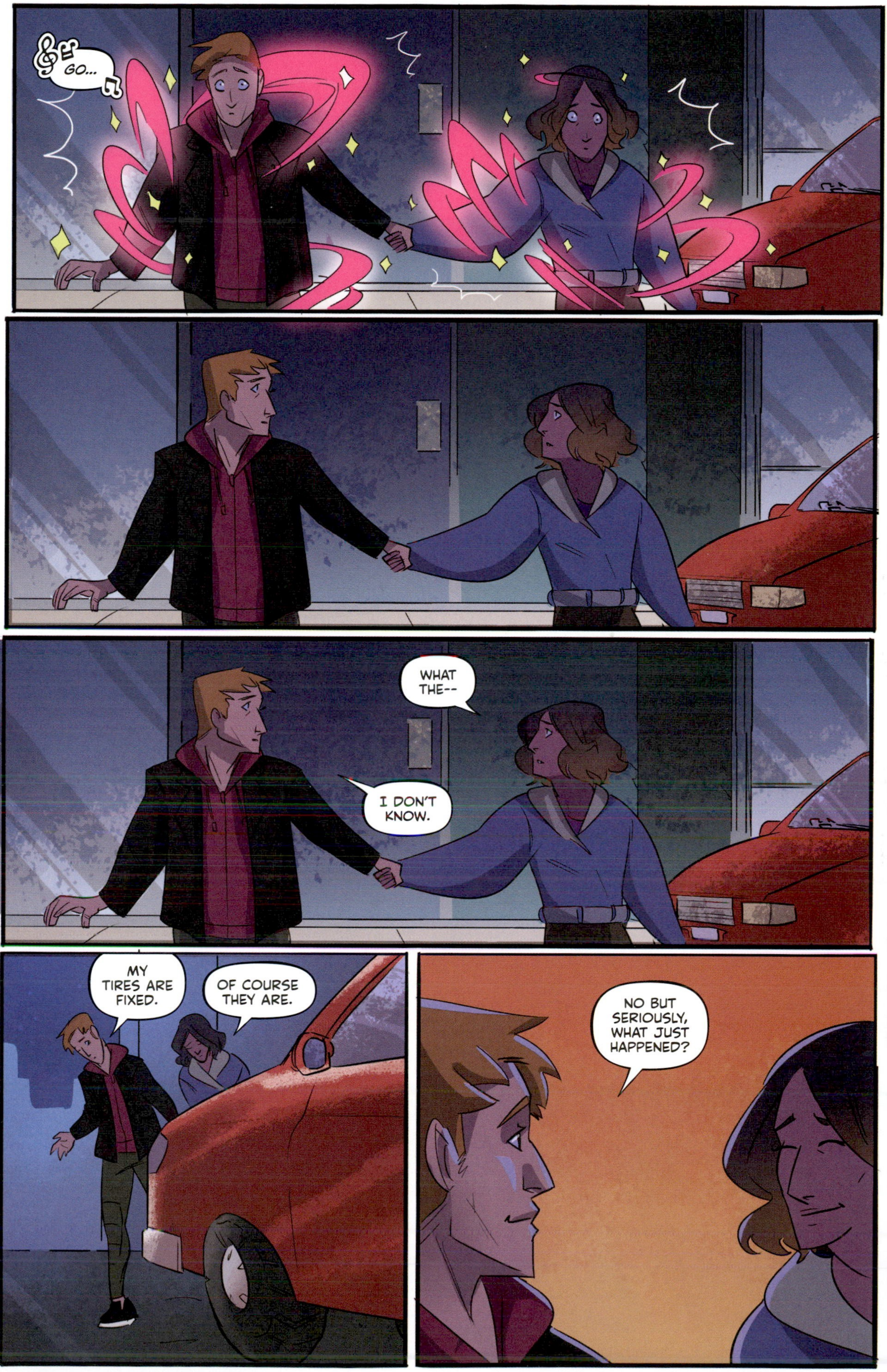
GO...
WHAT THE--
I DON'T KNOW.
MY TIRES ARE FIXED.
OF COURSE THEY ARE.
NO BUT SERIOUSLY, WHAT JUST HAPPENED?

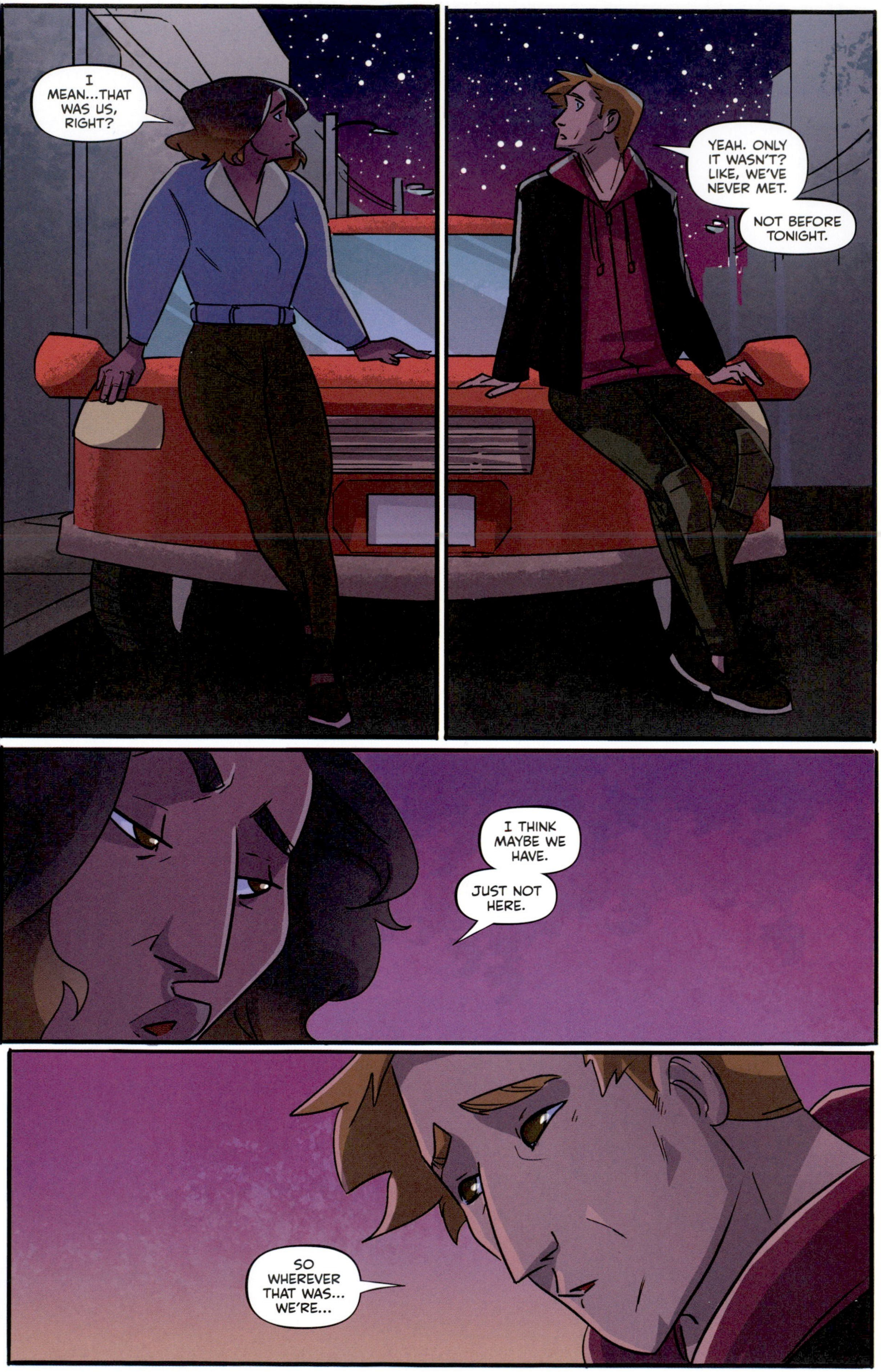
I MEAN...THAT WAS US, RIGHT?
YEAH. ONLY IT WASN'T? LIKE, WE'VE NEVER MET.
NOT BEFORE TONIGHT.
I THINK MAYBE WE HAVE.
JUST NOT HERE.
SO WHEREVER THAT WAS... WE'RE...

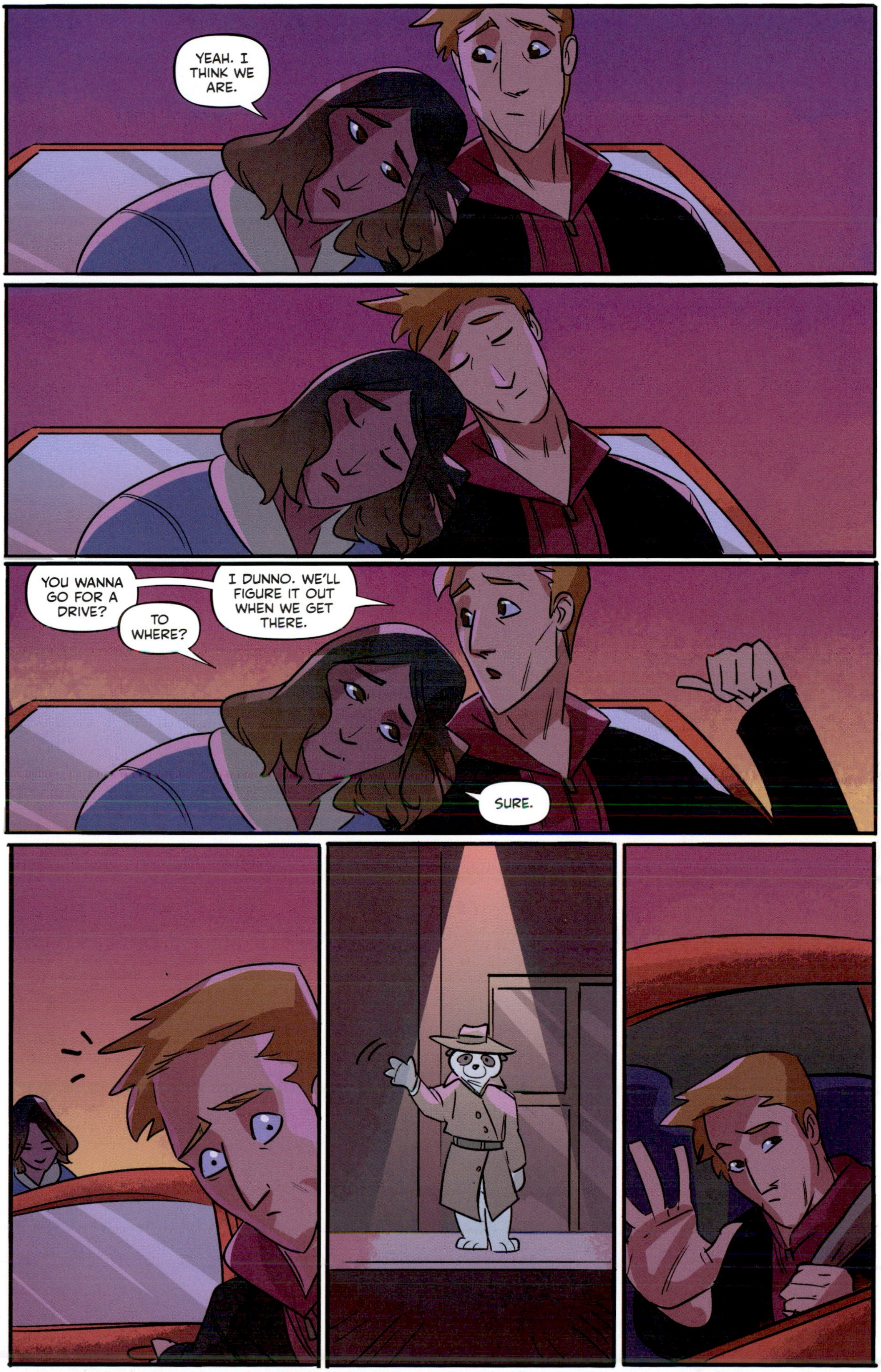

YEAH. I THINK WE ARE.
YOU WANNA GO FOR A DRIVE?
TO WHERE?
I DUNNO. WE'LL FIGURE IT OUT WHEN WE GET THERE.
SURE.

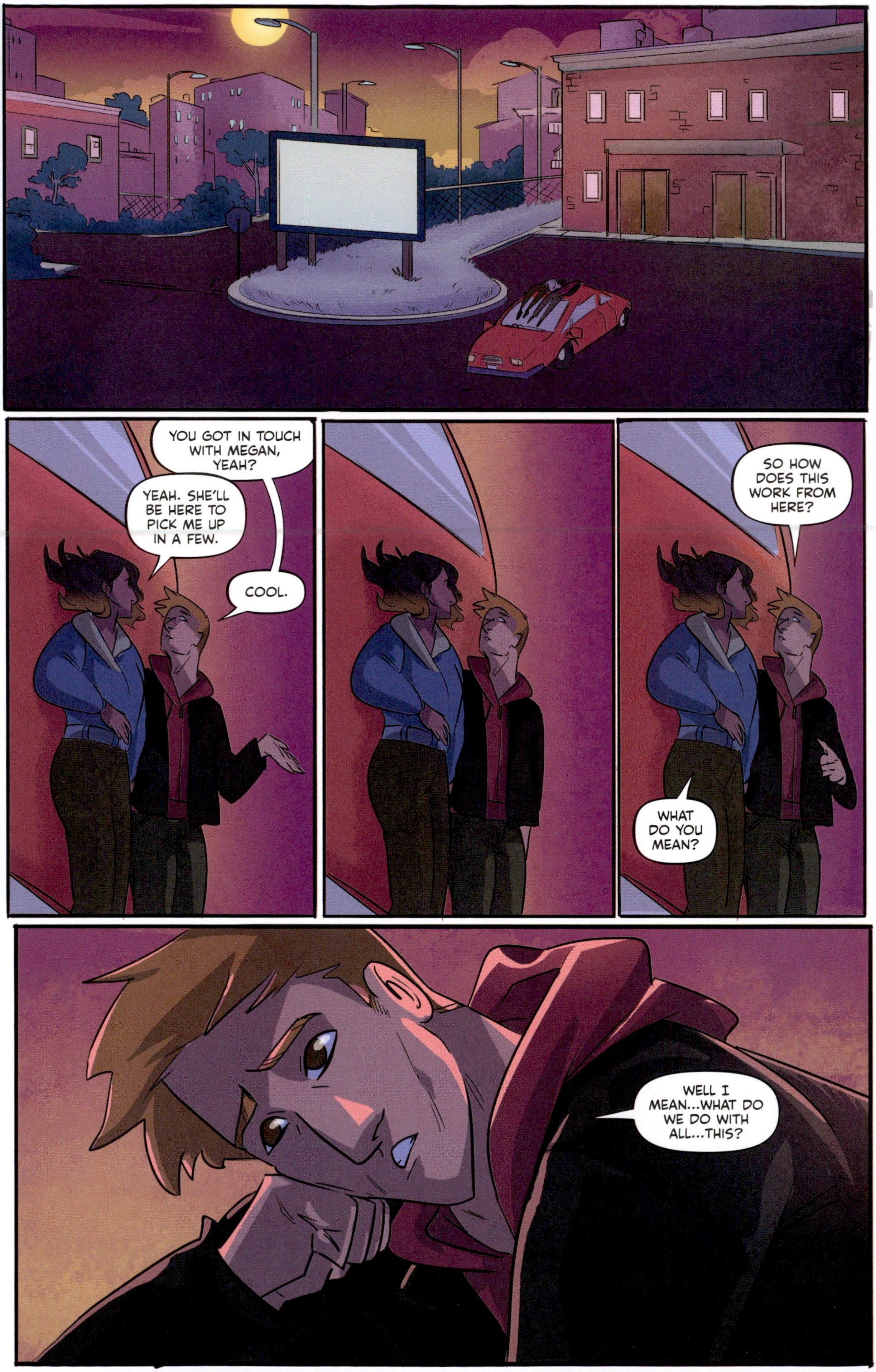

YOU GOT IN TOUCH WITH MEGAN, YEAH?
YEAH. SHE'LL BE HERE TO PICK ME UP IN A FEW.
COOL.
SO HOW DOES THIS WORK FROM HERE?
WHAT DO YOU MEAN?
WELL I MEAN...WHAT DO WE DO WITH ALL...THIS?

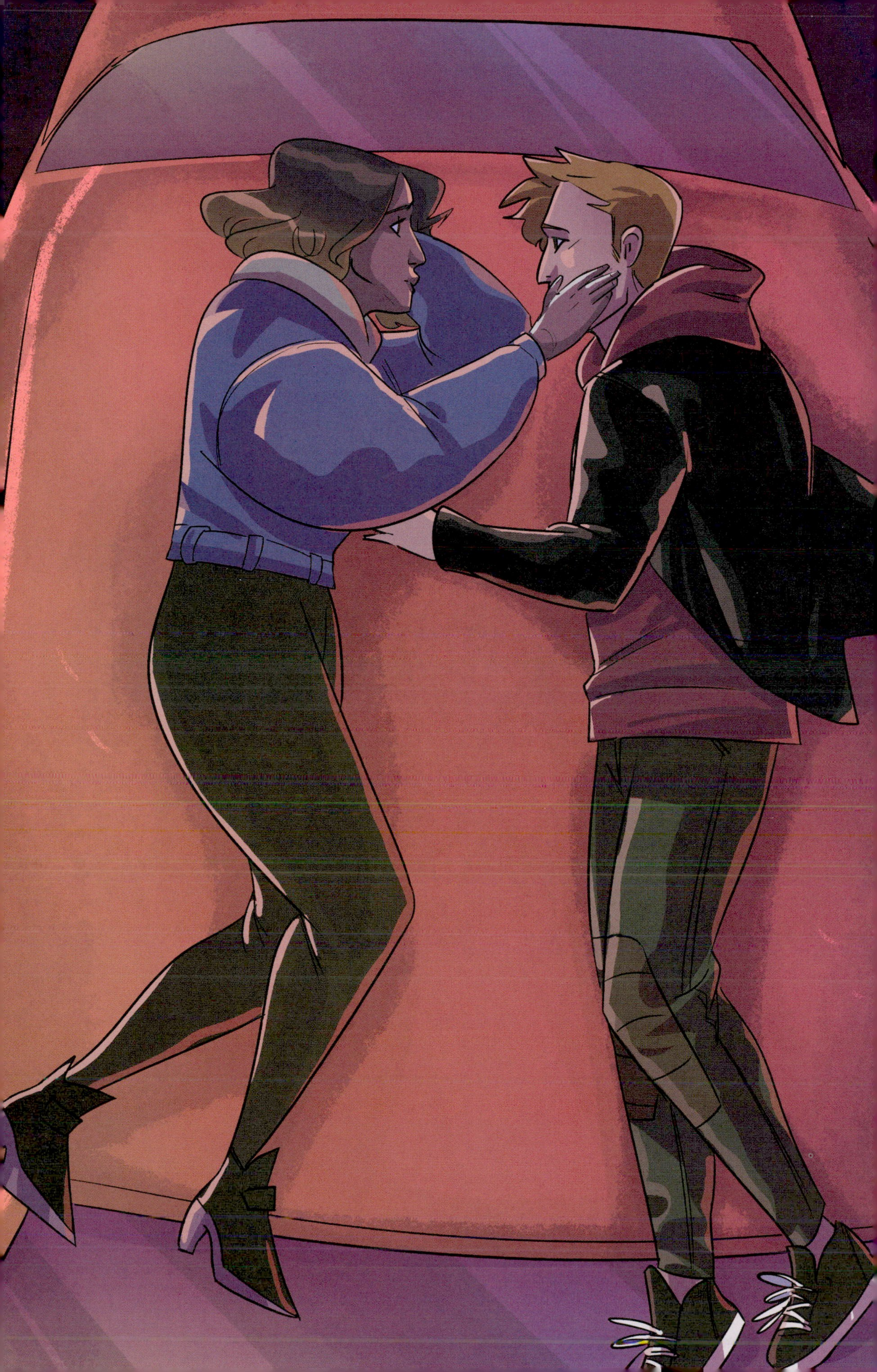

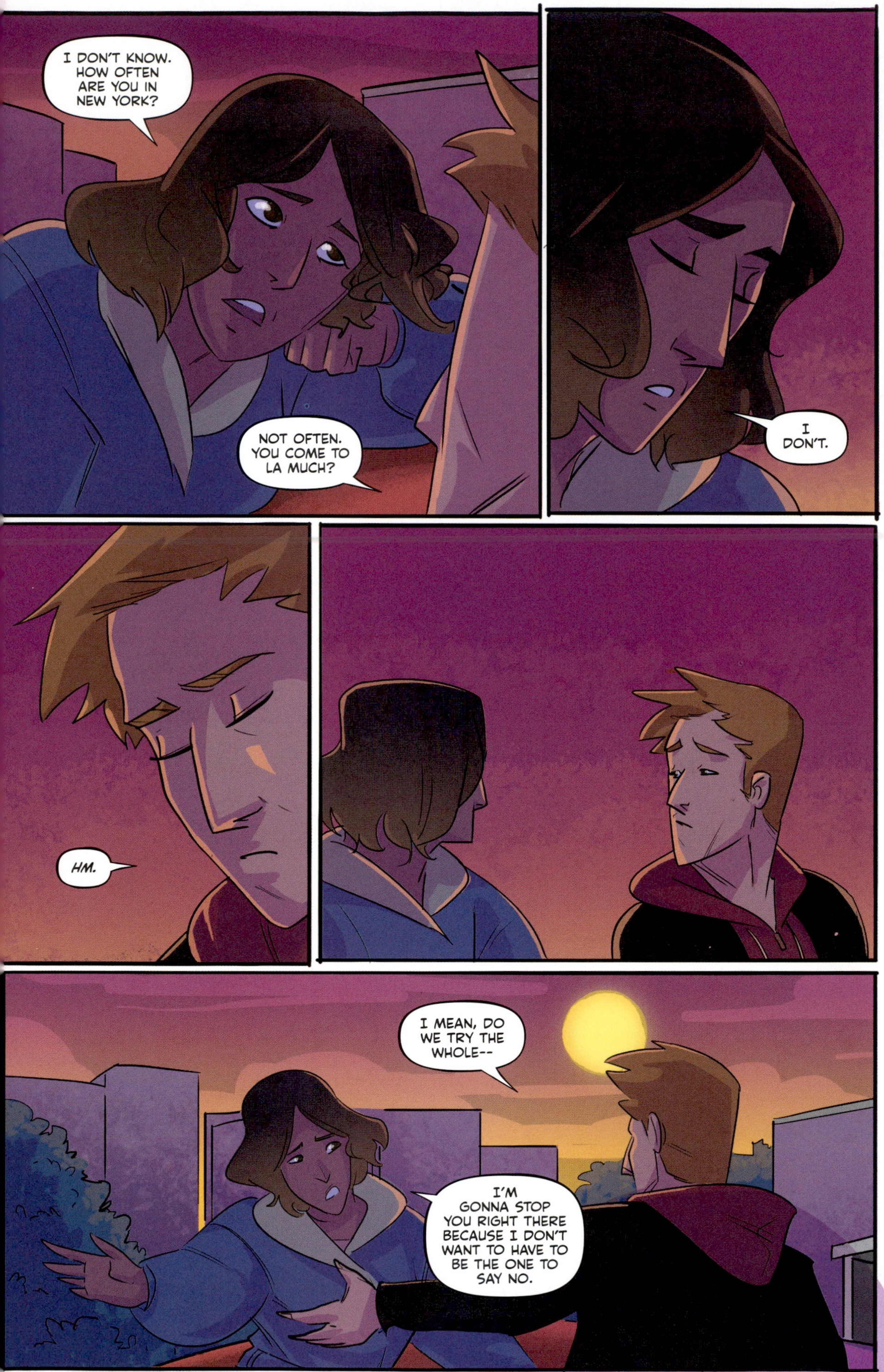
I DON'T KNOW. HOW OFTEN ARE YOU IN NEW YORK?
NOT OFTEN. YOU COME TO LA MUCH?
I DON'T.
HM.
I MEAN, DO WE TRY THE WHOLE--
I'M GONNA STOP YOU RIGHT THERE BECAUSE I DON'T WANT TO HAVE TO BE THE ONE TO SAY NO.

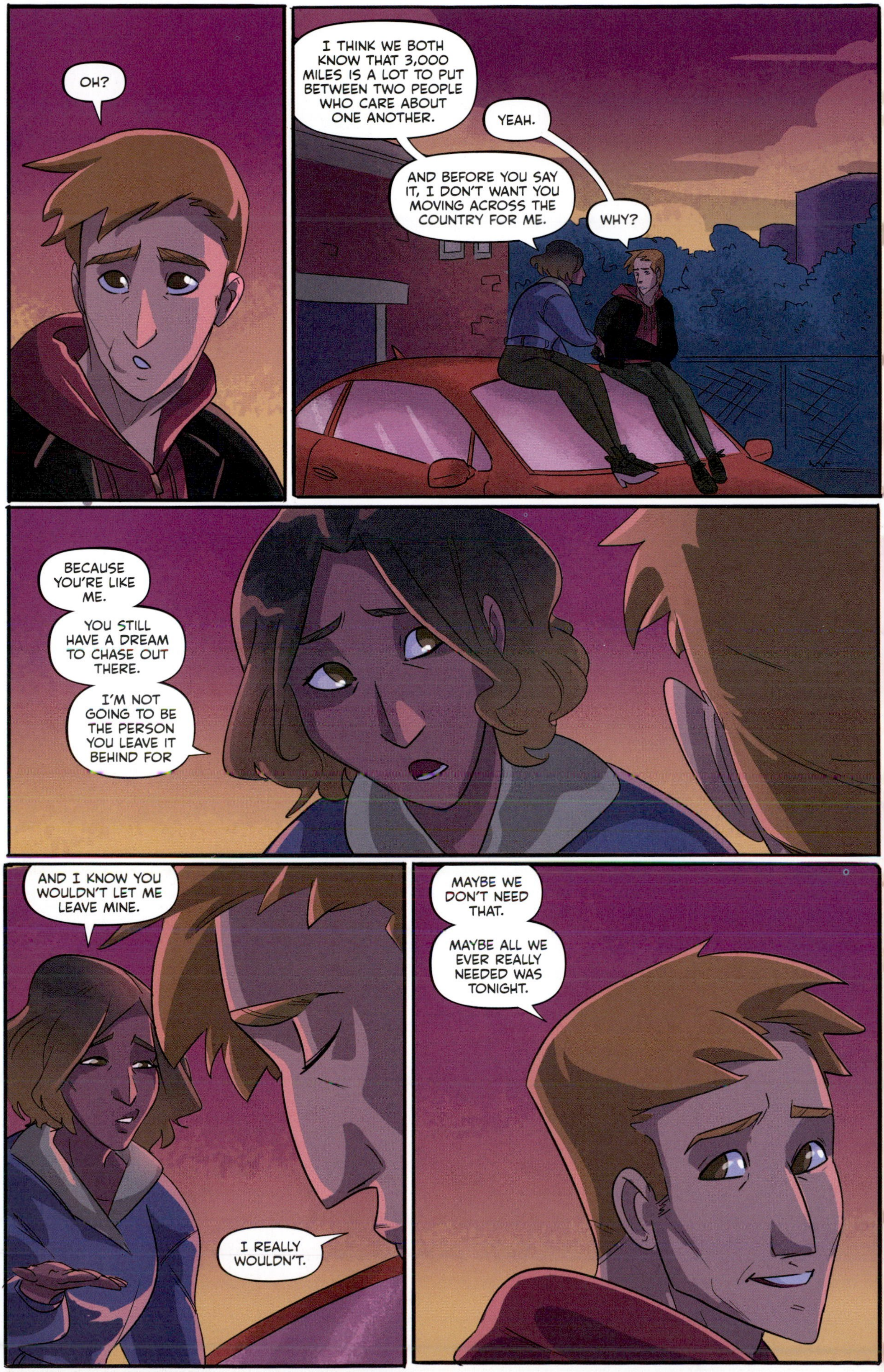
OH?
I THINK WE BOTH KNOW THAT 3,000 MILES IS A LOT TO PUT BETWEEN TWO PEOPLE WHO CARE ABOUT ONE ANOTHER.
YEAH.
AND BEFORE YOU SAY IT, I DON'T WANT YOU MOVING ACROSS THE COUNTRY FOR ME.
WHY?
BECAUSE YOU'RE LIKE ME.
YOU STILL HAVE A DREAM TO CHASE OUT THERE.
I'M NOT GOING TO BE THE PERSON YOU LEAVE IT BEHIND FOR
AND I KNOW YOU WOULDN'T LET ME LEAVE MINE.
I REALLY WOULDN'T.
MAYBE WE DON'T NEED THAT.
MAYBE ALL WE EVER REALLY NEEDED WAS TONIGHT.

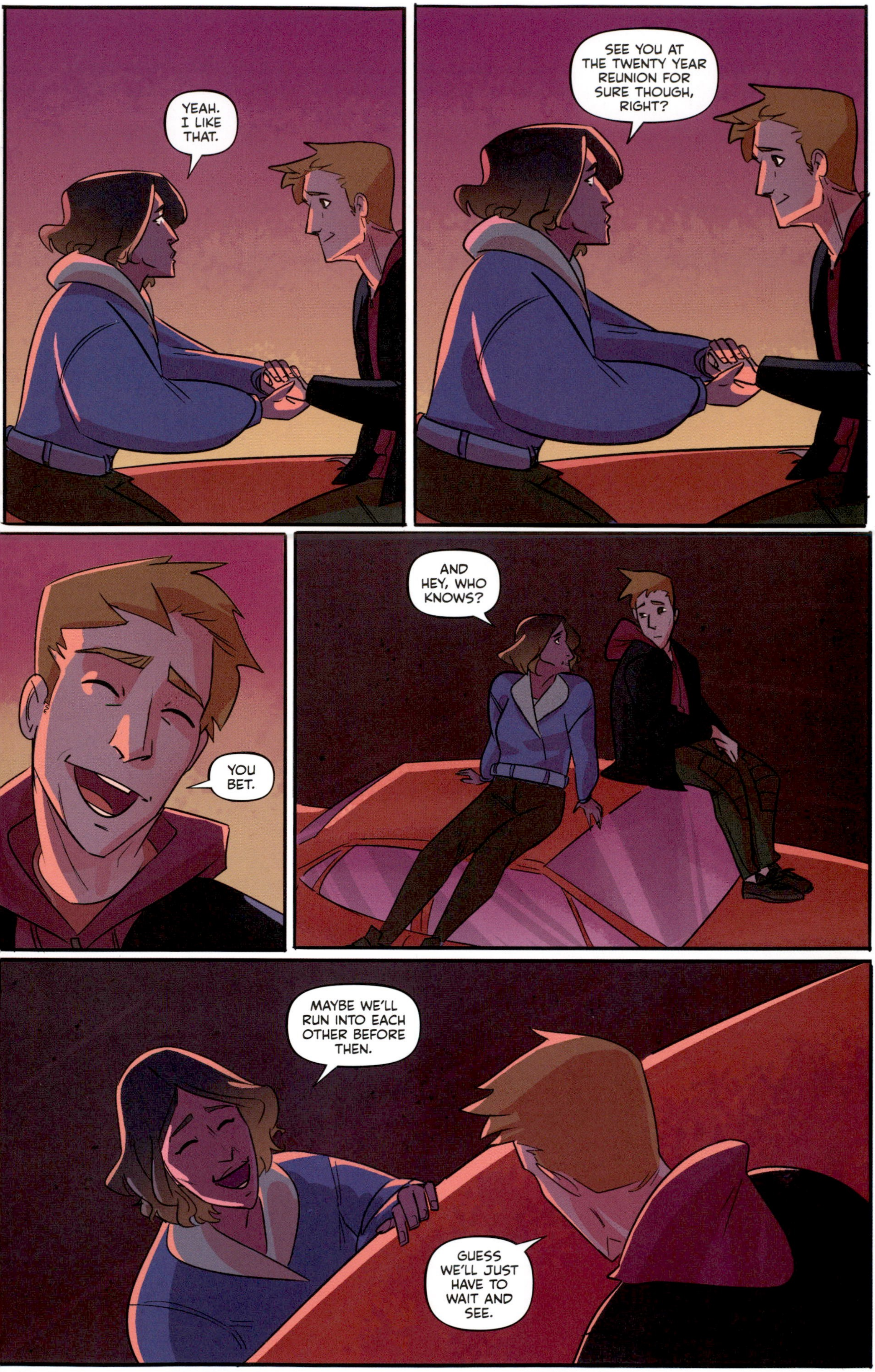
YEAH. I LIKE THAT.
SEE YOU AT THE TWENTY YEAR REUNION FOR SURE THOUGH, RIGHT?
YOU BET.
AND HEY, WHO KNOWS?
MAYBE WE'LL RUN INTO EACH OTHER BEFORE THEN.
GUESS WE'LL JUST HAVE TO WAIT AND SEE.

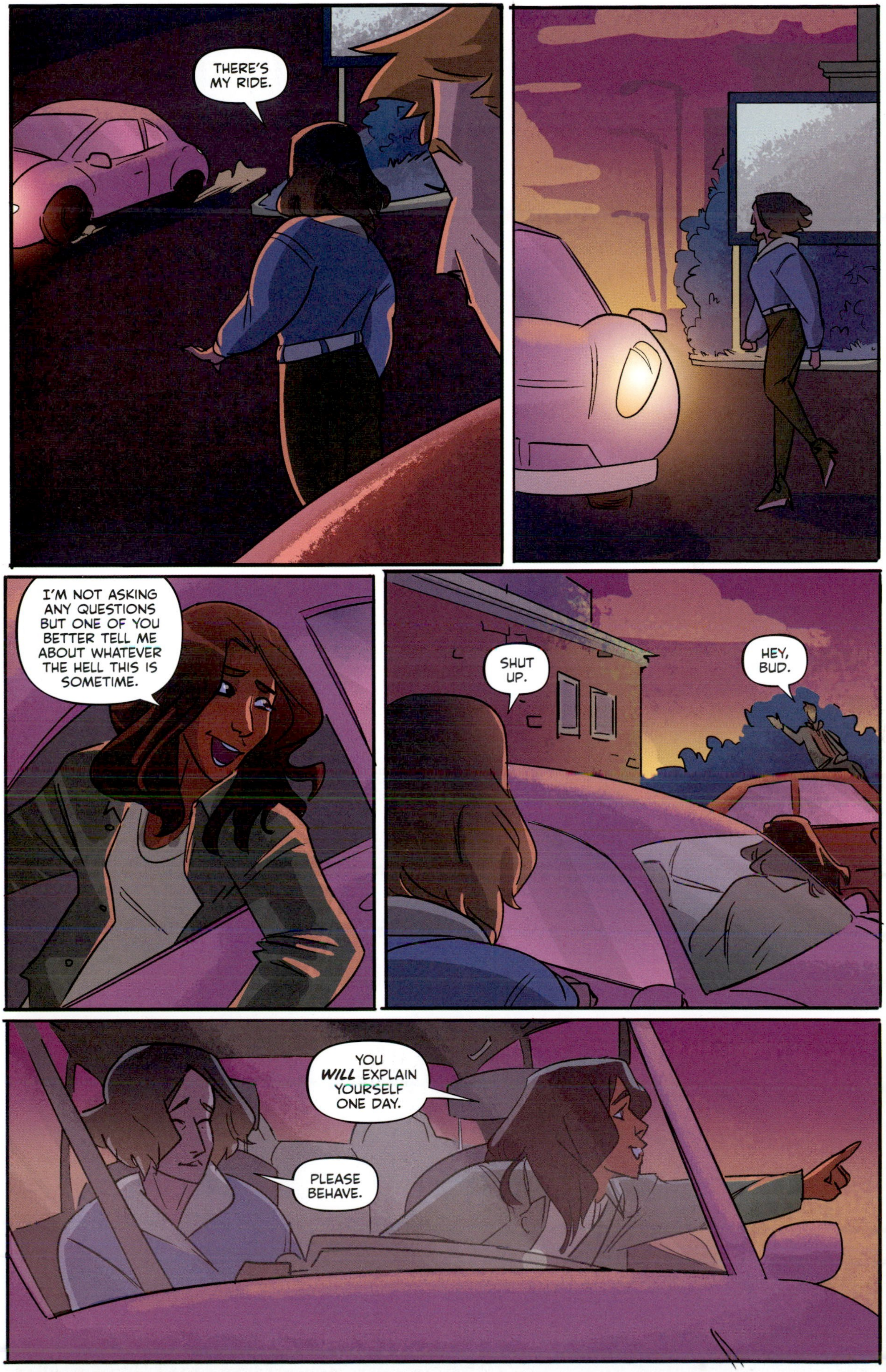
THERE'S MY RIDE.
I'M NOT ASKING ANY QUESTIONS BUT ONE OF YOU BETTER TELL ME ABOUT WHATEVER THE HELL THIS IS SOMETIME.
SHUT UP.
HEY, BUD.
YOU *WILL* EXPLAIN YOURSELF ONE DAY.
PLEASE BEHAVE.

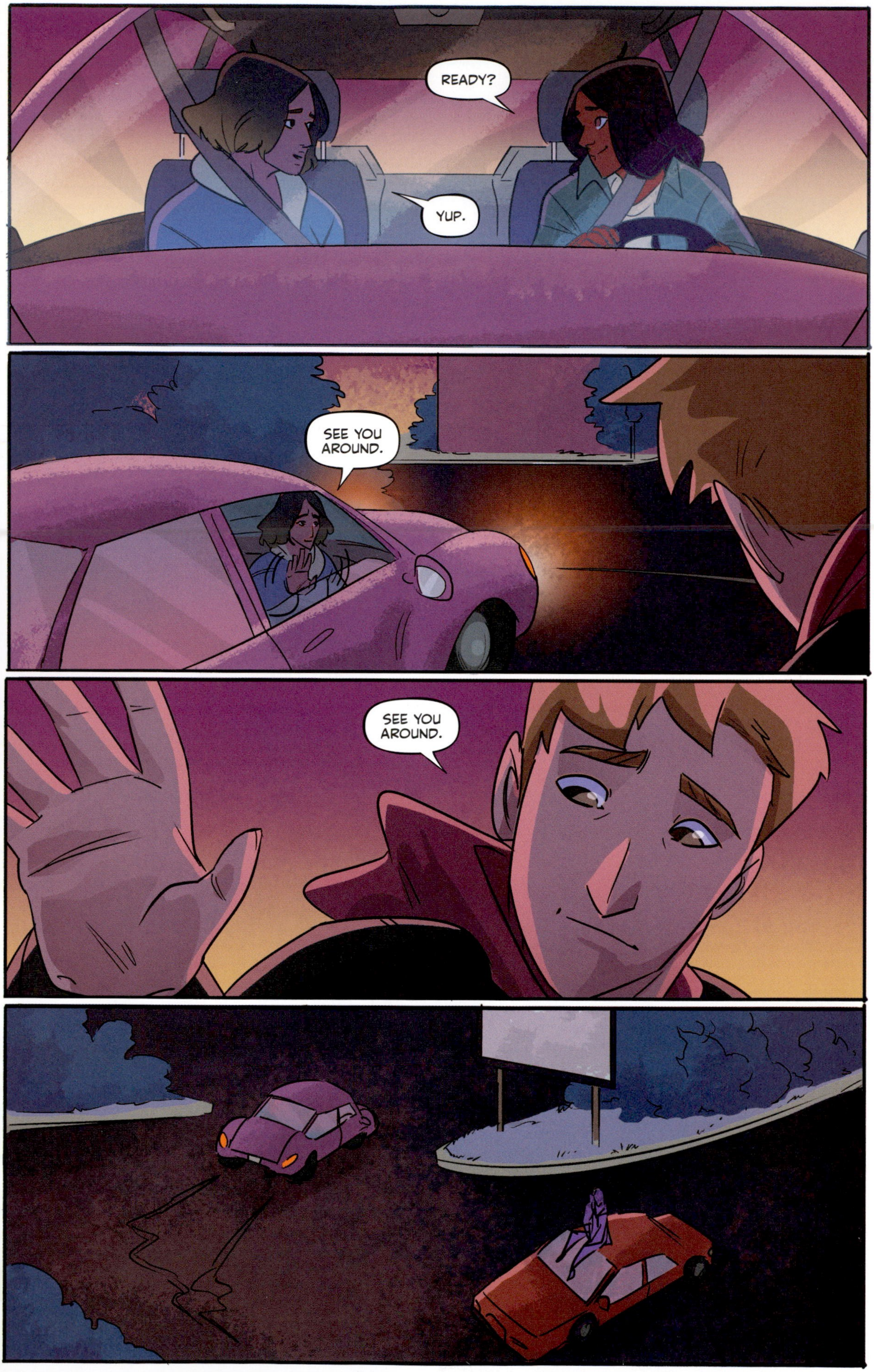
READY?
YUP.
SEE YOU AROUND.
SEE YOU AROUND.

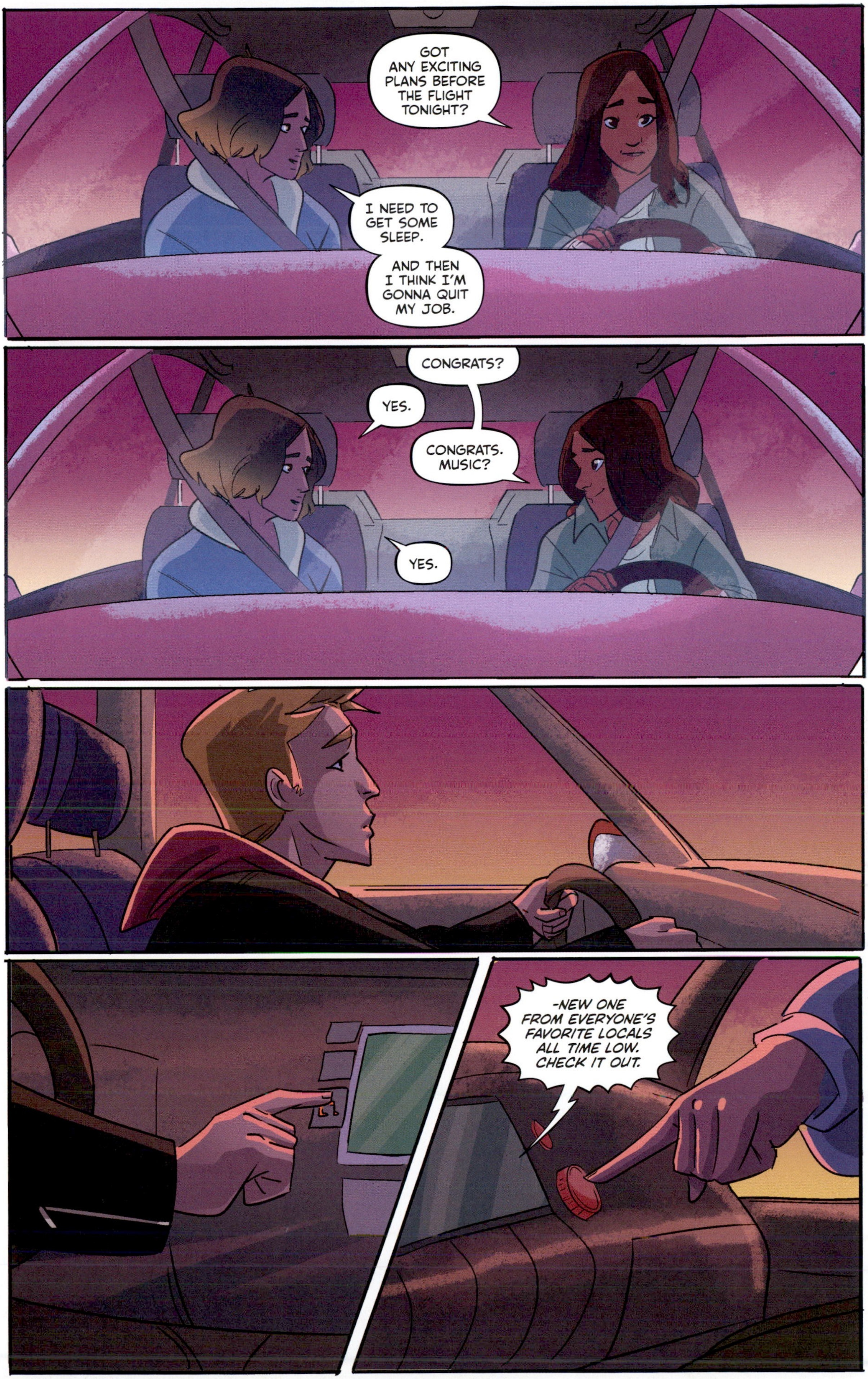
GOT ANY EXCITING PLANS BEFORE THE FLIGHT TONIGHT?
I NEED TO GET SOME SLEEP.
AND THEN I THINK I'M GONNA QUIT MY JOB.
CONGRATS?
YES.
CONGRATS. MUSIC?
YES.
-NEW ONE FROM EVERYONE'S FAVORITE LOCALS ALL TIME LOW. CHECK IT OUT.

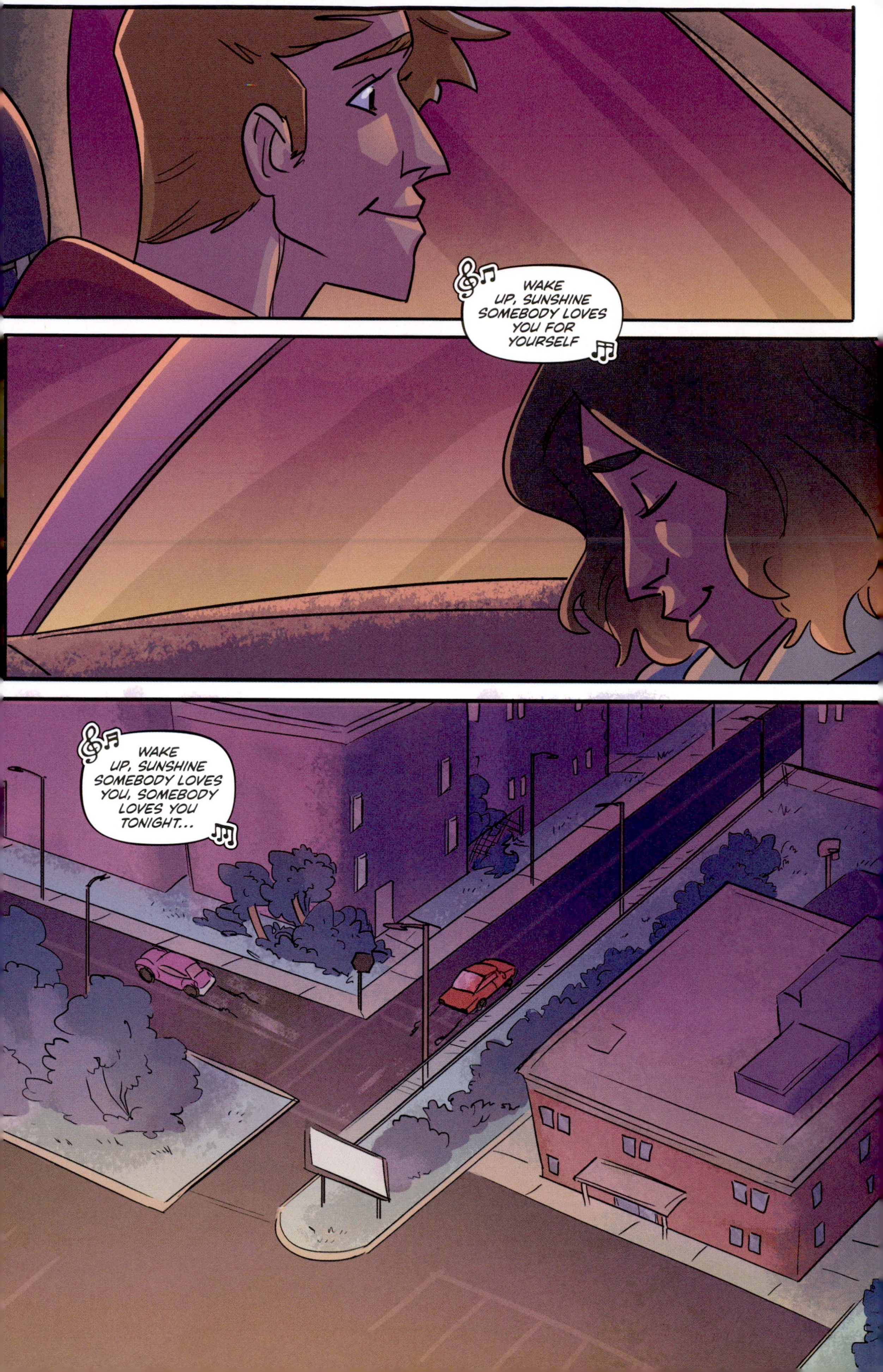
WAKE UP, SUNSHINE SOMEBODY LOVES YOU FOR YOURSELF
WAKE UP, SUNSHINE SOMEBODY LOVES YOU, SOMEBODY LOVES YOU TONIGHT...

GALLERY

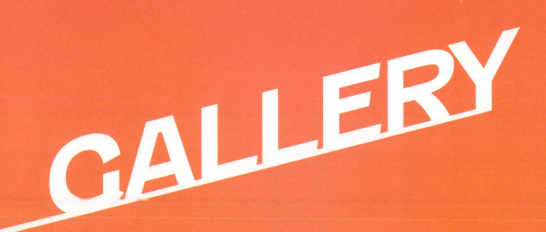

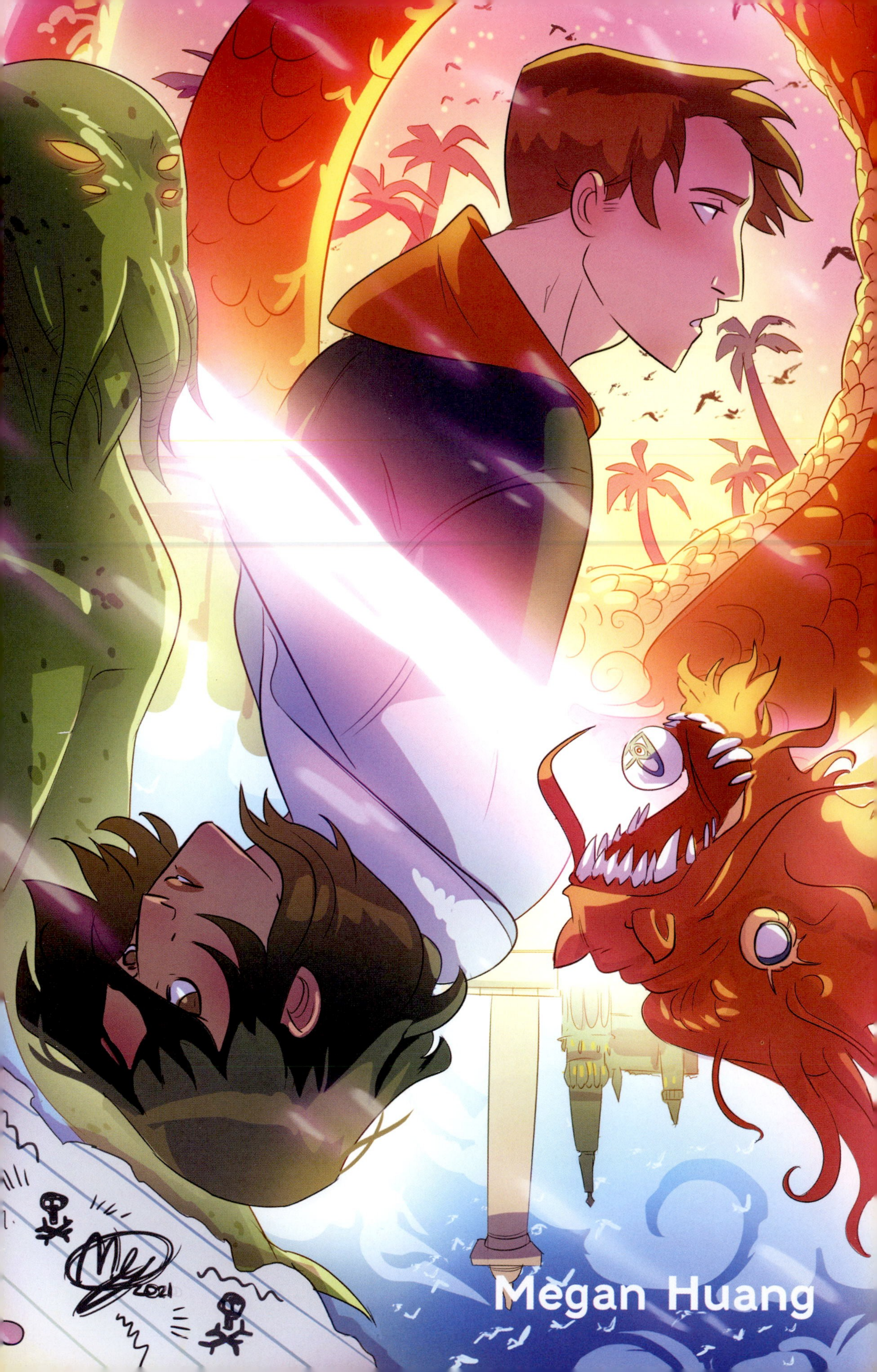
Megan Huang

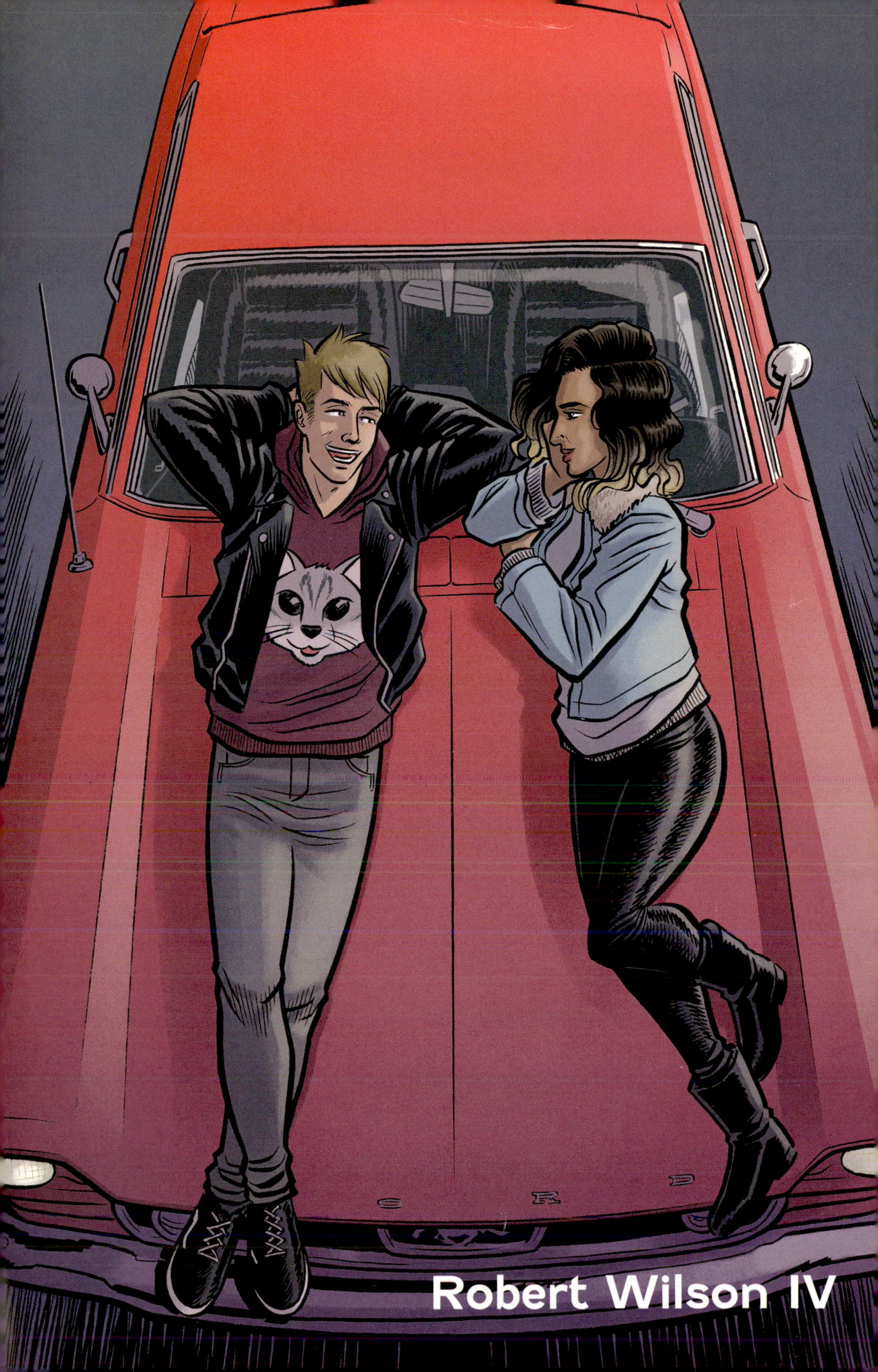
Robert Wilson IV

FOREWORD

PUBLISHERS	Joshua Frankel & Sridhar Reddy
CFO & GENERAL COUNSEL	Kevin Meek
SENIOR V.P.	Josh Bernstein
V.P., RETAIL SALES & MARKETING	Jeremy Atkins
V.P., DIGITAL	Anthony Lauletta
V.P., OPERATIONS	Dominique Rosés
V.P., MARKETING	Rebecca Cicione
PRODUCTION DIRECTOR	Courtney Menard
DESIGN DIRECTOR	Tyler Boss
RETAIL SALES DIRECTOR	Devin Funches
PROJECT COORDINATOR	Penelope Vargas

All Time Low PRESENTS YOUNG RENEGADES

WRITTEN BY TRES DEAN

INTERIOR ART BY MEGAN HUANG
& ROBERT WILSON IV

COVER ART BY ROBERT WILSON IV

COLORING BY MEG CASEY
& FRED C. STRESING

LETTERING BY ANDWORLD DESIGN

EDITED BY CAMILLA ZHANG
& RYAN CADY